WALTER CLARK
FIGHTING JUDGE

Sincerely Yours
Walter Clark

WALTER CLARK

FIGHTING JUDGE

By AUBREY LEE BROOKS

Chapel Hill
THE UNIVERSITY
of North Carolina
PRESS

Copyright, 1944, by

THE UNIVERSITY OF NORTH CAROLINA PRESS

Printed in
The United States of America

TO
THE SUPREME COURT OF THE
UNITED STATES
WHICH NOW REFLECTS THE VIEWS OF
WALTER CLARK

CONTENTS

CHAPTER		PAGE
I.	"Little Clark," the Soldier	3
II.	Family Tree, Its Roots and Fruit	23
III.	A Changed World	35
IV.	Love, Law, and Labor	47
V.	Country Judge	54
VI.	Premier Jurist	60
VII.	His Philosophy	75
VIII.	The Governing Power, Men or Money	85
IX.	Kilgo-Gattis Travesty Trials	102
X.	Impeachment of the Judges	122
XI.	Contest for Chief Justice	129
XII.	Attempted Larceny of a Railroad	142
XIII.	Prophet of a New Order	147
XIV.	The New Court	154
XV.	Women, Children, and Minorities	161
XVI.	The Political Machine Clicks	177
XVII.	Government by Judges	192

CHAPTER		PAGE
XVIII.	JUSTICE TO LABOR	206
XIX.	PARTING SHOTS	215
XX.	PERSONALITIES AND POWER	223
XXI.	"A BRAVE AND DETERMINED PEOPLE"	239
XXII.	THE FULLNESS OF TIME	247
	SELECTED LIST OF WALTER CLARK'S WRITINGS	257
	INDEX	267

ILLUSTRATIONS

Walter Clark. From an engraving in the *Biographical History of North Carolina* *Frontispiece*

Facing Page

Walter Clark at Tew's Military Academy in Hillsboro when he was fourteen. From a daguerreotype   6

Bronze buck still standing on the grounds at Albin. From a photograph by Charles Farrell   7

Officers of the Twenty-Second Regiment, with Walter Clark as Second Lieutenant and Drill Master. From *Histories of the Several Regiments and Battalions from North Carolina in the Great War 1861-'65.*   22

Walter Clark as lieutenant colonel in the Seventieth North Carolina Regiment. From a daguerreotype   23

Clark's maternal grandparents, his father, David Clark II, and his mother, Anna Maria Thorne Clark   30

The broad fields of Ventosa today. From a photograph by Charles Farrell   *Following page* 30

Dike along the Roanoke River at Ventosa. From a photograph by Charles Farrell   31

View of the Roanoke River from the old pier site at Ventosa. From a photograph by Charles Farrell   54

Two descendants of slave days and a section of slave quarters. From photographs by Charles Farrell   55

                                                       Facing Page

Susan Washington Graham (Mrs. Walter Clark) and her parents, Governor and Mrs. William A. Graham   70

Tester bed, one of the few things saved when Ventosa mansion was burned. From a photograph by Charles Farrell   71

The law office built by Clark at Halifax when he was twenty-two. From a photograph by Charles Farrell   182

The Supreme Court of North Carolina   183

Clark at his desk in the library of his home   198

Chief Justice Clark at seventy-two. From a portrait by Clement Strudwick   199

WALTER CLARK
FIGHTING JUDGE

Chapter I
"LITTLE CLARK," THE SOLDIER

"You may relish him more in the soldier than in the scholar." —Shakespeare

IN THE SPRING of 1860 a visitor at Ventosa, the Clark ancestral home overlooking the Roanoke River, saw from the broad piazza seventy plows drawn by seventy mules driven by seventy slaves. Behind this striking scene were generations of adventure and romance; immediately ahead of it lay tragedy and despair.

General David Clark took great pride in Ventosa with its five thousand acres and two hundred slaves, but his chief affection and that of his wife centered in their oldest child, who had been christened Walter McKenzie. At fourteen years of age Walter was still small and slender, but his large and well-formed head and piercing gray eyes gave evidence of a strong and active mind.

It was decided best for him to enter a military school where he could get both mental training and physical culture. In September, 1860, his father enrolled him as a cadet in Tew's Military Academy at Hillsboro, North Carolina. This school was modeled after West Point, from which its commandant, Colonel Tew, had graduated, and its student body was made up of boys drawn from the leading families of the state.

Walter had already learned how to study and how to make books his companions. His scholastic records show that he was from the first an apt student, particularly in Greek and Latin and in English composition. He entered with zest into the study and practice of military tactics and maneuvers, little realizing how soon he would be called upon to put them into practice.

Before his first year of instruction was completed, North Carolina, on May 20, 1861, took the fateful step and passed the ordinance of secession. The decision came unexpectedly soon. The people of the state did not want to engage in civil war and many of her ablest statesmen maintained up to the very last that the conflict could be avoided. But when President Lincoln called upon North Carolina for troops to join the Union Army she chose the alternative, as did General Lee—to fight with her neighbors and not against them.

North Carolina at this time was in a position very similar to that of the democracies at the beginning of the present global conflict, totally unprepared for war. Governor Ellis, realizing this state of affairs, called for volunteer troops to assemble immediately at Camp Ellis, near Raleigh. He requested Colonel Tew to assign one of his cadets to act as drill master for the first contingent of raw recruits then assembling. Colonel Tew and his staff designated Walter Clark for this undertaking. The lad was the youngest officer and smallest boy in the barracks, just fourteen years of age. His parents, on account of his extreme youth and slender physique, at first hesitated, but the boy was keen to go and they consented. The volunteers, many of them husky mountaineers and all much older than Walter, were soon impressed by his military knowledge and efficiency.

In July, 1861, the volunteer troops at Camp Ellis, numbering about a thousand men, were organized into the 22nd Regiment under the command of Colonel J. Johnston Pettigrew. Walter had so endeared himself to these men that they affectionately dubbed him "Little Clark," and by this name he was known throughout the war. Upon the organization of the 22nd Regiment he was elected second lieutenant and drill master, and went with his regiment to join the Army of Virginia. They encamped at Evansport on the Potomac River, and he continued there as drill master until November, when he was sent back to Raleigh to act as drill master for the 35th North Carolina Regiment stationed at Camp Mangum.

It is recalled by his fellow soldiers that it was both interesting and impressive to see this beardless youth, little more than a child, directing and commanding the military movements of men all older than he, some of them middle-aged and the fathers of families.

In the spring of 1862 the 35th Regiment was ordered to New Bern, and since there was little prospect of active military engagements Clark resigned from the regiment and re-entered Colonel Tew's Military Academy to pursue his studies.

In the early summer of 1862 the 35th Regiment was reorganized by electing Matt W. Ransom its colonel and "Little Clark" a first lieutenant. Colonel Ransom appointed Clark his adjutant, and in August of that year the regiment was ordered to join Lee's army preparatory to the Maryland campaign. This precocious and daring little soldier, who seemed to be spoiling for a fight, was soon to have his ambition gratified to the fullest. Within the next thirty days he was to see enough action and carnage to satisfy a Napoleonic guard. He, with his regiment, marched from Raleigh to Richmond and thence to Harper's Ferry, and after a desperate engagement there, marched double-quick to Sharpsburg, where on September 17 was fought the bloodiest one-day battle of the war.

Preparatory to Walter's joining the Army of Virginia his proud father equipped him for the undertaking. He gave him a bodyguard and two horses, for his rank as first lieutenant and adjutant entitled him to a suitable mount. The bodyguard was a Negro boy named Neverson, only two years older than Walter, but intelligent and devoted to his master.

The 35th North Carolina, to which Little Clark was attached, reached the Army of Virginia in time to see the successful conclusion of the Second Battle of Manassas, but was not engaged in it. Flushed with victory, General Lee prepared for his march into Maryland, and "when August with its trailing vines passed out the gates of summer," this noble army crossed the Potomac.

The bands were playing and the soldiers were singing "Maryland, my Maryland."

Walker's division, to which Clark's regiment belonged, was ordered to recross the Potomac and surround Harper's Ferry, while the balance of Lee's army moved on toward Hagerstown. At Boonesboro, on September 14, Lee's army was attacked and fell back to the village of Sharpsburg, with the Potomac at its back. Here Lee made his stand, while the Federal line of battle was drawn up along Antietam Creek—which accounts for the two names given to this battle, Sharpsburg and Antietam.

The Federal forces engaged here were approximately 90,000, while the Confederates had only 35,000 men and boys. In addition to the Federals' great superiority in numbers, General Lee had braved all rules of strategy by dividing his army and had sent his greatest general, Jackson, to invest Harper's Ferry. Fortunately for Lee, Jackson's corps, which included the 35th North Carolina, made quick work of Harper's Ferry by forcing the 12,000 Federal troops stationed there to surrender, and Jackson rejoined Longstreet's corps and Stuart's cavalry at Sharpsburg on the eve of the fateful day, September 17. The Confederate forces stationed in the bend of the Potomac had no way open to escape if the tide of battle should turn against them. A later-learned fact added to the extreme gravity of the situation. General McClellan had found at Frederick, Maryland, a dispatch from General Lee to General D. H. Hill, which had been dropped in the latter's encampment. This disclosed to him Lee's entire plan of campaign and the proposed division of his army.

Years afterward, when Adjutant Clark had become Chief Justice of the Supreme Court of North Carolina, he recorded his recollections of this never-to-be-forgotten battle and the part he took in it:

"I was then a mere boy, just sixteen a few days before, and have vivid recollections of the events of the day. About an hour before day, on the 17th, our division began its march for the posi-

Walter Clark at Tew's Military Academy in Hillsboro when he was fourteen years old. From a daguerreotype in the possession of the Clark family.

Charles Farrell

Bronze buck still standing on the grounds at Albin, where it was placed one hundred and twenty-five years ago. When Walter Clark as a boy visited his Uncle Colin at Albin, "he found great sport in mounting the bronze buck, holding to its horns, and playing horse."

tion assigned us on the extreme right, where we were to oppose the Federals in any attempt to cross either the bridge (since known as Burnside's) or the ford over the Antietam below it, near Shiveley's. Along our route we met men, women and children coming out from Sharpsburg, and from the farm houses near by. They were carrying such of their household belongings as were portable; many women were weeping. This, and the little children leaving their homes, made a moving picture in 'the dawn's early light.' On taking position, we immediately tore down the fences in our front which might obstruct the line of fire. About 9 a. m. a pressing order came to move to the left; this we did in quick time. As we were leaving our ground, I remember looking up the Antietam, the opposite bank of which was lined with Federal batteries. They were firing at the left wing of our army to the support of which we were moving. The Federal gunners could be seen with the utmost distinctness as they loaded and fired. Moving northwards, we were passing in the rear of our line of battle and met constant streams of the wounded coming out. Among them I remember meeting Colonel W. L. DeRosset, of the Third North Carolina, being brought out badly wounded, and many others well known in North Carolina.

"All this time there was the steady booming of the cannon, the whistling of shells, the pattering of fire-arms, and the occasional yell or cheer rising above the roar of battle as some advantage was gained by either side. Soon after passing the town the division was deployed in column of regiments. Around and just beyond the Dunkard church, in the center of the Confederate left, our line had been broken and was completely swept away. A flood of Federals were pouring in; we were just in time—ten minutes', five minutes' delay, and our army would have ceased to exist. We were marching up behind our line of battle, with our right flank perpendicular to it. As the first regiment got opposite to the break in our lines it made a wheel to the right and 'went in.' The next regiment, marching straight on, as soon as it cleared the left of the regiment preceding it, likewise wheeled to the right and took its place in line, and so on in succession. That is, we were marching north, and thus were successively thrown into line of battle facing east. As these regiments came successively into line they struck the Federal lines which were advancing; the crash was deafening. The sound of infantry firing at short distance can be likened to nothing so much as the dropping of a shower of hail-stones on an enormous tin roof. My regiment wheeled to the right about 150 yards north (and west) of the Dunkard church. In the wheel we passed a large barn, which is still standing, and entered the 'West Woods.' Being a mounted officer, I had a full view; our men soon drove the Federals back to the eastern edge of these woods, where the enemy halted to receive us. The West Woods had already been twice fought over that morning; the dead and wounded lay thicker than I have ever seen on a battle-field since. On the eastern edge of these woods the lines of battle came close together and the shock was terrific; here Captain Walter Bryson, of our regiment, was killed, along with many others in the Brigade. All the mounted officers in the division instantly dismounted, turning their horses loose to gallop to the rear. It being the first time I had been so suddenly thrown in contact with a line of battle, and not noticing, in the smoke and uproar, that the others had dismounted, I thought it my duty to stick to my horse; in another moment, when the smoke would have lifted (so the Federal line of battle, lying down fifty yards off, could have seen me) I should have been taken for a general officer and would have been swept out of my saddle by a hundred bullets. A kind-hearted veteran close by peremptorily pulled me off my horse. At that instant a minnie ball, whistling over the just emptied saddle, struck the back of my left hand which was still clinging to the pommel, leaving a slight scar which I still carry as a memento. The Federal line soon fell back. We then charged in pursuit as far as the post and rail fence at the turnpike. It was Gorman's Brigade, Sedgwick's Division, of Sumner's Corps our brigade was fighting. This was composed of troops from Massachusetts, New York and Minnesota, and from their returns they left 750 killed and wounded by our fire; this was about 10 a. m. A terrific shelling by the enemy followed, which was kept up for many hours, with occasional brief intermissions, caused probably by the necessity of letting the pieces cool. The shelling was terrible, but owing to protection from the slope of the hill, and there being a limestone ledge somewhat sheltering our line, the loss from the artillery fire was small.

"In the brief intermission, after the Federal infantry had fallen back and before the artillery opened, a cry for help was heard. Lieutenant (later Captain) Sanford G. Howie and myself going out in front of our line, found the Lieutenant-Colonel of a Massachusetts regiment—Francis Winthrop Palfrey—lying on the ground wounded, and brought him and others into our lines. With some reluctance he surrendered his very handsome sword and pistol and was sent to the rear. The sword bore an inscription that it had been presented to him by the town of Concord, Mass. He remarked at the time that he wished them preserved, and sure enough, after the war he wrote for them and they were restored; he was exchanged and became subsequently General Palfrey.

"There was another intermission in the shelling about 12 o'clock, when we were charged by the Second Massachusetts and Thirteenth New Jersey of Gordon's Brigade, who advanced as far as the post and rail fence at the Hagerstown turnpike, about 100 yards in our front, but were broken there and driven back, leaving many dead and wounded. There was another intermission about 2 o'clock probably. Word was then brought to us that we were to advance. It was then that Stonewall Jackson came along our lines; his appearance has been so often described that I will only say that I was reminded of what the Federal prisoners had said two days before at Harper's Ferry, when he rode down among them from his post on Bolivar Heights: 'My! Boys, he ain't much on looks, but if *we* had had him, we wouldn't have been in this fix.' Stonewall remarked to Colonel Ransom, as he did to the other Colonels along the line, that with Stuart's cavalry and some infantry he was going around the Federal right and get in their rear, and added 'when you hear the rattle of my small arms this whole line must advance.' He wished to ascertain the force opposed, and a man of our regiment named Hood was sent up a tall tree, which he climbed carefully to avoid observation by the enemy; Stonewall called out to know how many Yankees he could see over the hill and beyond the 'East Woods'; Hood replied, 'Who-e-e! there are oceans of them, General.' 'Count their flags,' said Jackson sternly, who wished more definite information. This Hood proceeded to do until he had counted thirty-nine, when the General told him that would do and to come down. By reason of this and other information he got, the turning movement was not attempted. . . .

"During the same lull, our Brigadier-General (Robert Ransom) received a flag of truce which had been sent to remove some wounded officers, and by it sent his love to General Hartsuff (if I remember aright), who had been his roommate at West Point; but Hartsuff, as it happened, had been wounded and had left the field. Soon after, our regiment was moved laterally a short distance to the right, and we charged a piece of artillery which had been put in position near the Dunkard church; we killed the men and horses, but did not bring off the artillery, as we were ourselves swept by artillery on our left posted in the 'old corn field.'

"Just to the right of the Dunkard church was the 'peach orchard' lying between the church and the town of Sharpsburg, where General D. H. Hill held our line for hours with a line of men four feet apart. A half mile in front of the orchard, early in the day, Anderson's Brigade had made the name of the 'Bloody Lane' forever famous. Its position thrust out in front resembled that of the 'Bloody Angle' at Spottsylvania later. It was overwhelmed by Richardson's Division, losing its Brigadier, Geo. B. Anderson, mortally wounded, Colonel Tew killed, Colonels Parkers, Bennett and others wounded.

"About 3 p. m., Burnside on our right (the Federal left) advanced, having crossed the bridge about 1 p. m., until which hour his two corps had been kept from crossing the bridge by Toomb's brigade of 400 men. Though it crossed at 1 p. m., Burnside's corps unaccountably did not advance till 3 p. m. Then advancing over the ground which had been abandoned by our division early that morning, utter disaster to our army was imminent. Just then A. P. Hill's division arrived from Harper's Ferry, where it had been paroling prisoners. A delay of ten minutes by Hill might have lost us the army; as it was, the division arrived just in time. The roll of musketry was continuous until nightfall and Burnside was driven back to the Antietam. Here General L. O'B. Branch was killed. . . . About dark our brigade was moved to the right a half-mile and bivouacked for the night around Reel's house near a burning barn. As we were moving by the right flank, we were seen by the Federal signal station on the high hills on the east bank of the Antietam. A shell sent by signal fell in the rear company of the 49th North Carolina Regiment, just ahead of us, killing Lieutenant Greenlea Fleming and killing or wounding thirteen others. It rained all next day. We were moved back that morning to our old position of the Dunkard church; neither army advanced. That night our whole army quietly moved off and crossed the Potomac, the passage of the river being lighted up by torches held by men stationed in the river on horseback. The army came off safely without arousing the Federal army, and left not a cannon nor a wagon behind us."

Freeman, in his life of Lee, recounting this battle, says that Lee in time became prouder of Sharpsburg than of any other battle he directed, because, as he believed, his men there faced the heaviest odds they ever encountered.

Clark, in recounting what occurred when he was peremptorily taken from his horse, toned down the account from what actually occurred. General Ransom, afterward recalling the circumstances under which Clark was wounded, said that what actually occurred was that a big mountaineer private ran up to him and pulled him off of his horse, exclaiming, "Git off'n this horse, you darned little fool! You'll git killed."

It is no wonder that Clark retained a vivid recollection of those moving and momentous days. As a sixteen-year-old boy, he experienced in sixty days more thrilling adventure than is given to most men throughout their entire lives. He joined Lee's army in time to witness the closing scenes of the Second Battle of Manassas; under Jackson he took part in the capture of Harper's Ferry; he was in the forefront of the Battle of Sharpsburg, and for three days he engaged in the Battle of Fredericksburg. And what a galaxy of distinguished military chieftains he was permitted to serve with and to know personally! In these engagements he fought under and with Lee, Jackson, Longstreet, Stuart, and the two Hills. Clark at that time never dreamed that in the years to come he would marry a first cousin of General Jackson's wife and be named as one of the executors of her will.

On October 23 Clark's regiment broke camp and marched through Culpeper Courthouse and Madison Courthouse, arriving near Fredericksburg on November 23. On this march orders were given to discharge all men in the regiment under eighteen and over forty years of age, and some fifty were sent home in this way.

The battle of Fredericksburg was fought on December 11, and Neverson rode with Adjutant Clark until the enemy opened fire at close range. Clark dismounted and directed Neverson to take the horses to the rear so as to be out of danger. In a letter to his mother he wrote that he didn't see Neverson or the horses for three days thereafter.

From Fredericksburg the 35th Regiment went with Lee into winter quarters near Richmond. Clark was troubled with his wounded hand, and the severe winter was a tax upon his strength. He wrote his mother asking for a pair of boots, telling her that the soles of his shoes, which he had worn continuously since August, had given way and that his feet were partially on the ground. "I have thought my feet would freeze in these low shoes for they keep no more water out than if I had none. It is folly to think that persons in the army can purchase at any time, anywhere, what they need."

On February 7 he wrote, thanking her for the boots. "If anyone wishes to become used to the crosses and trials of this life, let him enter camp life. There are millions of little petty crosses and trials in that kind of life which you can never imagine, even. I am quite bothered today. Someone came to my tent door and stole my oven and everything I had to cook in. Consequently I am without anything of the kind. I have sent miles out into the country trying to buy cooking utensils, but in vain. I am quite anxious to see you all, very anxious, but somehow I hate to leave the regiment and my companions in arms."

His mother's letters at this period show great concern over her boy's health, and she was urging him to resign.

The 35th Regiment, having become so badly depleted from losses in battle, was ordered back to North Carolina for local service. Clark accompanied it to the camp near Kenansville, North Carolina. While there he received a letter from his mother telling him that Major General Holmes had commissioned his father a brigadier general in the North Carolina Militia, charged with the obstruction of the Roanoke River, authorizing him to call as much of the militia of Bertie, Martin, and Washington counties as was necessary, and to impress Negroes, wagons, teams, and boats of every description into service. This letter disturbed Walter, and on February 6 he wrote his mother: "Tell Pa by no means to enter the service. One day of such service as we saw sometimes in Virginia would be sure to kill him. For instance (as we did before Fredericksburg) we had to lie in an open ditch, the rain pouring down, without blankets or a mouthful to eat (and the enemy picking off every man who raised up to stretch his benumbed limbs) for two nights and a day and the best part of another in succession, and then just as the day before we lay flat on our stomachs on the wet ground in an open field. The livelong day the enemy were firing at us from the housetops so that we had to wait till night to get a mouthful of dry bread to eat, and this after the heat and excitement of the battle the day before. Do you think he could stand that? ... Neverson's vaccination took finely at Fredericksburg when mine failed to take. My vaccination at Petersburg took very finely (in two places)."

This letter intensified his mother's concern over his health, and she again urged him to resign, but his father wrote him to exercise his own best judgment. His mother wrote: "Lay it all before the Good Being, my dear child, and ask His guidance and He will be sure to direct you aright. As for my part, when you left me to join the army I gave you up into His hands entirely, and scarcely feel as if you belong to me at all (not that I was weaned from you or loved you less, for you are doubly dear to me since you embraced the cause of Christ)."

Adjutant Clark remained with his regiment through February, 1863, when he resigned his commission in order to complete his education.

2

When Walter left the Academy and went with his regiment to Virginia, he took with him his school books, and it was facetiously said of him that he fought Yankees in the daytime and studied Greek and Latin at night. His enthusiasm for war and his love of the conflict did not weaken his determination to complete his education. In the spring of 1863 he entered the University of North Carolina, from which he graduated in one year with the first honors of his class. In August, 1863, he wrote his father: "I send by Willis my Political Economy which I have just completed. After Political Economy we take up Constitutional Law, which we will also recite to Governor Swain. I have commenced reading Law here under Judge Battle. Next June (if I should continue here that long), if I pass well upon what I recite to him, I will be entitled to a county court license though I would not be entitled to plead until I am twenty-one. I have finished Herodotus, having read in six lessons all that it took the Fresh class a session to read, as they had only two recitations a week in it. At that rate it will not take me long to make up the two years' Greek. If there is a Blackstone's Commentaries in the neighborhood please send it to me by Willis. I hope to be a full student by the end of the session, which will entitle me to a diploma next June just before the Supreme Court sits, when I would get my license. I have no idea of entering any profession except the army, but don't you think I am doing well enough to read Law, as the only possible disadvantage that could arise would be that I might injure my eyes. Let me know what you think of it. I thought you wouldn't care just so I was improving my time. Love to all. Your affectionate son."

On June 3, 1864, he wrote his mother: "I was graduated yesterday. Today I have been elected Major of the Fifth Battalion Junior Reserves. Need I say that my first thought on the announcement of my election was yourself, and that I hastened to write. I had strong opposition. A captain of cavalry and two or three enrolling officers were candidates against me. I received, however, sixteen votes out of the twenty. I have five fine companies, numbering nearly five hundred fine strapping western lads. There is hardly a small man in my Battalion. My Battalion is composed of picked men and picked officers."

He asked her to tell his father to "Please have my bay (not the gray) filly brought up to Airlie. Neverson will have to get ready to be 'off to the wars again.' I came off from home with only the shirt I had on and scarcely a cent of money, as I expected to go by Weldon. I have no army shirts. If you have no materials, I will get some here." He concludes his letter by saying that there was some opposition to his election because he was thought to be too young, and that the entire affair had been kept secret so that he did not know even five minutes before the election that he would be chosen.

On July 4 the First and Sixth battalions were organized into a regiment composed of ten companies, and Charles W. Broadfoot was elected colonel and Walter Clark lieutenant colonel. He was seventeen, probably the youngest lieutenant colonel in either army. The headquarters of Lieutenant General Holmes, which included the Junior Reserves, were removed to Weldon. Holmes communicated to the officers of this regiment his earnest wish that his chief-of-staff, Lieutenant Colonel F. S. Armistead, might be made colonel of the regiment, as thereby he felt confident that he would without delay be appointed brigadier general of the Junior Reserves Brigade, which was to be formed by President Davis. In deference to his wishes, the field officers resigned, and Armistead, who was a West Pointer, was elected colonel, Broadfoot lieutenant colonel, and Walter Clark major, the rank which he retained until the end.

The demand for the organization of Junior Reserves in order to protect and defend the home fronts had been so insistent that the Confederate Congress on February 17, 1864, passed a law placing in the Reserves those between the ages of seventeen and eighteen, and forty-five and fifty. The Act provided that they were not to serve out of their respective states, but the Junior Reserves of North Carolina served in South Carolina, Georgia, and Virginia.

The ranks of the army were being depleted by death on the battlefield and in the hospital, by wounds, by the growing volume of deserters, and by the necessity of detailing troops from the front to prevent depredations at home. The officers of the Junior Reserves, without exception, had seen previous service in the army. Major Clark was the only field officer in the Junior Reserves under eighteen years of age. He wrote his mother: "I am in good quarters, but cannot answer for our fare. One-third of a pound of bacon is the ration the government issues per man, and when I share that with Neverson you may be sure there is not much left. I have no plates, have to cook on a spider and eat with my hands. There is not a store in Weldon. Send me a couple of tin plates, two knives and forks, and a tin cup."

From the outset North Carolina had unsparingly given to the cause her men and boys; and her rich storehouses of food and material soon became the chief reliance of the Army of Virginia. Vance had shown himself an able and resourceful Governor in supplying war needs, and the rich valley of the Roanoke became the bread basket for Lee's armies campaigning around Petersburg and Richmond. To help protect this important source of supplies, the 70th North Carolina Reserves were organized, and at first were stationed at Weldon under General Baker. Major Clark and his command had occasional skirmishes with marauding enemy detachments, but his time for a few months was devoted largely to departmental duties.

In midsummer he wrote his mother from Camp Ransom near Weldon: "We are encamped about a mile and a half from Weldon in good log cabins, and I am drilling my battalion hard— five drills a day, and the officers recite on tactics twice a day. My hands are pretty full. Last Saturday and Sunday I lay in the trenches around Weldon. I was given a half a mile of breastworks to defend. The attack was expected every minute Saturday and part of Sunday. I had no troops to reinforce me."

On August 27 he wrote: "I have been on the Examining Board for over a month. We have examined between fifty and sixty officers. As junior officer of the Board I had all the records to keep and a great many cases take up two pages of foolscap. I am now ordered on a general court martial for the purpose of trying deserters."

In October his regiment was sent to repel a threatened Federal raid in Virginia, and toward the end of the month was sent to

Plymouth, to cover the approach to the eastern counties, from which large supplies were being drawn for the support of Lee's army. A part of this time Clark was in command of a post embracing cavalry, infantry, and artillery. For one so young this was an important command, and perhaps no other instance occurred during the war where an officer only eighteen years of age was entrusted with the responsible duty of holding such an exposed outpost defended by a force embracing every arm of the service.

His headquarters at Weldon were no great distance from his home, and frequent letters were exchanged between him and his mother. This correspondence reveals an interesting sidelight on young Clark's developing character and maturing mind. In October his mother warned him of a report that he was too attentive to one of Weldon's belles. In his immediate reply Clark displays the only irritation toward his mother that occurs in their frequent, intimate exchange of letters:

"Your caution in reference to the young ladies is quite amusing. I should have thought that caution in that regard would have been unnecessary from one who was as well acquainted with my opinion of the feebler sex as yourself. If I am but eighteen, as you hint in your letter, I am not a fool, and most certainly shall never entertain the most distant idea of tendering my 'hand and fortune' when the one has yet to achieve the other. With the profession that I have chosen it is not probable that I shall own any land beyond my sabre's length. With the total disbelief in the existence of such a passion as love—at least as far as myself is concerned—I am not the one to exchange the hopes of the future— delusive though they may be—for a few pieces of gold, as you would insinuate. I thought that you had long ago penetrated the secret that I fain would keep from others, for 'lowliness is young ambition's ladder'—that I have another aim in life than to 'live as my sires have lived and die as they have died.' In my opinion 'one crowded moment of glorious life is worth ten years of dull existence.' It has been my intention, and has been, should our young Confederacy go down in the billows which threaten to engulf it (which Heaven forbid) to collect a band of the brave around me and in a bright clime and more unclouded skies seek that which fortune denies me on my native shores. Maximilian of Mexico will not refuse a brave man's sword, and I trust I know how to wear one. I live in the future as I live for it. These are my sentiments known to none, suspected by few. Think you that they are reconcilable with the puling sentimentalism of love? The chords of my heart have been strung to a fiercer passion and echo not when struck by so unskilled a musician. I am as well aware as you are of the snares used to entice into matrimony. I am also pretty well versed in the duplicity of my own sex—you see I am fair, a blow at both sides of the question. But I fancy that an early and I might say bitter acquaintance with the world has taught me to beware of the one, while I can laugh at the other. It has also taught me another thing, to keep my own counsel. My real opinion on any subject is known to few or none, and while there is nothing that I would keep from you yet I suppose you are aware of my real sentiment on this subject, my usual reserve in regard to my opinions prevented any allusion to it."

In the closing months of the war North Carolina became a battlefield only less important than that of Virginia. Sherman, following his ruthless march through Georgia to the sea, was now headed north through South Carolina, burning and laying waste as he came. The war strategy of the Federals, as it unfolded, was for Sherman to destroy all supplies and military help to the Confederacy in Georgia, South Carolina, and North Carolina, and join Grant's army around Richmond for the final kill. The Confederate strategy was to stop Sherman, if possible, and leave General Joseph Eggleston Johnston free to join Lee's army in its desperate plight before Grant around Richmond. But Sherman could not be stopped, and finally General Wade Hampton and his dwindling forces retreated from South Carolina to North Carolina, and from Fayetteville joined General Johnston's forces then stationed at Smithfield. Near there, at Bentonville in Johnston County, was fought the last important battle in North Carolina, which Generals Hoke and Hampton later declared to be one of the most remarkable engagements of the entire war.

In this final carnage Johnston had at his command some fifteen thousand available men, while Sherman opposed him with an army seventy thousand strong, flushed with victory. On the morning of March 20 it was reported that the Federal right wing had crossed over to unite with the left wing which had been driven back and was coming up rapidly upon the left of Hoke's division. Hoke was directed to change front to the left. By this movement his line was formed parallel to and fronting the road. Here light entrenchments, made out of dead trees, were thrown up, and earth was dug with bayonets and filled in by the use of tin pans. From noon to sunset Sherman's army, now united, made repeated attacks upon Hoke's division of six thousand men and boys, but were uniformly driven back. The skirmish line of the brigade and the center were commanded by Major Walter Clark. The battle raged through March 20 and 21. The night of the 21st the Confederate army recrossed the creek by the bridge near Bentonville. The Federals made repeated attempts to force the passage of the bridge, but failed. At noon the retreat was resumed, and the troops camped near Smithfield. The Confederate losses in the battle of Bentonville were 2,343, while those of the Federals were nearly double that number. No bolder movement was conceived during the war than this of General Johnston, when he threw his handful of men on the overwhelming force in front of him, and when he confronted and baffled his foes, holding a weak line for three days against nearly five times his number. For the last two days of this fight, he held his position only to secure the removal of his wounded.

The Junior Reserves lost a number of officers and boys in this battle. It is reported that Major Clark time and again mounted the improvised breastworks and cheered his gallant men on until his left flank had been completely turned, and General Hoke commanded him to retreat. General Hoke wrote later of the Junior Reserves:

"The question of the courage of the Junior Reserves was well established by themselves in the battle below Kinston and at the battle of Bentonville. At Bentonville they held a very important part of the battlefield in opposition to Sherman's old and tried soldiers, and repulsed every charge that was made upon them with very meagre and rapidly thrown up breastworks. Their conduct in camp, on the march, and on the battlefield was everything that could be expected of them. It was equal to that of the old soldiers who had passed through four years of war. I returned through Raleigh, where many passed by their homes, and scarcely one of them left their ranks to bid farewell to their friends, though they knew not where they were going nor what dangers they would encounter."

General Johnston broke camp near Smithfield on April 10, and on April 12 reached Raleigh. There it was learned that Lee had surrendered to Grant at Appomattox. President Davis and his cabinet had abandoned the Confederate capital at Richmond and arrived at Greensboro on April 11. While not officially advised that the Army of Virginia was no more, Johnston and his officers knew that they were fighting a lost cause, and that Sherman and his devastating army could no longer be successfully resisted, but he did not surrender to General Sherman until April 26. On May 2, 1865, at Bush Hill, near High Point, Major Clark and what remained of the third Junior Reserves were paroled and turned their faces sorrowfully homeward.

The next day Major Clark and his faithful Neverson began their weary horseback ride one hundred and fifty miles to Ventosa. On their way home they passed through Hillsboro and in sight of the military academy from which Little Clark had gone so ambitiously and hopefully four years before. He knew that Colonel Tew had been killed at Sharpsburg, but did not know until afterward that every one of his instructors in the academy had gone to the war and had either been wounded or captured. The lonely trek of these two boys, their minds numbed by harrowing memories, was enough to chill their hearts, but there was worse to come.

When home was finally reached, there was no home—nothing but the land was there, and that covered with a tangled growth of bushes and briars. The once great cultivated fields of cotton and corn were now a wilderness of weeds. The slaves were wandering aimlessly through the neighborhood, and raiding Federal soldiers had stolen the livestock. The invading armies had burned to the ground the spacious Ventosa mansion, and its beautiful gardens had disappeared. All the happy memories of Walter's childhood here lay waste in ashes before his eyes. With an almost broken heart he turned to seek elsewhere for his father and mother, his sisters and brothers, in the hope that he would find them alive.

TWENTY-SECOND REGIMENT

1. J. Johnston Pettigrew, Colonel
2. Thos. D. Jones, Captain, Co. A
3. Graham Daves, 1st Lieut., and Adjt.
4. W. W. Dickson, 2nd Lieut., Co. A
5. Walter Clark, 2nd Lieut. and Drill Master

From *Histories of the Several Regiments and Battalions from North Carolina in the Great War 1861-'65,* edited by Walter Clark.—Volume II, facing page 161.

Walter Clark at seventeen as lieutenant colonel in the 70th North Carolina Regiment. This was the first regiment of Junior Reserves, and Clark was elected lieutenant colonel July 3, 1864. He is said to have been the youngest officer of his rank in either army. Note the two stars indicating his rank. From a daguerreotype in the possession of the Clark family.

CHAPTER II

FAMILY TREE, ITS ROOTS AND FRUIT

"Distinguished birth is like a cipher—it has no power in itself like wealth, or talent, or personal excellence, but it tells, with all the power of a cipher when added to either of the others." —John Frederick Boyes

COLONIAL CAROLINA was enriched by the immigration of many Scottish and Scotch Irish Macs from the lowlands and the highlands of Scotland. These sturdy settlers through the intervening years contributed so much to the economic, industrial, and religious life of the colony and afterwards to the State of North Carolina that they were given the appellation of "God Blessed Macs." There is a local tradition that among these early comers was Flora MacDonald, who is said to have lived for a while in the Scottish settlement on the Roanoke before she moved to Fayetteville, North Carolina. Another Mac, an Episcopal clergyman, McKenzie, settled about 1750 with his family at Plymouth, on Albemarle Sound. Here in 1770 a kinsman, Colin Clark, hailing from the highlands of Scotland, joined McKenzie. Within a few months Colin Clark married his cousin, Janet McKenzie, the clergyman's daughter, and remained at Plymouth for seven years. Then, wishing to visit the old home, he set sail for Scotland but was shipwrecked and lost. The widow and her four sons, left without means of support, were taken into the home of her brother as members of his family. She died soon afterwards, a brokenhearted woman, and the boys continued to be cared for in the McKenzie household until they reached maturity. When David, the oldest of the four boys, and grandfather of the Chief Justice, reached manhood he went to Plymouth, North Carolina, to make his own way in life. When he ventured forth, his only possession was a body servant given him by McKenzie.

At Plymouth, young David Clark soon engaged in the commission business, in which his success was remarkable. He developed an unusual capacity for business and, by industry and acumen, accumulated, within a span of ten years, an estate of $100,000. He acquired large areas of land along the Roanoke River in Halifax County, between the converging waters of the Roanoke River and Kehukee Creek. These rich lands had been temporarily settled by a number of enterprising Scots as early as 1710, and the section had become known as "Scotland Neck" because of this Scottish element and its unusual geographical formation.

The Indian name for Roanoke River was "Moratock," which meant "River of Death." The headwaters of the Roanoke drained a vast, fertile territory in North Carolina and Virginia; the broad lowlands on either side of the stream were repeatedly enriched by great freshets which overflowed the banks and deposited humus and alluvial soil along its whole course. These lowlands were likened to the Valley of the Nile, but, unlike the Nile, the river's flow could not be measured by a nilometer, and often great floods destroyed homes, stock, and other possessions of the settlers. They had not yet acquired the means, or learned how, to control these overflows by the construction of extensive dikes.

But the romance of rivers was again to play an important part in a new civilization. The rich valley of the Roanoke was inviting to hardy and courageous men from the old world, as well as from other portions of the colony. About 1725, Marmaduke Norfleet, who had earlier settled in Virginia, removed to Perquimans County, adjoining Halifax, and during his lifetime acquired vast landed estates in this territory, which is now known as Perquimans, Bertie, Edgecombe, Northampton, and Halifax counties. He accumulated a fortune for those days and became the progenitor of one of the most noted families in the colony. His grandson, Marmaduke Norfleet, inherited from him a large estate of lands and many slaves, and in 1786 married Hannah Ruffin, a member of the well-known Ruffin family. Their second child, Louise, with her personal charm and prospective dowry, became the belle of the colony.

In the meantime, David McKenzie Clark, on account of his business success, handsome appearance, and gracious manner, was regarded as the most eligible bachelor in the Roanoke section. In 1806, Louise Norfleet, who was then seventeen, and David Clark, thirty-four, were married. Her father settled upon her several thousand acres of land along the Roanoke and gave her a hundred slaves. The young couple established their home in Clarksville, which later took the name of Scotland Neck. Here they built a colonial mansion, for generations one of the show places of the colony. They named it "Albin," after the Clark ancestral estate in Scotland.

Years afterward an observant visitor at this home described it as a large white house with Ionic pillars and a massive front door with a brass knocker. The entrance was guarded by two life-size bronze lions, couchant. The front hall was lighted by a transom of stained glass, and a wide spiral iron stairway led to the second floor. The halls and rooms had rich wainscoting, with scenic wallpaper purchased in France, that in the parlor picturing Watteau figures and bow bridges. The house throughout was furnished with handsome mahogany; oil portraits adorned the walls, and tall bookcases were filled with rare books. The mantels were of gray marble with bronze ornaments. On the spacious lawn, among the trees and shrubs, were two large Norway firs, and in the shrubbery stood two life-size bronze deer. To the north of the house was a large oak grove with a small stream of water fed by several springs from the hillside. David built picturesque springhouses above these springs and, over the stream, a bow bridge copied from the scenic paper in the parlor.

By frugality and good business judgment, David added to the family fortune until he became one of the wealthiest and most successful planters in the state. He operated a line of boats on the

Roanoke River, which, by river and sound, carried the commerce of many plantations to the markets at Norfolk, and as far as New York and the West Indies.

The Clarks had eleven children, two of whom died in infancy. Their eighth child was named David and before he was ten years old his mother died; a year later, in 1830, he lost his father, whose will, recorded in Halifax County, shows that he bequeathed to his sons 376 slaves and 20,000 acres of land. Young David Clark II was placed in the care of his guardian, who lived in Raleigh, and there he attended school; later he was sent to Boston to be educated, and remained in school there for seven years. During a part of this time he was under the tutelage of George Bancroft, the historian.

David Clark II married Anna Maria Thorne, a granddaughter of Dr. Thorne, a distinguished physician from New York. The Thorne family was closely related to the Van Wycks of New York City, and Anna, when a girl, was sent to New York to finish her education. She returned a charming and intelligent woman. After their marriage, David built a home on the Roanoke plantation, which he named "Ventosa," and this he made his winter residence. It was a spacious house of three stories, ample to accommodate their growing family, which ultimately numbered thirteen children, four of whom died in infancy. Ventosa is remembered for its splendor in appointments and furnishings, its well selected library, and especially for its flower gardens which Anna developed and supervised.

The climate on the plantation was hot and humid in summer, and so in the late spring of 1846 David took his wife some fifty miles away, to Prospect Hill, the family home of her parents, where it was cooler. There, on August 19, their first child, Walter McKenzie Clark, was born.

Prospect Hill was one of the most impressive mansions in the state; artisans from England had been engaged to carve by hand hardwoods, which were made into priceless mantels, doors, and stairways; exquisite paneling, extending from floor to ceiling, adorned the halls and a number of the great rooms. A large ball room was constructed in one wing of the house.

The ruling families of the South at this period drew their financial power and social prominence from the possession of land and slaves; by intermarriage this supremacy was maintained from one generation to another, and such possessions brought leisure, and leisure afforded an opportunity for culture and learning.

As the Clark family increased, a summer home was built near Prospect Hill, and the Scottish influence was indicated by the name given it, "Airlie."

The Ventosa plantation, where Walter was to spend his early boyhood, was an estate self-sustained and self-sufficient, and represented the best of antebellum plantation life. It was fortunately situated in an arm of the Roanoke River, which lent itself to the construction of a great levee or dike, thus deflecting from the broad lowlands the flood waters of the river. This levee was built of earth by hand labor, and its dimensions were, on an average, forty feet broad at the base, twelve feet high, eight feet across the crest, and seven miles long. At its western end it connected with another similar levee extending ten miles up the river. This levee was located, in the main, about a mile from the riverbed so as to afford a leeway for the storage of high water. A snake-rail fence forming a crescent was built along the outer boundary of the plantation, connecting at each end with the levee. This fence was ten miles long and ten rails high; each rail was ten feet long, and riven from clear pine. The terrain of the four thousand acres so enclosed was slightly undulating, its elevation sloping to the east as the river ran, affording perfect drainage. Considering the lack of machinery in those days and the fact that the construction of this levee had to be done by hand with farm labor when such labor was not needed for cultivating the crops, it is estimated that its building required the toil of two hundred slaves working six months each year for a period of ten years.

The wide strip of land lying between the levee and the river was heavily wooded with a growth of pine, gum, ash, cypress, and oak. In this forest wild game abounded—deer, turkey, squirrels, racoons, and 'possums, while the river in season was visited by wild geese and duck. Colonel William Byrd in his account of the running of the dividing line between Virginia and North Carolina in 1728, reports killing wild turkey weighing as much as forty pounds while passing immediately north of this plantation. In the river were black bass and white perch, delectable for the master's table, and catfish and eels to furnish additional food for the slaves. In the springtime a great delicacy was the shad which visited this river in the spawning season and were taken from its waters by the thousands.

The slaves at Ventosa numbered more than two hundred. Their quarters composed two villages about two miles apart, of well-built houses, consisting of two rooms, each sixteen feet square, with a chimney between and a porch across the front, all kept whitewashed—very similar in character to many of the tenant houses used today by textile manufacturers for their white help throughout the South. Some of these houses are still in use, showing the excellence of the material used in their construction. The houses were built in a row in the shape of an ell, all fronting on a street. The overseer's house was located near by, in easy access to both villages. Each house had a garden of sufficient size to provide vegetables for the family. On the plantation were blacksmiths, carpenters, cabinet makers, laundry women, nurses, and cooks in abundance. The descendants of slaves, still to be found on this estate, a part of which remains in the ownership of the Clark family, are unanimous in their testimony to the effect that the slaves were always well fed, well clothed, and kindly treated. When they were sick a physician was provided, and at death they were given decent burial. Families were not separated, and there is no evidence of miscegenation.

James Truslow Adams points out that the Negroes found in Virginia and North Carolina seem much superior physically and mentally to those found farther south. This observation is confirmed by a visit to the Ventosa plantation today, where one hundred and twenty-five descendants of those slaves still live as tenants and laborers. There are to be found among them no receding foreheads, blue gums, or ill-formed bodies, such, for instance, as are to be seen in certain parts of South Carolina. On the contrary, one is impressed with their well-shaped heads, faces, and bodies, and the apparent purity of their African blood. The children are as black as the ace of spades, but have regular features and intelligent eyes.

A major portion of the soil at Ventosa consists of dark sandy loam especially adapted to the growth of cotton and grain. Cotton, corn, wheat, oats, rye, and clover grew here in abundance, unaided by artificial stimulant. Large apple, peach, and pear orchards furnished fruit for all, as did melons, berries, and grapes of many varieties. The famous scuppernong grape grew wild in the woods. A roadway was built along the levee bordered by a row of apple trees, extending its entire length of seven miles.

The clothes of the slaves were made from cotton and wool grown on the plantation. The young children carded the yarn by hand and it was spun and woven by the women with their spinning wheels and looms. Hides taken from cattle grown on the plantation were tanned and made into shoes for the slaves and harness for the teams.

There was no railroad in that section of the state. The Roanoke River was the great highway upon which the surplus crops of the plantations could be easily and cheaply transported by boats to market, and David Clark's two steamboats and numerous tugs formed the principal means of transportation for his own produce and that of other planters of the region.

Here was a principality, apparently a human paradise, comparable to the haciendas of Mexico and South America, but like them it had its shadows. The flood waters of the river, notwithstanding the dikes, occasionally did serious damage to the crops, and the stagnant pools of water left by the floods produced mosquitoes and malaria. The slaves who remained on the plantation throughout the year seemed to become practically immune to the chills and fevers, but the masters had to spend their summers in the highlands to avoid illness.

The Clarks and most of their relatives were devout Episcopalians, but Anna before her marriage had become a Methodist, and ever afterward was devoted to and active in the cause of Methodism. They employed a young Methodist minister to preach to the slaves, took him into their home as a member of the family, and built a church upon the plantation for them to worship in. A Methodist minister, writing years afterwards of his experiences while visiting and holding a meeting for the slaves, recounts that he was greatly impressed with their religious fervor and physical well-being, and that at these meetings some of the older members would lead in prayer and invariably close their supplications with a "God bless marster and mistress."

Amid these scenes and surroundings Walter spent his childhood. More and more he became the idol of his mother. Other children came, but to her, like most mothers, the firstborn, a boy, gave sublimity to motherhood and life. This attachment grew with the passing of the years. To her forever thereafter, whether he was on the battlefield or on the bench, Walter was still her adored boy, and throughout life he manifested a never-failing affection and tenderness for her.

Walter in childhood was small for his age and rather frail, but he loved outdoor life. His playmates at Ventosa were mostly Negro boys of his own age and older. One who has never shared such an experience cannot possibly understand the thrill and joy of a white boy privileged to play, hunt, and swim with Negro

Upper left, Walter Clark's maternal grandmother; upper right, his maternal grandfather, William Williams Thorne, who lived at Prospect Hill; lower left, his father, David Clark II; lower right, Anna Maria Thorne Clark, his mother.

Charles Farrell

The broad fields of Ventosa today. "In the spring of 1860 a visitor at Ventosa, the Clark ancestral home overlooking the Roanoke River, saw from the broad piazza seventy plows drawn by seventy mules driven by seventy slaves. Behind this scene were generations of adventure and romance; immediately ahead of it lay tragedy and despair."

Charles Farrell

Dike along the Roanoke River at Ventosa. It is seven miles long, twelve feet high, and forty feet wide at the base. It was built about a hundred years ago by slaves, who moved the dirt in wheelbarrows.

urchins who obeyed and adored him and called him "Master." Indeed these playmates possessed all the virtues of the Negro without many of the vices of the whites.

David Clark loved fine horses and kept a stable of well-bred saddle and carriage horses. A change of residence with the seasons between Ventosa and Airlie was accomplished by the use of carriages and phaetons, accompanied by a large retinue of trained servants. The distance was only about fifty miles, but because of the condition of the roads it required two days for the journey.

Walter, from the first, showed an interest in reading, which his mother encouraged, particularly along religious lines. The Clarks engaged a governess to aid with the care and tutoring of the children but the mother directed their religious instruction, and by the time Walter reached the age of six he had read the entire Bible.

When he was eight, Walter was sent to school at Vine Hill Academy, located near Clarksville, on a tract of land which his grandfather had given for school purposes and on which about one-third of the present town of Scotland Neck is built. Colin Clark, his uncle, owned Albin near by; he had no children, and Walter soon became a favorite in his household. During his frequent visits there as a youngster, he found great sport in mounting the bronze deer standing in the front yard, holding to the buck's horns and playing horse. In 1857, when he was eleven years old, Walter was sent to school at Ridgeway, in Warren County, under the care of Professor Bass, where he remained for two years. There are still preserved among the Clark papers reports of his progress at school, some of his original essays, and letters from his mother. In December of that year, Professor Bass wrote to Walter's father: "He is very studious and, what is rather remarkable in a boy of his age, seems to be so from the love of study. If I had a school of such boys, most of the troublesome part of the business would be avoided."

In April, 1858, Walter, then twelve, wrote his mother: "I hasten to reply to your kind and affectionate epistle of the 15th ultimo, which I received Saturday evening too late for me to reply. I like Greek as well as ever, but it's harder than it was at first. I have commenced reading it right well, I think, considering the time I have been reading. I am the only boy in school studying Greek." In the frequent letters to his mother during this time, he often closed with the request, "Kiss all the children for me." His letters were long and newsy—"I went to Warrenton Tuesday last to hear the famous renegade, Old-Line Whig (as he is facetiously styled by the 'know nothings' up this way) deliver a first rate speech. Everybody that I heard speak of it said that they had never heard the like before. It was excellent. Even the 'know nothings,' hard as it was for them, confessed he delivered no second rate speech. Henry W. Miller is the gentleman I refer to. I reckon you are tired of this trash, though I remember a proverb, 'A single fact is worth a shipload of arguments,' but arguments and writing trash are different. I attended the Episcopal service in Warrenton last Sunday. I suppose you know it is the first time I ever attended any church whatever except the Methodist Church." In a postscript he added: "I have finished the second book of Caesar this week. The reason I finished it so soon is because I had no algebra. I got two lessons in Caesar every day, and finished it in five and a half days." A few weeks later he wrote: "I read three chapters in my Bible regularly every day and five or ten every Sunday, like you requested me to do. I go to Sunday School and church, and also clean my teeth every morning, and everything else you requested me to do. I have 'most finished Caesar." On September 24 he wrote: "I have finished the first book in Ovid and have a prospect of finishing the whole this session. I expect to finish my Greek sometime also this session, and possibly my algebra. I will be in geometry soon, I hope." Professor Bass reported to Walter's father upon his progress at school, "In orthography very superior, in composition, besides writing a nice hand, he manifests considerable faculty in composing, as well as facility of expression for one of his age."

Walter took time off from his strenuous work on Greek, Latin, and his devotional exercises to engage in sports with his schoolmates and to write amusing squibs. In September he wrote an essay on "The Bull Frog" and dedicated it to one of his class friends, Old:

> "Humbly I dedicate my composition bold
> To Mr. William Walter Raleigh Old,
> Who lives near the famous river Pasquotank,
> Where bullfrogs jump from bank to bank."

The essay ends with a poem which he called "Animals and Their Countries, or the Wind-up":

> "O'er Afric's sand the tawny lion stalks.
> On Phasis' banks the graceful pheasant walks.
> The lonely eagle builds on Hilda's shore;
> Germania's forests feed the tusky boar.
> From Alp to Alp the sprightly Ibex bounds;
> With peaceful lowings Brittania's isle resounds.
> The Lapland peasant o'er the frozen meer
> Is drawn in sledges by his swift reindeer.
> The River-horse and scaly Crocodile
> Infest the reedy banks of fruitful Nile.
> Dire Dipsas hiss o'er Mauretania's plain.
> Seals and spouting Whales sport in the northern main.
> At last but not least the humble Frog
> His home he has beneath the moss-cov'r'd log—
> But should I not say on the bank
> Of the muddy, of the renowned Pasquotank,
> Where turtles and crokers in numbers untold
> Raise up their heads, all besmeared, and look at Mr. Old."

In the fall of 1859, Walter was placed under the tutelage of Professor Graves, principal of Belmont Select School in Granville County. A report of his studies has been preserved, along with the method of grading; the grades of scholarship numbered from 1 to 7, 1 indicating the lowest and 7 the highest mark. Each report shows a mark of 7 for every course of study and deportment, except the course in speaking which was a 6. Walter's minus in speaking ability is both significant and prophetic. His strength, like Jefferson's, was independent of oratory.

Walter, while yet a child, became interested in Napoleon Bonaparte and wrote an essay on him. When he was twelve years old he wrote an essay on "Hope," which contained phrases of the boy foreshadowing the philosophy of the man to be: "When in the hour of adversity everything else is gone, friends, kindred, property, all—throw everything into the scales, soul and head, and abide the results and be a man. Give fair play to enemies and leave no stone unturned that may further your cause, and in a good cause, such a man, with such resolution, never failed."

It was customary in those days for the oldest son of families that could afford it to have a body servant, and Walter's father in 1859 purchased a Negro boy two years older than Walter to attend and wait on him. The receipt for the purchase price is indicative of the times, and the price paid shows how highly the boy was regarded:

> "Received of David Clark Nine Hundred & Fifty Dollars in full for negro boy Neverson, aged about fifteen years. I warrant said boy sound in body & mind & the title good this October 29th, 1859.
>
> "Levi Howell"
>
> "Witness:
> "Wm. G. Biggs"

The summer of 1860 was a happy one for the Clark family, and particularly for Walter, who, accompanied by his ever faithful Neverson, with fishing poles and a can of worms, often invaded the Roanoke; with guns these two roamed the fields and woods for wild turkey, deer, quail, squirrel; and on horseback they rode to fox hounds; and later together they rode away to battle.

CHAPTER III

A CHANGED WORLD

> "New occasions teach new duties;
> Time makes ancient good uncouth;
> They must upward still, and onward,
> Who would keep abreast of truth." —Lowell

WHEN THE HOME at Ventosa was burned, General Clark took his family to their summer cottage at Airlie. Here Major Clark found them; but, as he had feared, the demands of army life had been too great a tax on his father's health, and, added to this, an attack of camp fever had left him a physical wreck. General Clark had been a proud man, but now with his health ruined, his fortune gone, his home destroyed, and his hopes blasted, he welcomed surrendering all that was left to his adored son.

Walter, then only eighteen, became the head of the family and accepted the responsibility of supporting it from the earnings of a five-thousand-acre abandoned farm.

After the emancipation proclamation most of the Negroes had quit work and left the plantation; they were now roaming aimlessly around the country. Walter was confronted with a major problem, a common one which was staggering the wisest and most experienced men throughout the South. It was not only the problem of reconstruction; for him it was the task of providing food and clothing for his invalid father, his mother, and eight younger brothers and sisters.

With a determination and courage equal to that which he had repeatedly displayed upon the battlefield, young Clark faced the facts and finally mastered the situation by rehabilitating the plantation and keeping the family together. He performed this task so well that his parents, as long as they lived, and his brothers and sisters afterwards, insisted that he should continue to supervise and manage the plantation, which he did continuously for fifty years, until his death. One of the most impressive facts in Clark's long career was his ability to do so many things at one time and do them all skilfully and well. This trait of character, appearing in his early youth and continuing throughout his entire life, elicited repeated expressions of amazement from his contemporaries, admirers and critics alike. Although not physically robust he apparently never tired, and his recreation and diversion consisted in turning from one difficult job to another one equally arduous.

Near the close of the war General Clark gave his son a large plantation, known as Riverside, near New Bern, and he undertook the management and control of this in addition to the Ventosa plantation. For several years Walter kept a diary in which he briefly recorded his movements and the happenings from day to day. This diary is interesting and illuminating, reflecting a strenuous and varied life. There were no railroad connections between the two plantations one hundred and fifty miles apart, and he records traveling back and forth between them, sometimes on horseback and sometimes partly by train and by boat. On several occasions while traveling on horseback he became lost and spent the night in the woods without shelter, and once he rode his horse into a swollen stream, where both were nearly drowned.

On both estates he undertook the task of rebuilding the destroyed barns and houses and collecting laborers to till the soil, even though the crop year of 1865 was already far advanced. All this required the expenditure of money, and he had none. His diary discloses that he met this problem by establishing connections with commission merchants in Norfolk and Baltimore, through whom he secured supplies for his laborers and food for his livestock, pledging as security the products of the two plantations. He kept an itemized account of all receipts and disbursements, now and then noting a loan of cash from his uncles, Colin and Ed. He recounts buying young mules and trading in old, worn-out ones, left as useless by the Yankee invaders. He also had his labor problems, which were far more baffling than the question of whether an employee shall work forty or forty-eight hours a week. With the exception of a few old and dependable family servants the former slaves were thoroughly confused. These Negroes were being deceived by the report that Lincoln had promised to give each family a mule and forty acres of land and that they as free citizens would not have to work for anyone. Thus demoralized and imbued with false hopes, they staged the first great "sit down strike." In an effort to secure dependable labor for the plantation, Clark visited Raleigh, Baltimore, and even New York, but with little success.

The scope of his education was increasing and his interests multiplying. His convictions were forming into a philosophy based on the belief that a new order was at hand and that the public welfare demanded a changed attitude on the part of the ruling classes, very different from that which had dominated the old South.

In December, 1865, he contributed to the *Raleigh Sentinel* two communications which show that he fully appreciated the seriousness of the problems confronting him and his fellow countrymen and that he had no illusions about how they should be solved. His appraisal of the past and his prophecy for the future evinced a striking maturity of mind and a clarity of judgment remarkable for a youth still in his teens. On December 2 he wrote:

"The picture of abandoned farms, stagnated business, a dejected people and open lawlessness is fearful to contemplate. Gentlemen may go to Raleigh and legislate, but what does their collective wisdom amount to if the plow stands still in the furrow and the anvil rests on its block? We are told that the state is suffering from want of capital. How then do you propose to get it? It is out of the ground that our capital must come. We must rid ourselves of the dead body of slavery, and with it dispose of the perplexing problems of negro suffrage and negro equality forever. We have fertile lands, navigable rivers, inexhaustible mines, and a brave and generous people. We need labor to develop these resources and improve our advantages. To do this, however, the labor must be dependable. The conduct of the newly emancipated freedmen is a problem yet to be solved by the future. The prosperity of a great state should not depend upon a contingency.

"The 'peculiar institution' (slavery) has indeed been a curse to the country that gave it domicile and to the land that has witnessed its sudden extinction. Our magnificent country is unimproved, our factories unbuilt, our wants supplied from without, and the South, like the sun upon Gibeon, has stood still in the onward race. We must encourage energy and industry. *Our people are indolent.* This is our besetting sin. It is work, **WORK, WORK** that we need. This is the great panacea for all the ills that society is heir to. This will efface the ravages of war, suppress crime, organize and consolidate society, and cover our fields with harvests."

On December 12, in an article signed "L'Orient," he wrote: "While slavery existed the brain was cudgeled and reason was put to the rack to convince our people that the prosperity of the South depended upon its future maintenance. The hidden leaf in the book of fate has at last been turned, and there in unmistakable characters the doom of slavery has been written by the hand of destiny."

Clark pointed out that if the resolution for the abolition of slavery introduced in the Virginia and Kentucky legislatures in 1831 and 1832 had not been defeated by the menacing tide of fanaticism, our own interests would have long since led us to abolish a system which is "at variance with the spirit of our institutions and the genius of the age and has been fraught with the most baneful effects."

He strongly urged the importation of free white labor and advocated the industrial development of the state, saying: "The broad fertile fields, unexplored mines, unimproved waterpower and dwarf cities of North Carolina are imperiously calling for the influx of population."

The spirit of the reformer was stirring in this ambitious youth of nineteen. He presumed to criticize the antebellum system of buying up immense tracts of land to provide for the increase of Negroes, a practice which now resulted in the ownership by prominent families in the state of five or six times as much land as could be worked by the labor available. Such lands, he maintained, had been rendered worthless to the owners and to everyone else through the abolition of slavery, and these conditions were driving the industrial part of the population to seek more congenial homes in other states. "Our legislature now in session at the capitol would do well to consider this matter, and by laying a heavy tax on all unimproved land either force the proprietors to make them productive of some good to the country at large, or part with them to those who will. The state has too long suffered herself to be drained of her wealth and population by this narrow-minded policy."

Such views foreshadowed the reasoning of Henry George and the measures employed half a century later by Lloyd George, while Prime Minister of England, to break up great landed estates.

During this period Clark was as busy as a shifting-engine, but he was succeeding at a task that was appalling to his elders, and he enjoyed it. His diary discloses a strong family attachment; he records visiting the homes of his many kinspeople, especially frequent visits to Albin, indicating the growing attachment which existed between him and his Uncle Colin. In later years he spoke of this uncle as one of the ablest men he had ever known. During these visits he made free use of his uncle's extensive library, which was regarded as one of the best in the state.

As we have seen, at seventeen he completed the law course at the University of North Carolina under Judge Battle and was entitled, but for his minority, to receive his license to practice law in the county courts. In August, 1866, after the crops were laid by, he determined to pursue further the study of law, since he was still too young to be licensed to practice. He confided to his father and mother that he was going North to study so that he might improve his general knowledge and "see how the Yankees did it." The first recorded mention of this subject occurs in his diary in 1866: "Rode down to Prospect Hill; saw Uncle Ed about money to go to New York." He left home the next day, stopping off in Norfolk to see his commission merchants on business connected with the plantations. From there he went to Washington to consult a physician both about his eyes and about the malaria from which he had seriously suffered. Upon arriving in New York he found no law school open; so he entered the law offices of Weeks and Foster, 58 Wall Street, and began the study of law. He also enrolled as a night student in the Bryan & Statton Commercial College, later securing a diploma from that institution. While in New York, his diary records, after office hours he often visited the libraries and museums, and he called upon the French Consul. Each Sunday he attended a different church, the Catholic, Presbyterian, Baptist, Methodist, and Episcopal.

Learning that the Columbian Law School at Washington was open, he decided to go there, and in a few months he completed its law course. He seems to have had an insatiable desire for all kinds of knowledge; while in Washington he spent hours in the Congressional Library, and he called on numerous statesmen, including the despised Thaddeus Stevens. During the months when he was carrying on his law studies, he communicated frequently with newspapers in North Carolina, and in one article he sought to encourage the people of the South, imparting to them some of his concepts, ideals, and enthusiasm: "True, however, to the republican faith of our ancestors, we cannot but believe that the masses of the people mean well. They may be mistaken; they may be deceived; they may be misled by designing and unprincipled leaders, but sooner or later the popular mind will discover the truth and the great popular heart will throb in unison to the true principles of liberty and right. For the present, however, the will of the predominating section, and with that the policy of the government, has been unmistakably settled. The only course, then, for the South is to develop her resources, encourage immigration, and bide her time." The influence of Jefferson's teachings is here reflected, and Clark thus early espouses the doctrine of popular government and expresses a belief in the ultimate composite wisdom of the people.

During all of this time he personally handled the financial accounts for both Ventosa and Riverside plantations, but he also found time to do an almost unbelievable amount of collateral reading. A memorandum attached to his diary records a list of the books read by him during the year 1866: *"Life of Douglas; Reminiscences of Lord Holland; Letters of Junius; Battlefields of the Revolution; Maxims of Napoleon; Review of Burns' Poems;* three volumes of *Peloponnesian Wars; Recueil Choisi Oissian;* four volumes of *Gil Blas; Lancelot Greaves;* first four volumes of *Don Quixote; Paradise Lost; Paradise Regained; Milton's Other Poems; Lives of Southern Generals;* ten volumes of the *Spectator;* Stevens on *Pleadings and Commercial Law; Life of Napoleon and his Errors; Fifteen Decisive Battles of the World; Chitty on Pleadings; Lewellyn's Nisi Prius; Smith on Contracts; Greenleaf on Evidence; Adams' Doctrine of Equity; Dean's Commercial Law; Blackstone's Commentaries; Fern on Remainders; In Vinculis; Party Leaders; Storey on Partnership;* and the *Life of Marion."*

While he was in Washington, his Uncle Colin placed with him for collection a claim for $25,000 against the Government on account of cotton confiscated during the last year of the war. He also handled at that time a claim of his father on account of the destruction of his two Roanoke River boats.

On the last day of December his diary records that he had paid off all of his hands, and concludes: "On review of the year, I have much cause to be thankful. The Lord be praised for His manifold mercies. May He remember not my iniquities against me on that great and final day of settlement."

In January, 1867, though not yet twenty-one he was admitted to the practice of law in the county courts of Halifax and opened his office in Scotland Neck. Upon coming of age he was licensed by the Supreme Court as a full-fledged lawyer, and his diary and the records disclose that he was soon employed as counsel in important cases and engaged actively in the practice of both civil and criminal law. His practice increased, and after two years' residence in Scotland Neck, he moved his office to the county seat at Halifax and formed a partnership under the firm name of Clark & Mullen, which did an extensive law practice in Halifax and adjoining counties.

By blood and marriage Clark was connected with most of the great families of northeastern Carolina, notably the Johnstons, Blounts, Grays, Norfleets, McKenzies, Hilliards, Davises, Smiths, Alstons, Williamses, and Ruffins. One line of his ancestors was connected with the Bryans of Virginia, the same family from which William Jennings Bryan descended.

It is estimated that at this time Clark had one hundred and thirty cousins living in that section of the state, many of whom had important business matters which they confided to his care. Later, when his Uncle Colin died, the widow qualified as executrix of her husband's large estate and she employed Clark as her counsellor and business adviser. At Halifax he built a commodious brick law office fronting on the court green, as was customary in those days, which is still standing and is still in use. He took an active part in the public affairs of the county and became locally prominent in politics; he was twice nominated for the legislature but, on account of the Negro vote, was defeated. He was made chairman of the judiciary committee for his district, composed of Halifax and a number of other counties.

After beginning the practice of law, he sold his Riverside plantation but continued to manage Ventosa, which was about twenty-five miles from his office at Halifax. He kept a pair of fine driving horses and used them in going to and from the farm and in his practice of law throughout that section.

In 1870 Clark became disturbed about the action of the legislature in not properly supporting the State University and wrote an open letter to the *Raleigh Sentinel* in which he made clear his views with respect to the importance of education and the necessity of the state's supporting both the University and the common schools: "The cause of learning is the cause of civilization. Should North Carolina neglect her University she cannot be expected to provide for her common schools. The plea now abroad to excuse neglect of the one can as easily be urged for the abolition of the other." Here we see advanced the thought that the University is the natural head of the state's school system.

These and other manifestations by Clark of an aggressive aptitude for reform, together with his bold criticism of the old order, aroused resentment on the part of those who had been unable to adjust themselves to the new order. In 1871 he wrote a letter to the *Roanoke News,* signed "Notes By the Way," dealing with the faults and shortcomings of the unreconstructed. It gave offense to one of the old-timers, H. P. Pugh, who answered it with a publication in the *Norfolk Journal,* signed "Veritas," in which he reflected upon the author of "Notes By the Way." Clark resented this article and demanded of Pugh an apology, which was refused, and there followed a challenge by Clark to a personal duel. Dueling was unlawful in North Carolina, but it was permitted in the adjoining states of Virginia and South Carolina. The following correspondence between Clark and Pugh was later published:

>Scotland Neck, Halifax Co., N. C.
>November 18, 1871.

Sir:

I beg leave to inform you that I wrote the letters in the Roanoke News over the signature of "Notes By the Way." I respectfully desire to know if you wrote the article signed "Veritas," which appeared in the Norfolk Journal of the 14th inst., and if in that article you intended in any respect to reflect upon my character as a gentleman.

This note will be handed you by my friend, Capt. W. H. Day.

>Yours respectfully,
>WALTER CLARK.

To H. P. Pugh, Esq.,
Hotel, N. C.

>Hotel, Bertie County, N. C.
>November 19, 1871.

Walter Clark, Esq.
Sir:

I received your note this morning desiring to know whether I was the author of the article over the signature of "Veritas." I am. Of your character I know nothing. I care to know nothing. If you take any exceptions you can do so.

>Respectfully,
>H. P. PUGH.

This will be handed you by my friend, W. E. Savage.

>Scotland Neck, N. C.
>November 19, 1871.

Sir:

Your note of this date is received. I beg leave to request that you will meet me at your earliest convenience, at such point in Virginia or South Carolina as you may designate.

>Very respectfully,
>WALTER CLARK.

H. P. Pugh, Esq.,
Hotel, N. C.

Hotel, Bertie Co., N. C.
November 19.

Walter Clark, Esq.,

Sir:

I will meet you at Fair Bluffs, South Carolina, on December 8th.
This will be handed you by my friend W. E. Savage, Esq.

Respectfully

H. P. PUGH.

Scotland Neck, N. C.
November 20, 1871.

Sir:

I have to acknowledge yours of yesterday, appointing Fair Bluffs, South Carolina, and December 8th, as time and place of meeting.
My friend, Capt. W. H. Day, will arrange the particulars of the meeting with any one you may select to act for you.

Respectfully,

WALTER CLARK.

H. P. Pugh, Esq.,
Hotel, N. C.

Hotel, N. C. Nov. 22, 1871.

Sir:

In reading your first note I misconstrued the tenor of it, as I was very much excited about other matters at the time, and did not give it due deliberation. I considered it altogether in a different light then from what I do now, after my friend, Col. W. E. Savage, and I have read it over and sifted the matter thoroughly between ourselves. The article in the Norfolk Journal was intended in no wise to reflect upon your private character. I only attacked it as I would any other public paper or correspondent of a public paper.

Respectfully,

H. P. PUGH.

To Col. Walter Clark.

                                            Scotland Neck, N. C.
                                            November 23, 1871.
Sir:
Your note of the 22d instant is received. I beg leave to say that your disclaimer of any intention to reflect upon my character as a gentleman in the article signed "Veritas" comes late, but it is satisfactory.
I have the honor to be, very respectfully your obedient servant,
                         WALTER CLARK.
To H. P. Pugh

In the years that followed, Clark was to be involved in several bitter conflicts where passions ran high, but it is not recorded that there was ever again any challenging to a duel.

Captain W. H. Day, who acted as Clark's second in the threatened conflict, was a lifelong personal friend; they had served together in the Confederate Army. In later years, as we shall see, they were to meet on a political battlefield, arrayed against each other, and the resulting breach in their friendship was deeply regretted by both.

Notwithstanding Clark's youth, his talents seem to have attracted the attention of his elders and impressed them with his business capacity. In 1869 the University of North Carolina conferred upon him the degree of Master of Arts. As early as 1870 he was elected director of the Raleigh and Gaston Railroad, and two years later was sent to Atlanta by the Governor as a delegate to a convention of southern representatives who were considering the construction of the Atlantic and Great Western Canal. The Governor also appointed him honorary commissioner for the state to the International Exposition at Vienna and colonel on his staff.

In Clark's diary repeated mention is made of arguing cases before the State Supreme Court; at one term he argued five cases, two of his own and three for other lawyers. He appreciated the high compliment of being employed by older practitioners to argue their cases before the State Supreme Court.

CHAPTER IV

LOVE, LAW, AND LABOR

"All brave men love; for he only is brave who has affections to fight for, whether in the daily battle of life or in physical contest." —Hawthorne

"Go up to Company Shops [Burlington] today to the Tournament—go for the purpose of seeing Miss Sudie Graham."

Company Shops, mentioned in this diary entry was about one hundred and fifty miles away, and a day's journey, but Miss Sudie was calling, and the business of law and plantation must wait.

Walter Clark was then twenty-five years old, no longer "Little Clark" but a man five feet eight inches tall, weighing one hundred and seventy pounds, with the manners of a Chesterfield and the attire of a Beau Brummel. The contempt which he at seventeen expressed in a letter to his mother for the sentimental passions of love had long since been forgotten, and he was on his way to an unconditional surrender to a lovely member of that "weaker sex," which in his youthful arrogance he had scorned. He had many friends among the girls of his acquaintance and enjoyed being with them, but he seems never to have had a serious love affair until he met the winsome Susan Washington Graham.

The tournament at which he was to meet her was a contest between expert horsemen in a game which had originated in England centuries ago and had long prevailed in the South. It afforded an opportunity for the display of well-bred horses and skill on the part of the riders. It was made colorful by the regalia of the contestants, each of whom was panoplied in striking attire to represent some ancient knight-errant.

These tournaments were proverbially festive occasions which drew immense crowds from far and near. Lovers of fine horses and beautiful women met at the tournament to make it a gala day. The contest was usually held about midday, with bands playing and crowds cheering. The course to be run by the horsemen was about 400 yards long on a straight track. Along and near the side of the track were planted three upright posts fifteen feet high, spaced about one hundred yards apart, and from the top of each upright post a bar was extended at right angles, giving the appearance of an inverted "L." To the end of the bar a large leather cord was attached so that it hung down immediately over the center of the course where the horsemen ran, and fastened to the end of each cord was a small hook on which a ring about two and one-half inches in diameter was loosely hung. The length of the cord was so arranged that each ring came about even with the shoulders of the mounted horsemen as they rode by, and the riders were furnished lances about ten feet long tapered to a point at one end. The sportsmanship and the excitement of the contest consisted in each rider's running his horse at full speed along the entire course, and, while guiding his mount with his left hand, carrying the lance in his right, so evenly balanced and accurately aimed as to run the point of the lance through each ring as he approached it. Some riders were so expert that they were able to collect all three rings a number of times in succession. As one after another of the riders failed to get all the rings, each dropped out of the contest until the surviving knight was declared King of the Tournament. Every girl in attendance hoped that her favored knight would win the tournament and crown her queen. The selection and crowning of the queen was attended with pomp and ceremony, and was followed by a supper and dance.

Susan, the only daughter of Governor William A. Graham, of Hillsboro, North Carolina, was born in Washington, D. C., while her father was Secretary of the Navy. She received her early education at Misses Nash and Pollock's Female School at Hillsboro, and later attended Madame Roustan's French School in New

York City. Susan was a favorite of her father, who took pains to direct her education; his official position, too, gave her an opportunity to meet the most prominent men and women of the times. Governor Graham was the political idol of the people of the state. They elected him speaker of the House of Representatives, governor of the state, United States senator, Confederate States senator, and after the war again elected him to the United States Senate, but he, along with other Southern senators, was not allowed to take his seat. In 1852 he was nominated for vice president of the United States on the Whig ticket. Susan's mother, Susannah Sarah Washington, was a blood relative of George Washington.

The romance between Walter and Susan, which began at the tournament, resulted in an ardent courtship lasting three years. In his diary Walter mentions frequent visits to see "Miss Sudie" at her home in Hillsboro, and tells of catching midnight freight trains on his return trips.

Clark had become a director and general counsel for North Carolina of the Raleigh and Gaston and the Raleigh and Augusta railroads, and later of the Seaboard Air Line when these roads were merged, and this employment made it more convenient for him to live in Raleigh. Susan preferred the capital as a home, for she had relatives and friends there; consequently, a few months before their marriage in January, 1874, Clark moved to Raleigh. The Clarks had a comfortable but inexpensive home in the capital city, where they entertained their many friends and reared their growing family. Both Clark and his wife were fond of children and eight were born of this union, five boys and three girls—Susan Washington, David, William A. Graham, Anna M., who died in infancy, Walter, John Washington, Thorne McKenzie, and Eugenia Graham.

Busy as he always was, the father found time to help the youngsters, as they came along, with their lessons, while the mother took pains with their religious instruction. A Sunday afternoon custom grew up at the Clark home; the neighborhood children would gather to play on the lawn and later would go into the house, where Mrs. Clark would read them a chapter in the Bible. Frequently, Clark would take the boys for a long ramble through the countryside, ending at the old swimming hole on Crabtree Creek some miles away. Occasionally these jaunts included a visit to the place where Ellis Camp had been located, and he would tell them of his experiences there as a boy when he was drill master, and other thrilling stories of the war.

Mutual affection and intellectual companionship characterized the Clarks' home life. In religion they differed in name only, she a Baptist and he a Methodist. Fortunately for him, his wife was fond of reading and studying, keeping abreast of the times and encouraging him in his struggle for liberal reforms. This adventure in love remained fresh and unimpaired until her death in 1909. When the time came for him to join her, he requested his children to take their love letters from his lock box, where he had kept them all these years, and place them beside him in his casket. His wishes were carried out.

2

Clark's life in the capital city from the beginning was characterized by incessant work in many directions. He wasted no time on frivolous amusements, and he had not a single hobby. His capacity for sustained intellectual labor over long hours every day except Sundays set him apart from his fellows. He early discovered that to labor efficiently one should have up-to-date implements, and this led him to purchase the first typewriter that was ever owned in Raleigh and to assemble the most complete legal library owned by a practicing lawyer in the state. Later when be became superior court judge he was frequently requested by other judges holding court at the capitol to leave the key to his library with the clerk of the court so that they might have the benefit of it.

He was barely settled in Raleigh before he got printer's ink on his fingers; he induced Governor Holt to become associated with him in purchasing control of the *Raleigh News,* a daily newspaper which he managed and directed for a number of years. He put new life into this publication, advocated numerous reforms in government which attracted public attention, and, what proved to be equally important for his future, became a favorite with the newspaper guild. Soon after removing to Raleigh he was elected a member of the Democratic State Executive Committee and continued in this position until 1885, when he was appointed judge.

His newspaper soon attained political importance, and his editorials cracked like a new saddle. He made considerable reputation by a series of letters which he wrote for his paper, known as the "mudcut letters," criticizing an improvident legislature for embarking the state on an expensive and wasteful undertaking in extending the Western North Carolina Railroad across the Blue Ridge Mountains. Large sums had been expended upon the project, and the work had bogged down from serious mud slides which had been encountered in getting across the mountains. Clark advocated the sale of the road to a railroad company. Such a company, he asserted, could construct the road more cheaply and with great savings to the state. His agitation was an important factor in determining the outcome—the calling of a special session of the General Assembly in 1880, which sold the unfinished road to private interests. Later it was completed by these interests.

For the next ten years Clark was very busy in many ways, and his restless mind was working like a ten-day clock. In addition to his exacting law practice he wrote and annotated *Clark's Code of Civil Procedure,* the first of its kind in the State. This work, involving great labor, was so thoroughly and accurately done that every practicing lawyer in North Carolina found it necessary to have a copy, and the Supreme Court, in its opinions, cited it with approval. It went into three editions.

When he moved to Raleigh Clark transferred his membership to the Methodist church there and took an active part in its religious work; he prepared an interesting and valuable historical summary of Methodism in North Carolina and was the moving spirit in consolidating all of the Methodist churches of the state into two conferences, the Eastern and the Western. He was several times a delegate of his church to its national conferences, and the College of Bishops of the Southern Methodist Episcopal Church named him in 1881 a lay delegate to the Ecumenical Conference of Methodism which met in London. After attending that conference, in which he took an active part, he traveled extensively through Europe studying economic, social, and political conditions in the countries visited. While abroad he wrote a series of letters to his newspaper, giving an account of his experiences and observations.

A never-ending problem to which he gave thought and time was the cultivation of the Ventosa plantation a hundred miles away. The farmers during this period were finding it hard to "make both ends meet," and absentee landlordship added to Clark's difficulties. The tenants and their families, numbering a hundred and twenty-five, looked to him for direction and aid; and he worked out an arrangement to save them from the curse of the time store system, which imposed upon them the necessity of paying excessive prices for supplies purchased on credit, with heavy interest added. This usually resulted in the creditors' consuming all of the income from the crops at the end of the year to satisfy their exorbitant charges. Such a credit system was so disastrous to Negro tenants that a saying became current among them, that when the accounts were balanced with the merchant at the end of the year it meant,

"Nought's a nought, and a figger's a figger
All for the white man and none for the nigger."

Clark's interest in agriculture drew him close to the farmers of the state, and he sought to improve his and their condition by encouraging the rotation of crops and introducing the use of improved methods of cultivation. His correspondence at this time discloses that he was making inquiries of America's consuls located in England, Germany, and Italy, asking for government publications dealing with agriculture and the improvement of the soil, seeking to secure new seeds, plants, and trees which might be used to advantage in North Carolina. While visiting London he established credit with a bookshop with directions to furnish him desired books, magazines, and papers appearing in England and on the continent.

An incident occurred in 1885 which laid the foundation for one of the most important friendships in Clark's life. He received this message and request from Judge H. G. Connor: "I write you to call to your attention and ask your good offices in the way of kind words, etc. for my young friend, Josephus Daniels, who begins his career as a metropolitan editor." Clark cordially responded to this request and aided Daniels in every way he could. Out of this grew an intimate friendship which continued unabated for twenty-five years. Judge Clark's subsequent able opinions and striking dissenting opinions blazed the pathway for a new order in which both he and Daniels were deeply interested. These deliverances of Clark's were broadly publicized through Daniels' paper, *The News & Observer*. This combination became awesome to the growing power of trusts, railroads, and political machines, while at the same time it gave a definite and able leadership to the advanced liberals in the state. The relationship, so long as it lasted, proved invaluable to both men in many ways.

Clark was by now so well and favorably known throughout the state that political leaders began urging his nomination for attorney general of the state, but this he discouraged. With him lay the choice of continuing a growing, lucrative law practice, entering the political field, or becoming a jurist. He deliberately chose the bench for his life work, which at that time carried the munificent salary of $2,250 a year.

CHAPTER V

COUNTRY JUDGE

> "*It is provided in the essence of things that from any fruition of success, no matter what, shall come forth something to make a greater struggle necessary.*" —Walt Whitman

IN 1885 A VACANCY occurred on the superior court bench, to which Governor Scales, at the request of the Raleigh bar and other prominent lawyers of the state, appointed Clark. He was elected to the position in 1886 and held the office until 1889, when Governor Fowle appointed him to fill a vacancy on the Supreme Court.

The position of superior court judgeship was in some respects the most important office in the state's judicial system. The superior courts had wide and general jurisdiction, including the trial of practically all civil and criminal cases—from carrying concealed weapons to murder. The people regarded this court as their peculiar forum and attended its sittings in great numbers. The judges rotated from one district to another, from the mountains to the sea, so that in a few years each judge held court in most of the counties of the state and became acquainted with the leaders of the bar who regularly practiced in these courts. There were no real cities in the state, and court week in each county was an occasion looked forward to when people from the countryside could meet together, discuss their neighborhood problems, and "swap horses and lies." The patent medicine vender with his jokes, "Cheap John" with his wares, and the venders of ginger cakes and cider were always in attendance.

A custom had long prevailed for the judge to deliver a charge to the grand jury on the opening of court, and the citizens from the remotest sections attended to hear these charges, which embraced a dissertation upon the criminal law, duties of citizenship,

Charles Farrell

The Roanoke River. A view from the old pier site at Ventosa, from which the river boats operated.

Upper left, a present-day onlooker at Ventosa; upper right, a descendant of slave days living as a tenant on Ventosa plantation. Below, these cabins, still standing, illustrate the arrangement and construction of a section of the slave quarters at Ventosa, which were destroyed by fire. Photos by Charles Farrell.

and obligations to the state. The charge offered free range for the judge to display his learning and views upon government and society, and Judge Clark took advantage of it. The daily and weekly press soon began publishing his wise sayings, applauding the ability and dispatch with which he conducted his courts. Up to his time the judges and practicing attorneys had treated "court week" as something of a social affair. In the evenings they would gather for a sociable time around the bottle, usually winding up with a game of poker. These diversions sometimes lasted into the wee small hours of the night, and as a result judge and lawyers were often late the next morning for the opening of court.

Judge Clark rudely disturbed this ancient and honorable custom by indicating a preference for a good book rather than a bottle and declining to enter a game of poker. Each morning at 9:30, on the minute, he opened the court for business and called the calendar of cases for trial. If lawyers, litigants, or witnesses were not present and ready to proceed, their cases were dismissed; tardy jurors and witnesses were fined, and absent counsel found their cases out of court when, an hour later, they appeared with flimsy excuses for their absence.

Many of the county seats in the state were located long distances from the railroad, and this necessitated a horse-and-buggy trip over unimproved roads to reach the courts. It was a trying ordeal and most of the judges, after finishing one court, leisurely traveled to the next county; sometimes they arrived as late as Tuesday or Wednesday the following week, although court was due to open Monday morning. These delays entailed heavy costs upon the counties and litigants, since jurors, witnesses, and other interested parties had no way of knowing when the judge would arrive. Judge Clark ordered the county commissioners in each county in which he held court to place a clock upon the walls of the courtroom so that all might know the time. The canard was circulated that he once fined himself for not opening court on time. In his papers, however, there is a memorandum noting that he never fined himself for being late because during his four and one-half years' service as superior court judge he was never absent a day or late a minute in opening court. Years afterward, Governor Glenn wrote him, recalling a trip which they took together from Winston-Salem to Dobson, the county seat of Surry, driving all Sunday night so that the Judge could open court Monday morning at 9:30; they arrived drenched with rain, but the Judge opened his court on time and remained upon the bench until the noon hour without breakfast or change of clothes.

Judge Clark was even-tempered and courteous, but intolerant of slovenly practice and needless delay. So long as there was business to be done he kept his court open and remained to clear the docket wherever possible. In the enforcement of the criminal laws he was a terror to evil-doers. White and black, rich and poor fared alike in his court. His reputation preceded him from county to county. Some of the lawyers criticized him (always behind his back) but the people applauded. During a session of his court at Greensboro an unusual circumstance occurred. Two of the most eminent lawyers of the state—ex-Judges Schenck and Ruffin —who were engaged on opposite sides in the trial of an important case, became involved in a violent dispute which threatened a personal encounter. The Judge ordered them to take their seats, and when they did not heed him he attached them both for contempt of court and imposed on each a fine of one hundred dollars. Decorum restored, they started to proceed with the trial of the case, whereupon the Judge announced, "No, gentlemen, you cannot proceed until the fine is paid."

One of the most sensational cases handled by him during his career as superior court judge was the one tried in the state's capital. A man by the name of Miller was indicted for maintaining a gaming house on the main street of Raleigh. His saloon and game rooms were located next to the Yarborough House, where all the visiting statesmen and members of the legislature gathered, as well as attorneys appearing before the Supreme Court. Here

Yarborough House colonels were made, legislation drafted, and party candidates for office agreed upon. A connecting door opened from the hotel lobby into Miller's saloon, where convivial spirits met and lingered, the proprietor becoming personally acquainted with the great and near-great of the state. Gambling games in this anteroom had been played among gentlemen for years without police disturbance, and the place had become notorious for wild parties. Clark, in his charge to the grand jury, told them that it was unlawful in North Carolina to maintain a gambling house and that it was their duty to indict all such offenders. They took his seriously, and indicted Miller. When the case was called for trial, able counsel for defense, by agreement with the solicitor for the state, entered a plea of guilty to one count in the indictment, assuming that the court would, as was customary in such cases, impose a small fine. To their amazement, the court directed the solicitor to present his evidence, which showed a long and continuous violation of law and revealed that Miller had accumulated considerable wealth from the operations of his gambling house. Calmly, Judge Clark did the unusual—he entered his findings of fact upon the court's record and pronounced his judgment: "Two thousand dollars fine and thirty days in prison." The press of the state heralded it as a triumph of justice, a vindication of law, and the Judge was praised in editorials, telegrams, and letters.

Clark's experience as a trial judge had its humorous side also. Once while holding court in a rural mountain county, a number of lawyers and others attendant upon the court were having a party in the courtroom one night, since this was the only assembly hall in town; they had a keg of whiskey upon the Judge's stand, and after celebrating until late in the night they decided to have a committee call on the Judge and invite him to make a speech. The committee found him asleep; they got him out of bed and insisted that he accompany them to the courtroom. He, good-naturedly, took in the situation, ascended the Judge's stand and told them he was delighted to see them so happy and having such a good time. He begged that they excuse him from taking a drink, but assured them they were free to use the courtroom and continue the party as long as they liked, since he would not need it until the next morning at nine-thirty. The crowd was so pleased that they adopted a resolution thanking him for coming, excused him from making a speech, and had a committee escort him back to his room.

He enjoyed a good story and was amused at the one told on "Colonel" Watlington, an inoffensive ex-Confederate soldier who spent most of his time following the sittings of the court from county to county, sponging on his friends for board and lodging. The story went the rounds that Colonel Watlington was fishing one day on a stream near a railroad track; a passing train struck a bull that was crossing the track near by, throwing him on the Colonel, precipitating both the Colonel and the bull into the creek. Colonel Watlington sued the railroad for damages, but the court held that his suit had been improperly brought—that he should have sued the bull instead of the railroad.

The Judge's poise and self-restraint were put to the test in a case tried before him in Charlotte. A woman who was being prosecuted for keeping a bawdy house, took the witness stand in her own behalf, and Judge Osborne, the Solicitor, began asking her embarrassing questions. She became irritated and asserted that "it is none of your damned business." The Judge said to her that the question was a proper one and told her to answer it, whereupon, in a fury, she turned upon him. "You bald-headed son of a bitch, what have you got to do with it?" Without batting an eye and with perfect composure, the Judge directed the clerk of the court to make the entry that the witness was guilty of contempt of court and ordered that she be confined in the common jail for ten days. "Mr. Sheriff," said he, "take her from the courtroom. Mr. Solicitor, call your next case."

Fifty years have elapsed since Clark was judge of the superior court, but there still remain with the bar and among the older citizens traditions of how ably he conducted his courts and made the lawyers work. It is recounted that without the aid of a statute or rule of court he would save hours of time by suggesting to lawyers in the presence of the jury that they agree upon the number of speeches to be made and limit the length of their arguments. This mild intimation usually had the desired effect. A statute has since been enacted empowering the presiding judge in certain cases to limit arguments to the jury. England had already adopted a much saner system in this respect than even yet obtains in America. In 1899 a vacancy occurred on the Supreme Court. Governor Fowle, on account of Clark's great reputation as a superior court judge, gave him the appointment.

As the nominating convention for Supreme Court judges approached, friends of McRae, another superior court judge, brought his name forward for the vacancy to which Clark had been appointed by the Governor. A spirited contest was in the making when an anonymous circular was distributed over the state charging that Governor Fowle and Clark had made a deal in 1888, whereby Clark agreed not to allow his friends to press his name for the nomination for governor in competition with Fowle. The circular charged that the two had agreed that if Fowle became governor he would appoint Clark to the first vacancy occurring on the Supreme Court. Color was given to this charge by the fact that a strong movement had been on foot throughout the state to nominate Clark for governor in 1888, but he had written an open letter announcing that he did not care to be a candidate, since he preferred to remain on the bench. Judge McRae, as soon as the anonymous circular appeared, wrote Clark that he knew the charges were false, and that his own name would be immediately withdrawn lest it be construed as a reflection upon Clark and the Governor, and this he would not be a party to. Clark was unanimously nominated and elected for four years to fill out the remainder of the unexpired term to which he had been appointed.

CHAPTER VI
PREMIER JURIST

"Justice is truth in action."—Joubert

WHEN CLARK became an associate justice of the Supreme Court he was just forty-three, the youngest member of the bench of five judges, in perfect health and known to be a glutton for work. For the next thirty years, except for rare instances of sickness and two deaths in the family, he was not to miss a single session of the court or to be late a minute from the bench when it convened for business.

Clark's personal appearance gave the impression of power and poise. He stood erect; he was stockily built, with piercing steel-gray eyes, high forehead, well-shaped head, a mustache and small goatee. When approached he looked one straight in the eye, replying in an agreeable manner. He had a pleasant smile and a sense of humor; yet his innate dignity and reserve did not encourage familiarity. He was always gracious and considerate in personal intercourse and never lost his temper or became garrulous in argument. His personal habits were as orderly and as well disciplined as his mental operations; he ate prudently and never drank or smoked. He had many friends but few intimates; most of his friendships grew out of a common interest and devotion to causes.

Clark brought to the Court not only a trained and cultivated mind, but also five years' experience in the actual trial of cases in the superior courts. He had a disdain for the inexcusable delays of the law, the inadequacy of the rules of Court governing their proceedings, and the failure of the older lawyers and judges to administer the Code of Civil Procedure in its true spirit. His subsequent career upon the bench demonstrated that he regarded the

Code of Civil Procedure as the legislative declaration against the rigidity of the old common law, and an adaptation by the people of the principle of obtaining reforms in the law and procedure by legislative enactment rather than by reliance upon the judges to make the law. In one of his earliest opinions he wrote: "The 'law's delay' is assigned by Hamlet as one of the great evils of life, and the barons at Runnymede thought it so great a one that they exacted the insertion of a guarantee against it in Magna Charta—a guarantee which has been copied into the Constitution probably of every American state and which is to be found in Section 35 of our own Declaration of Rights. This guarantee, so notably won, so carefully retained for so many centuries, and still incorporated into our organic law, that 'justice shall be administered without delay' is not a mere rhetorical flourish—it is a constitutional right."

Clark's insistence throughout his entire judicial career upon efficiency and promptness in the dispatch of business set him apart from most administrators of the law. He induced the Court to permit him to rewrite the rules of practice for the courts, which up to that time had been meagre and, he thought, inadequate. In this undertaking he was so completely successful that a third of a century later, Hoke, his successor as Chief Justice of the Court, in accepting his portrait for the Court, declared: "I am justified in saying that it is due to his great diligence and the methods established by him that the Court has thus far been able to efficiently dispatch its business and keep abreast with its docket."

All of the other judges, while men of ability, were distinctly the product of a past age. Their legal education consisted chiefly of a few months at a law school where Blackstone's Commentaries was the chief textbook, or in law offices where little attention was given to the history of jurisprudence. These judges, like most of the older lawyers, had never become completely reconciled to the changes in law and procedure which the Code of Civil Procedure had introduced. To many of them it was anathema because it undid most of what they had been taught, prescribing a different method of procedure, from the manner and time of starting an action, through the trial, and to the Supreme Court to final judgment.

The monumental labor that Clark had put on his Code of Civil Procedure, collecting in one volume all of the statute law and annotating it, had made him the recognized authority in North Carolina upon this subject. The result was that his associates designated him to write most of the opinions of the Court construing and applying the new system of procedure. The importance of this assignment will be appreciated when it is considered that, according to estimates, more than fifty per cent of all the cases sent back by appellate courts to the lower courts for retrial result from some alleged error in not observing the rules of practice and procedure.

No one now questions that Clark vitalized the Code practice in the courts of North Carolina, which did much to speed justice, clear congested dockets, and discourage the bar and judges alike from employing worn-out technicalities which had grown up under the old common-law practice.

It would naturally be expected that a man who so unreservedly put his trust in what Mr. Lincoln called the "common people," who fought their battles against the strong and insisted that they, through legislation, should make the laws rather than the judges, would allow his humanitarian sympathies to influence him as a judge when administering the criminal law. But not so—on the contrary, in his four years' service as trial judge and thirty-five years as Supreme Court justice, there is not a recorded instance in which he ever sacrificed the rights of property in favor of a criminal, little or big, or withheld the penalty of the law for sentimental reasons.

In one of his first dissenting opinions he wrote: "The primary object of the criminal law is not to secure liberty or privilege, but to take them away from those who have shown a contempt of the law by violating it."

In another dissenting opinion, in a capital case, he declared: "It should be borne in mind that a trial for a capital offense is a solemn, serious proceeding, which society has decreed is necessary for its safety and well being. It is not to be approached from the sentimental or humanitarian side. The sole object should be the cold, impartial ascertainment of the facts."

And again: "If the Courts can be tempted to abrogate the law whenever the Judges in any given case think it would bear harshly, then the law would be swallowed up and the courts would become mere boards of arbitration, which are a 'law unto themselves.'"

His inflexible sternness against all violators of the law was so universally recognized that he gained the reputation among some of being the coldest blooded judge on the bench. He began applying his philosophy as a jurist, and wherever the public interest was involved, either in the enforcement of the law or in the advocacy of needed reforms, he was wholly detached from the influence of friends, party, creed, or race. Throughout his strenuous and sometimes stormy career it was never suggested, even by his enemies, that his judgments were unduly influenced by lawyer or litigant, or that it made the slightest difference to him whether they liked his decisions or not.

During the thirty-five years that Clark was to remain on the State Supreme Court bench he wrote 3,235 opinions, nearly a hundred a year. Of these, 182 were concurring, and 371 were dissenting opinions. It had long been a custom among judges on courts of last resort occasionally to write dissenting opinions, briefly assigning their reasons for not concurring with the majority of the court. Clark was the first jurist in America to employ extensively the technique of writing dissenting opinions, bolstering his arguments with documented extra-legal matters, such as government bureau reports, statistics, scientific discoveries, and occasionally reports of American Bar Association committees. This innovation, which two decades later was to be adopted and popularized by Justices Holmes, Brandeis, and Stone of the Supreme Court of the United States, was criticized in Clark. It was even whispered that some of his brethren on the bench complained that such methods were unfair, since it sometimes made the majority of the Court look rather ridiculous in the public mind. Taking note of this in one of his dissents, he stated what he regarded the office of dissenting opinions to be:

"Every dissenting opinion is necessarily a declaration that, in the opinion of the dissenting member of the Court, the law has been erroneously declared by the majority. It is not every time, however, that a Judge who disagrees with the majority is justified in dissenting. The matter should either be of enough importance to justify putting his dissent on record, on the prospect that on some future occasion the Court may change its views, or the matter should be of such a nature that the dissenting Judge deems it in the public interest to point out the injurious consequences which in his judgment will result from the principles laid down in the opinion of the Court. The purpose to be served in filing opinions is to give the reasons actuating the Courts, and this applies as much to dissenting opinions and to opinions on a divided Court as where there is unanimous opinion. If the reasons given cannot be sustained, upon examination, by the bar and by public opinion, as sound, sooner or later the ruling is reversed by the Court itself, or is cured by legislation."

It soon developed that the press and public showed more interest in these dissenting opinions than in the opinions of the Court, and this often resulted in the legislature's changing the law (when such law concerned needed reforms and the public policy of the state), in accordance with Justice Clark's views, or in the Court's adopting his as the better reasoning the next time the question was presented. It is beyond the scope of this book to specify the astonishing number of instances in which his dissenting opinions, by adoption of the Court or through legislation, became the settled law of the land.

The writing of nearly one hundred opinions each year while he was a member of the Court resulted in his handing down more opinions than any other jurist in the United States; yet his restless spirit and inexhaustible energy drove him to labor in other fields—to wage war for overdue reforms in government and society.

In the archives of the North Carolina Historical Commission there are many hundreds of letters of Clark's correspondence, and members of his family still preserve three or four thousand other such letters, which were made available for the preparation of this work. In the University Library at Chapel Hill is to be found a large volume of addresses made by him on various subjects, and there are indexed numerous magazine articles which he contributed to the leading law and public opinion magazines of the nation.

After becoming a Justice of the Supreme Court, outside demands upon his time increased. There were invitations to deliver commencement addresses at the University of North Carolina, Trinity, Wake Forest, Davidson College, and before bar associations in several other states. His learning and erudition were so universally recognized that in 1890 the University of North Carolina conferred upon him the degree of Doctor of Laws, and as early as 1893 the trustees of the University and of Trinity College were both soliciting him to become their president, while Wake Forest law school sought to make him its dean.

Justice Clark manifested great pride in the tradition of his Court and the reputation of his predecessors in office by writing an appreciative history of the Court and its members for *The Green Bag,* a nationally known law magazine, which attracted favorable attention from other like publications. The editors of *The American Law Review* wrote: "We will welcome anything from your pen. Your sketch of the Supreme Court of North Carolina and its judges in *The Green Bag* is very far above the generality of sketches of that kind." The editor of the *Magazine of American History* in New York City asked permission to publish this sketch, saying, "The sketch is of national interest." Clark soon followed this with an extended sketch of North Carolina's great Chief Justice Thomas Ruffin, which was published in *The Green Bag*.

Amid all these multiplied activities Clark, at the request of the state, began the work of compiling and editing, without compensation, the State Records of North Carolina, in sixteen volumes. As a pleasant intellectual diversion, in which his wife, who was an accomplished French scholar, joined, he translated Constant's life of Napoleon from the French, in three volumes.

But with all his engagements he never forgot his first love, the Confederate soldier who was so dear to his heart, and he cheerfully responded to frequent invitations to deliver memorial addresses on the Lost Cause in different parts of the state.

In the field of North Carolina history Clark came to be regarded as a walking encyclopedia. Students and college professors alike wrote him for historical information. A typical example of such letters was one from Dr. George Winston, President of the University of North Carolina, thanking him for some historical matters and adding, "I do not see how you find time for such researches. Truly, we all owe you a deep debt of gratitude."

Among his correspondence are numerous letters from admiring friends, admonishing him not to undermine his health by incessant labor. Among them, Judge David Schenck, division counsel for the Southern Railroad, wrote, warning that he was doing more work than he could possibly bear; that his spirit was stronger than his body, and that the state needed his services too much for him to destroy his health.

2

But this remarkable man still had time to write magazine articles calling specific attention to needed reforms. Two of the most important of these appeared in 1895, one for *The American Law Review* on "The Legal Aspects of the Telegraph and Telephone—Essential Parts of an Efficient Postal Service," and the other in *The Arena* entitled "The Telegraph in England." He advocated the Government's taking over control of the telegraph and telephone system as a part of the postal service. These addresses attracted nation-wide attention and both were republished as a senate document by the Fifty-fourth Congress. He pointed out that the Supreme Court of the United States had held "the power of Congress over the post office and the carrying of the mails to be exclusive"; that "the first telegraph line was built under a 'strict construction' administration (Polk's), and the telegraph belonged to the Government from 1844 to 1847; and when, under mistaken notions of economy, it was then turned over to private ownership, Henry Clay, and Cave Johnson, Postmaster General, were among the public men who went on record as earnestly protesting such a step." In support of his contention Clark quoted a statement of Justice Brown of the United States Supreme Court appearing in *The Forum,* in which he said: "If the Government may be safely entrusted with the transmission of our letters and papers, I see no reason why it may not also be entrusted with the transmission of our telegrams and parcels, as is almost universally the case in Europe."

Clark maintained that this privilege of carrying mail for hire, whether sent by electricity or steam or stage or on horseback, is an exclusive governmental function and no corporation or monopoly can legally exercise any part of it; that it is the duty of the Government to do it and to do it in the quickest and most efficient manner and at the lowest possible rate consistent with the cost. He supported these contentions by citing as an example Great Britain, which had extended the use of the telegraph and telephone as a part of its post office and made an actual profit from its operations instead of incurring a deficit. This was his argument: "With telephones at all country post offices and all villages and the smaller towns, few additional employees would be required, and those few would be added at centers which require the telegraph and where civil service rules obtain. The telephones and telegraph would be put in the post office buildings already owned or rented by the Government, thus saving the rent on all the buildings now used by the private companies" and saving the large salaries to officials of corporations and the dividends on their largely watered stock, which, he prophesied, would result in reducing the tolls to the uniform rate of ten cents per message. He supported these contentions from a report of one of our English consuls: "The service is performed with the most perfect punctuality. It is calculated that the average time employed today in the transmission of a telegram between two commercial cities in England varies from seven to nine minutes, while in 1870 (under private ownership) two to three hours were necessary. The rate of one cent a word includes delivery within the postal limits of any town or within a mile of the post office in the country."

Clark in these articles advanced the contention, which many years later has grown in favor, that utilities by fixing lower rates and extending their service could and would attract the support of a greatly increased number of people, which in turn would yield a revenue more than sufficient to take care of the cost of the extended service. He pointed out that in 1870, under private ownership in England, seven million individual messages and twenty-two million words of press dispatches were sent annually, while the telegraph operated by the post office delivered annually seventy million individual messages and over six hundred million words of press dispatches; that the rates had been reduced so low that every weekly country paper could afford to print the latest telegraphic dispatches as it went to press, and a telephone and a telegraph were now available at every country post office.

He maintained that the existing system was burdensome to the masses, exacting oppressive tolls and a tax levy on knowledge; that it was illegal because it was contrary to the Constitution in that it left this essential function of a modern up-to-date postal service in the hands of private corporations.

By 1894 Clark had made an enviable place for himself on the Court, he enjoyed the complete confidence of the people, and he was gaining national attention. But his term of office was ending that year, and the Democratic party was confronted with a dangerous political situation which threatened to end its control of the state, including the retirement of Clark from the bench. The greatest peace-time political revolution in the history of the state was in the making. It came about in this way: The agrarian unrest and revolt, which had its origin in the Middle West, against both old parties, the Democratic and the Republican, had now swept over the South, including North Carolina, and a national organization resulted, known as the Populist party, which became the movement's mouthpiece. Two of the most conspicuous national leaders of this movement lived in North Carolina: one, Colonel L. L. Polk, editor and owner of a widely circulated publication, *The Progressive Farmer,* and the other, Marion Butler, who was soon to become a United States senator from North Carolina. Both of these men, who had formerly been Democrats, were very able; Polk had long been the friend of the farmers and was deservedly popular among them, while Butler was a great organizer of the discontented and as wily and daring a politician as ever scuttled a political ship. The Populist party in North Carolina had attracted to its banner thousands of farmers who had been lifelong Democrats but were now extremely bitter toward the "Cleveland Democrats," who, as they were told and believed, were the cause of all their woes—particularly 4-cent cotton, the adoption of the Gold Standard, and the unrestrained organization of trusts, monopolies, and combines.

The tobacco farmers of North Carolina were especially resentful of the American Tobacco Company, which had been organized in their midst. Having absorbed or ruthlessly destroyed all competitors, it was, they charged, in the absence of competition, robbing them of their leaf tobacco by fixing the price below the cost of production, while piling up untold millions in profits from its manufacture and sale to the public.

In this situation, when political bitterness and rancor was at its height, the state conventions of all three parties were called to meet in the spring of 1894 at Raleigh to write their platforms and nominate candidates for state offices. The Democratic Convention as a matter of course renominated Clark for an eight-year term on the Supreme Court. Like a clap of thunder out of a political sky, the Populists and Republicans did the totally unexpected—endorsed Clark's nomination, which assured his unanimous election. A few conservative Democrats advised him not to accept the endorsement, but the overwhelming sentiment of his party was that he should do so. Clark sensed the possible embarrassment in the situation and promptly gave out a statement that he had no previous notice of their endorsing him and was not a party to the arrangement. He also consulted the leaders of his party, who, with practical unanimity, advised his acceptance; among them was Senator Simmons, and in the files of Clark's correspondence is a letter from J. P. Caldwell, editor of the conservative *Charlotte Observer,* urging his acceptance and concluding with the statement, "No one can question your democracy."

Reviewed in retrospect it is perfectly understandable why the Populists wanted to have his name on their ticket. In the first place, the rank and file of the Populist party were farmers and Clark, too, was a farmer, who like them was suffering from the ruinous low prices at which farmers were forced to sell their products. And secondly, nearly every member of the party was an ex-Confederate soldier, or a son of one who had worn the gray, and to them the valor and daring of "Little Clark" upon the

Susan Washington Graham, the "Miss Sudie" whom Walter Clark married in January, 1874.

Governor William A. Graham, Mrs. Clark's father; and Susannah Sarah Washington Graham, Mrs. Clark's mother.

Charles Farrell

This tester bed is one of the few things saved when Ventosa mansion was burned. It is still in the possession of a member of the Clark family.

battlefield had enshrined him in their memories as a hero of the Lost Cause. Finally they knew from Clark's opinions and writings that he was just as ardent a progressive as they were and that he subscribed to many of the reforms and demands contained in their Ocala national platform. In truth Clark was more popular with Populist voters than many of its newly selected leaders, and they did not want to see him retired from the bench, while as a practical proposition the leaders did not believe they could defeat him. His unanimous nomination and election under these circumstances made Walter Clark the premier jurist of the state.

3

When the Democrats met in Raleigh in 1896 to nominate a candidate for governor and other state offices, they were more confused and dispirited than at any time since the Carpetbaggers and Negroes had taken charge of the state during Reconstruction days. The Fusion victory in 1894 by which they acquired control of the election machinery and elected both United States senators, plus the growing discontent among the farmers and laborers, was a flaming political danger signal of what was likely to happen in the 1896 election. The stakes were high. A governor, complete state ticket, and most of the county officers were to be elected, which, if the Fusionists were successful, meant a complete sweep of Democratic control in the state from top to bottom.

A number of delegates felt that the wise and smart thing to do was to wean back the Populists by effecting a fusion arrangement which would result in giving them a division of offices, while other delegates insisted that such a course would be ruinous to the morale of the party and hurtful to the state.

Amid this confusion of counsel the convention opened, and after the usual preliminaries, Bob Glenn, a noted political orator, later to become governor of the state, was called on for a speech. Sensing the situation and not knowing whether a majority of the delegates were for or against fusion with the Populists, he threw out a feeler, performing a magnificent political straddle with the opening statement that, coming to the convention, on the train he had talked with many delegates from various sections of the state, all of whom were greatly disturbed over the present situation and the outlook for the future; that the party was in desperate straits which, in the opinion of some, could be met only by fusion with the Populists. At the very mention of the word "fusion" a roar of dissent and boos came from the delegates. When the tempest subsided, Glenn, in a stentorian voice, boldly proclaimed: "Fellow-Democrats, I care not how others may feel, but for me, I despise fusion and all its works; I am a lifelong Democrat who intends to abide in the Democratic ship and to fight it out under our own flag, untainted with Populism."

Great roars of applause followed, but when it was over the convention was still at a loss to find a man to head the ticket for governor who it was thought had a chance to win. The names of several prominent Democrats were placed before the delegates in eloquent speeches, but the response was lacking until Colonel Bennett, a distinguished Confederate veteran, mounted the platform and declared, "If you want to nominate a man who can certainly be elected governor, and the only Democrat in North Carolina who in my opinion can, I will give you his name—Walter Clark." The suggestion electrified the convention and a stampede began to nominate him then and there, without knowing whether or not he would accept the nomination. To meet this situation the leaders quickly had the convention take a recess, after appointing a committee to visit Justice Clark and learn if he would accept the nomination.

The committee, accompanied by a large number of other delegates, found Clark at work in his library at home. The spokesman told him that the Democratic State Convention wished to nominate him for governor of the state and had sent them to urge his acceptance, while it had temporarily adjourned to await his answer. Many in the delegation were his personal friends, among them a number of Confederate soldiers with whom he had served in the army. He was deeply stirred by their confidence, and with emotion expressed his appreciation for the honor his party wished to bestow upon him. Addressing the gathering he assured them of his willingness at all times to serve his state, but that he had two years before been unanimously elected a Justice of the Supreme Court for eight years, and that he felt it his duty to serve out his term. In reply to their insistence he reviewed certain personal reasons which also deterred him from accepting the nomination. He reminded them that his salary as judge for the last ten years had been only $2,500 a year, that he had seven children to care for and educate, that his plantation was no longer a source of profit, and that frankly he was financially unable to bear the expense of a campaign.

Disappointed, the convention turned to another distinguished Confederate soldier, Cyrus B. Watson, an eminent lawyer, and friend of Clark, whom they nominated to wage a forlorn battle against the Republican nominee, Daniel Russell, and the Populist nominee, Major William A. Guthrie. In this three-cornered contest Watson lost the election by less than ten thousand votes. It was universally believed that if Clark had accepted the nomination he would have been elected.

The Chairman of the Democratic State Executive Committee, James H. Pou, who prior to the convention had urged Clark to head the ticket, wrote him that in his opinion he was the only Democrat in the state who could be elected. Later, probably knowing Clark's feelings, he wrote that he wished to see the convention endorse him for vice president of the United States; that he would gladly go to the National Convention and work for his nomination. The convention enthusiastically instructed their delegates to present his name for vice president to the National Convention meeting in Chicago, which was done, and he received a substantial number of votes from a number of other states.

Bryan's nomination for president made Clark's nomination for vice president a logical one, but for the fear of putting a southern Democrat and ex-Confederate soldier on the national ticket. Bryan's philosophy and revolt against the existing order fitted perfectly with Clark's known views, and his great "cross of gold" speech preceding his nomination, which swept the delegates off their feet, was typical of Clark's philosophy: "You shall not press down upon the brow of labor this crown of thorns; you shall not crucify mankind upon a cross of gold.... Burn down your cities, but leave us our farms, and we will build them up again in a day; destroy the farms and grass will grow in the streets of the cities."

During the free silver campaign in 1896 Clark visited Mexico and wrote several articles dealing with this question. The most important one was in the November issue of *The Arena;* in this he declared that free coinage, while necessary, was not a panacea for the existing ills.

In the years to follow, Bryan repeatedly expressed admiration for Clark's devotion to the cause of the common people and for his relentless fight against monopolies, trusts, and combines.

Chapter VII

HIS PHILOSOPHY

"The most important thing about a man is still his view of the universe . . . his philosophy." —Chesterton

BEGINNING WITH his services in the army as drill master, continuing through his election as lieutenant colonel, his elevation to a seat upon the Supreme Court of the state, and until 1896 when he was tendered the nomination for governor of his state and endorsed for vice president of the United States, Clark's career in both law and politics was an uninterrupted honeymoon of success. But now this universal adulation ceased, and for the next six years he became the central figure in a series of bitter conflicts that shook the state from center to circumference.

The first conflict resulted from his denunciation of the organization of the American Tobacco Trust and its practices; the second, from his exposure of evils resulting from the consolidation of the Southern Railway Company, the Seaboard Air Line, and the Atlantic Coast Line into three powerful systems which he alleged were violating the law and dominating the politics of the state. In these conflicts a number of valued friends of a lifetime and many old political associates joined the opposing forces, turned upon him with unprecedented bitterness, and sought to destroy him and to drive him from public life. This change of attitude and apparent paradox was grounded in the belief that Clark had become radical in his political thinking, tainted with Populism and dangerous to the existing economic order. There was much truth in this conclusion except that his critics were mistaken in thinking that he was a recent convert to liberalism. A study of Clark's life from youth on clearly shows that he was never a conservative either in thinking or in acting. His bold and fearless denunciation of the landed and slave oligarchy of the old South while still in his teens, his challenge of Pugh to a duel for questioning his integrity, gave notice to the world that here was a man of extremely liberal views and one who was willing and ready to fight for them.

But these and other manifestations of liberalism had to do largely with the economic and social order of the past and with suggestions how to rebuild a new South along truly democratic lines. His advocacy of legal reforms and improvement in the administration of justice was accepted as harmless because this was an old story, and the conservatives had no idea that he would do any more than talk about it, as many early would-be reformers had done. But a new Richmond had come into the field. The times had changed, and new problems had arisen seriously affecting the economic, social, and political life of both the state and the nation. Clark realized this more clearly than any other jurist of his generation, and from his exalted position as the acknowledged head of the judiciary of the state he began a crusade against those institutions and organizations which he believed were wrongfully organized and criminally operated at the expense of the public. There is no evidence that Clark had changed his principles, but conditions had changed, and this aroused in him the deep-seated conviction that the public welfare is the supreme law and that all offenders, great and small, against the common interest should be unhorsed. In other words, he already had an established philosophy of life, law, and government which dominated his every public action and reaction and made him an outspoken liberal and reformer.

To understand Clark it is necessary to know his philosophy, particularly of religion, law, and government, for this is the key to his character both as citizen and as judge. Clark's faith in religion, his belief in democracy, and his trust in the people made of him a crusader for righteous measures. William James, in his work on Pragmatism, quotes with approval Chesterton's observation: "The most important thing about a man is still his view of the universe ... his philosophy," and Justice Cardozo, in his noted lecture on the Growth of the Law, declares that the more he reflects upon a judge's work the more he is impressed with the belief that Chesterton's observation is true.

2

At the very foundation of Clark's philosophy was his implicit belief in the teachings of Christ. His devoted mother, by precept and example, instilled it into him as a child, and he had the daily association of a wife who was equally religious. Clark never advertised or paraded his religious views, but he was a thorough student of the Bible and religious literature—a fact known only to his mother, his wife, and a few associates. The meaning of Christ's teachings to him was not only a plan of salvation for the soul of man but he also regarded it as the Magna Charta of a democratic system of government.

As early as 1880 Clark disclosed his philosophy of religion in a commencement address at Trinity College (now Duke University):

"There is an active principle at work fermenting in the bosoms of mankind which will not let them rest—whose motion is Progress, whose advance is Civilization, whose form is Republicanism, and whose ultimate achievement is universal Christianity. I call your attention to the nature of this grain of leaven which is working so great a ferment in the masses of mankind. No man in this intelligent audience needs to be told that the history of our present civilization is that of the ideas which were incarnated in Bethlehem, and which were lifted up to the eyes of all succeeding centuries at Calvary. How profoundly those ideas have penetrated every domain of life—social, educational, religious, legal—it is not necessary for me to say, for civilization is a reflex of and a constant approximation of Christianity. . . .

"In treating this subject of the influence of Christ on politics, it is naturally divided into the effect on the form of government and on the mode of administration. In speaking of the influence of the teachings of the great Master in this connection, I shall view Him simply as a man. I would have no one misunderstand me. I would not for a moment intimate the slightest doubt upon that mysterious revelation, which I so little comprehend but most reverently and devoutly believe, of His being God in the flesh. The central idea in the teachings of Christ is that between the supremest of supreme powers and the humblest individual the dignity of manhood needs no human intermediate. In that idea is the germ of the political equality of men, and before its irresistible force the forms of government established by kings and oligarchies, with their artificial and burdensome inequalities, become vain barriers against the might and majesty of popular rights."

Clark then goes on to declare that "Christ taught neither agrarianism nor sedition, but so far as the influence and spirit of such a religion could leaven human society it was impossible for it not to promote liberty and brotherhood and equality among men. From such teachings come the freedom of thought, freedom of speech, freedom of conscience, freedom of action. The highest type of a Christian State is 'government of the people, by the people and for the people.' Well might the old Roman emperors recoil from a religion whose teachings would strike off the fetters from subject races as well as from subject men. The progress of Christianity ethically means morality, but politically it means Republicanism. Other forms of government cannot abide the doctrine it teaches. The perpetuity of our free institutions depends on our public morals and an enlightened public sentiment."

In an address delivered, after he became a member of the Supreme Court, before a Methodist Sunday School Convention, Clark emphasized his beliefs in the influence of the teachings of Christ. Of "the great thought of the equality of mankind" he said:

"No heathen philosopher ever dreamed it. In every pronouncement He ever made He taught the nothingness of human rank, the worthlessness of distinctions of wealth. Jesus was the first true gentleman that ever lived. His teachings, viewed from a political standpoint alone, have undermined the governments which were based upon force and fraud, upon rapine and injustice, upon wealth and corruption, and have shaken the forces of tyranny with more fatal effect than the spears of the phalanx at Marathon or the serried columns of liberty at Morgarten."

To a war-torn world today his declarations of half a century ago are as vibrant with truth as when he uttered them.

As a student of both sacred and profane history, Clark had become established in his philosophy and frequently employed the ideas of great teachers of the past. He was fond of Kossuth's statement that "Justice is immortal, eternal and immutable, like God himself, and the development of the law is only then a progress when it is directed towards those principles which, like Him, are eternal." This philosophy had so permeated every fibre of his being and so dominated his thinking that when confronted with injustice or challenged by wrongdoing, his beliefs compelled him to action without evading the issue or retreating from the contest.

The sum total of his religious philosophy as affecting his daily life was bound up in a declaration made in an address at Wake Forest College: "For my part, resistance to evil is obedience to the will of God." His enemies were ere long to learn—to their sorrow —that fortified with such a faith he was a man who could not be frightened or intimidated, and was as hard to whip as a rattlesnake.

3

Clark's philosophy of law and government was just as definitely settled in his mind as was his philosophy of religion. He embraced Jefferson's trust in the common people, Jackson's willingness to fight for them, and Lincoln's devotion to them. As for the law, he had an unvarying definition oft repeated in his opinions from the bench: "The public welfare is the supreme law." He was familiar with Justice Holmes's observation that "the life of the law has not been logic; it has been experience," and with Samuel Johnson's abstract definition, "Law is the last result of human wisdom acting upon human experience for the benefit of the public."

It will be observed that Holmes spoke of what kept the law alive, and Johnson of what law is, but Clark was primarily concerned with who had the power to make the law and for whose benefit it was written. If, as he proclaimed, the welfare of the public was the supreme law, then it necessarily followed that the people should write the law by legislation and into codes, and not the judges by opinions based on precedents established by earlier judges, whose opinions were in turn the result of still earlier judges' opinions, ad infinitum.

This philosophy of law and the law-making power was first developed by Jeremy Bentham in England in the latter part of the eighteenth century, and was primarily directed against the fetish of what was known as the common law of England. Up to that time the laws of England had been made by the judges, whose opinions from one generation to another were compiled and served as a binding precedent upon succeeding judges; and the substance of their rulings and reasoning was collected by Sir William Blackstone in his *Commentaries on the Laws of England* (1765-1769). The school of Bentham revolutionized in England its old method of judges' making the law, and succeeded in having Parliament enact long-needed reforms in its archaic system of practice and procedure, abolishing much of the common law which was still slavishly being followed by the courts in America.

Clark accepted this philosophy of law, espoused it, and in the closing years of the nineteenth century became the most insistent and conspicuous judge in America in advocating its adoption as a cardinal part of our law-making system. Familiar, historically, with the struggle of his masters in overcoming the dogmatic prejudices of the old order in England against reform, and knowing that American jurisprudence had adopted the common-law concept, he realized that these reforms could be had in this country only by fighting for them. He sought by opinions, writings, and addresses to educate the people of the state and nation to the need of this method of making new laws and reforming old ones and to arm them against the criticisms of judges and lawyers who were wedded to the old order.

One of the sources of his inspiration which helped make him "a fighting judge" was Rudolf von Jhering's brilliant lectures, copies of which he gave to a number of his legal friends. Jhering's philosophy fitted perfectly with Clark's philosophy, temperament, and disposition:

"The end of the law is peace. The means to that end is war. So long as the law is compelled to hold itself in readiness to resist the attacks of wrong—and this it will be compelled to do until the end of time—it cannot dispense with war. The life of the law is a struggle—a struggle of nations, of the state power, of classes, of individuals.
"All the law in the world has been obtained by strife. Every principle of law which obtains had first to be wrung by force from those who denied it; and every legal right—the legal rights of a whole nation as well as those of individuals—supposes a continual readiness to assert it and defend it. The law is not mere theory, but living force. And hence it is that Justice who, in one hand, holds the scales in which she weighs the right, carries in the other the sword with which she executes it. The scales without the sword is the impotence of law. The scales and the sword belong together, and the state of the law is perfect only where the power with which Justice carries the sword is equalled by the skill with which she holds the scales."

Accepting this appraisal of law and justice, no course was left open to Clark but to challenge to mortal combat the god of the status quo. His experience at the bar and on the bench had satisfied him that no substantial reforms in the adjective or substantive law were possible so long as the profession worshipped at the feet of Blackstone's common law and revered the precedents established under it. It may be well said of Clark what Lord Campbell wrote of Lord Mansfield: "He formed a very low, and I'm afraid a very just, estimate of the common law of England which he was to administer." In one of his ablest opinions he wrote, "Every age should have laws based upon its own intelligence and expressing its own ideas of right and wrong. Progress and betterment should not be denied by the dead hand of the past. The decisions of the Courts should always be in accord with the spirit of the legislation of today, which should not be misconstrued to conform to the views of dead and forgotten judges of centuries long over past who were not always learned and able, and who, if wise were really wise beyond the narrow vision of their own age."

The Bentham philosophy which Clark adopted assumed that the law must be reformed, if at all, by parliamentary enactment rather than by the courts. Simply stated, this process exalted the will of the people, as expressed through legislation, over the opinion of judges. Such a doctrine was obnoxious to the staid and conservative members of the legal profession in North Carolina and throughout the nation, but this did not deter Clark. He was satisfied that the "public welfare" urgently demanded that justice be not delayed or denied; that antiquated practice and procedure be abolished; and that substantive law should be modernized and streamlined to make it in keeping with the age in which he lived—and that this could be accomplished only by the people through legislation. He agreed with Lord Brougham's observation that Bentham was the first legal philosopher of his period in the world and that "the age of law reform and the age of Jeremy Bentham are one and the same. He is the father of the most important of all the branches of reform, the leading and ruling departments of human improvements."

Clark's philosophy of religion and law, coupled with his philosophy of government, formed a trinity of convictions which impelled his every action in dealing with the problems of society and government. With respect to government, Clark embraced unreservedly Jefferson's philosophy as set forth in the Declaration of Independence, his subsequent teachings, and the Bill of Rights. To apply this philosophy and translate it into action he relied implicitly upon the informed judgment and will of all the people. He asserted the conviction that unless our form of government is a mistake, the more the people know the surer they are to go right. The people can be trusted with their own government, else our Republican form of government is a failure. Hence, Jefferson's creed—"Whoever expects the people to be ignorant and free expects what never was and never will be." He agreed with Gladstone: "The people are not always right but they are seldom wrong," and with Lincoln, "Why should we not have a patient confidence in the ultimate justice of the people? Is there any better, is there any equal hope in the world?"

In an address in 1897 before the University College of Medicine at Richmond, Virginia, Clark stated his ideal as to the form of government. Said he, "An anarchist is one who is opposed to all government. He is a *ne plus ultra* of individualism. Society has nothing to fear from the few hundred throughout the union professing that faith. At the very opposite pole are the communists who believe in government for everything, in the community of goods. This system failed under the Apostles themselves, who gave it a trial, and is not likely to be tried again with any success while poor human nature remains what it is. Between these opposite poles anarchism, or no government on the one hand, and communism, or government in everything on the other, lies socialism. Every civilized government is to a large extent, and almost in proportion to its degree of civilization, socialistic."

The form of government to which Clark unqualifiedly committed himself is what is now known as socialized democracy. He pointed out in this address that taxes were levied on the property of all persons, whether they have any children or not, in order to educate other people's children, and that in like manner public taxes are levied to maintain hospitals for the sick, the poor, the insane, the blind, the deaf, and the dumb, all in a measure socialistic. "Government," said he, "exists for the people and not the people for the government," but in the functioning of a democracy he approved the Jeffersonian mandate: "Equal rights for all and special privileges for none." In both the writing of laws and the administration of government he insisted that the "public welfare" was the sole and supreme factor. In the midst of a world dominated by monopolies, trusts, and transportation combines, Clark understood that his philosophy concerning religion, law, and government was repugnant to the thinking and interest of the governing forces in the state and nation. He fully realized that his course meant alienating some lifelong friends whose financial interests would be disturbed, but here again he adopted the philosophy which Bentham had proclaimed more than a century before: "Would you appear actuated by generous passion, be so—you need then but show yourself as you are. I would have the dearest friend I have to know that his interests, if they come in competition with those of the public, are as nothing to me. Thus I will serve my friends—thus I would be served by them. Has a man talents? He owes them to his country in every way in which they can be serviceable."

Chapter VIII

THE GOVERNING POWER, MEN OR MONEY?

"We do not take possession of our ideas, but are possessed by them. They master us and force us into the arena, where, like gladiators, we must fight for them."—Heine

WITH THE DEFEAT of Bryan for the presidency and the triumph of money over men under the aegis of Mark Hanna, the masses, particularly the farmers and laborers, believed they had been sold down the river. Clark by now was convinced that the control of the national government had passed from the people to the railroads, trusts, and bankers. As a historian, he knew that the causes which had produced this political result lay in a vicious combination of evil forces that were operating under cover and through aliases. He had before him the recent statements of two of the world's famous statesmen of the time, President Cleveland's address to Congress, and Lord Bryce's *American Commonwealth*, graphically picturing the growing evils of corporate greed and monopoly ruthlessness in America:

From President Cleveland's Message to Congress, December, 1888:
"We discover that the fortunes realized by our manufacturers are no longer solely the reward of sturdy industry and enlightened foresight, but that they result from the discriminating favor of the Government, and are largely built upon undue exactions from the masses of our people. The gulf between employers and employed is constantly widening and classes are rapidly forming, one comprising the very

From Lord Bryce's *American Commonwealth:*
"He who considers the irresponsible nature of the power which three or four men, or perhaps one man, can exercise through a great corporation, such as a railroad or telegraph company, the injury they can inflict on the public as well as on their competitors, the cynical audacity with which they have often used their wealth to seduce officials and legislators from the path of virtue, will find nothing unreason-

rich and powerful, while in another are found the toiling poor. As we view the achievements of aggregated capital we discover the existence of trusts, combinations and monopolies, while the citizen is struggling far in the rear, or is trampled to death beneath an iron heel. Corporations, which should be the carefully restrained creatures of the law and the servants of the people, are fast becoming the people's masters. . . . The communism of combined wealth and capital, the outgrowth of overweening cupidity and selfishness, which insidiously undermines the justice and integrity of free institutions, is not less dangerous than the communism of oppressed poverty and toil, which exasperated by injustice and discontent attacks with wild disorder the citadel of rule." able in the desire of the American masses to regulate the management of corporations and narrow the range of their action. The same remark applies, with even more force, to combinations of men not incorporated but acting together, the so-called Trusts, i.e. commercial rings, or syndicates. . . . It may therefore be conjectured that the railroad will long stand forth as a great and perplexing force in the economico-political life of the United States. It cannot be left to itself—the most extreme advocate of laissez faire would not contend for that, for to leave it to itself would be to make it a tyrant. It can hardly be taken over and worked by the National government; . . . The railroads illustrate two tendencies specially conspicuous in America,—the power of the principle of association, which makes commercial corporations, skilfully handled, formidable to individual men; and the way in which the principle of monarchy, banished from the field of government, creeps back again and asserts its strength in the scarcely less momentous contests of industry and finance."

Theodore Roosevelt was later to brand the wielders of these powers as malefactors of great wealth, but Clark was the first jurist in high place to join in exposing their means and pointing out their baneful influence upon the nation. The situation had become so aggravated that in 1890 the Congress passed the Sherman Antitrust Act, but nothing was immediately done to enforce it.

Within four years after Clark went upon the Supreme Court there developed a situation in North Carolina which he regarded as alarming and fraught with the very evils which Cleveland and Bryce had decried. All of the principal railroads in North Carolina and throughout the South were consolidated in the '90's into three grand trunk systems, the Southern Railway, Atlantic Coast Line, and Seaboard, all headquartered in North Carolina. The tremendous influence which these railroads and the Tobacco Trust exercised upon the economic and political life of the people of North Carolina was so far-reaching and devastating that it formed a sensational chapter in high finance and low morals, which attracted the attention of the nation. Since Clark was soon to become their severest critic and most hated enemy, it is historically important to understand how these institutions came into being and the methods employed to accumulate unearned fortunes and to dominate the state.

The structure of the Southern Railway system was made in the '90's by consolidating into a great trunk system the ownership and control of many existing lines of roads located from the Potomac to the Gulf. The consummation of this ambitious scheme was accomplished primarily by J. P. Morgan and Company, together with London bankers, taking advantage of the financial panic which at the time had prostrated the South. The means employed were foreclosure proceedings of first mortgages through Federal court receiverships by bond-holding committees, which in turn were controlled by the bankers. By this method not only were the properties wanted for the system acquired, but all junior bondholders, other creditors, and the entire stock ownership, most of which was held by the public, were wiped out.

The Atlantic Coast Line and the Seaboard Air Line were soon to follow a similar procedure, which, in a few years, resulted in the establishment of the giant railway systems mentioned above.

So passed forever from the states affected and from their citizens the last vestige of ownership in these properties, into the building of which they had put millions of dollars. A notable example of what was done and how they did it was the rape in

1893 of the Cape Fear & Yadkin Valley Railroad Company, located in North Carolina, with a branch line extending into South Carolina. For forty years the enterprising business people along this line of road had put much of their fortunes into its building, from Mount Airy near the Virginia line, across the state through Greensboro, to Wilmington, North Carolina. Its charter declared that the purpose of its construction was to establish direct connection with the coal fields and granaries to the west and to make available the commodious seaport at Wilmington. The State of North Carolina invested more than a million dollars to help along this enterprise, but in order to finish the road's construction a mortgage was given upon all of its property, subordinating prior indebtedness, and the bonds secured by it were taken by the bankers. This road crossed at right angles the main line of both the Southern and the Atlantic Coast Line, thus creating serious competition by a locally owned and independently operated road.

This road had scarcely been completed when the depression and panic of the early nineties struck, causing a default in the interest on its bonds. A proceeding was immediately instituted by the first mortgage bondholders, in the Federal court, asking for the appointment of a receiver for the entire system and all of its property; the Southern and Coast Line intervened, filing a supplemental petition asking that the receiver be instructed to dismember the road and sell it in two sections, so that the Southern could acquire that portion of the line lying in the western part of the state, where it was supreme, and the Coast Line, the eastern portion lying in its territory. Federal Judge Simonton declined to allow the road to be dismembered and the case was taken to the circuit court of appeals, which affirmed his decree, denying the dismemberment of the road. Notwithstanding these decisions, Samuel Spencer, president of the Southern, and Harry Walters, president of the Atlantic Coast Line, met at Fayetteville, North Carolina, on the day appointed by the court for the sale of the property in its entirety, and then and there entered into a secret agreement to suppress bidding; Walters was to purchase the property as a unit as cheaply as he could, and thereafter they would divide the road as previously sought, in defiance of the court's decree.

As a result of this scheme the Cape Fear and Yadkin Valley, 284 miles long, was cut in two and its disjointed parts absorbed into the Southern and the Coast Line systems. Under the terms of the sale it was provided that the bonds secured by this first mortgage might be used in satisfaction of the purchase price. The bankers had looked after this detail by previously purchasing these bonds at a heavy discount from the public and then rebonded the road for more than the face value of the old bonds and passed the new issue out to the public, which resulted in the two roads' acquiring the ownership and control of this valuable property without expending a single dollar.

This and similar kinds of high financing in disregard of the rights of others later became an open public scandal which was the inspiration for Brandeis' pamphlet, *Other People's Money,* written years later, naming the railroads, including the Southern and the Atlantic Coast Line, which had exploited the public and enriched themselves by means of such consolidations. With respect to the bankers' connection with such transactions, Brandeis wrote: "The great banking houses came into relation with this enterprise either after success had been attained or upon reorganization after the possibility of success had been demonstrated, but the funds of the hardy pioneers who had risked their all were exhausted."

In this pamphlet he severely condemned the Atlantic Coast Line for issuing fifty millions of securities to acquire control of the Louisville & Nashville Railroad, which was already a successfully operated road with gross earnings nearly twice as large as those of the Atlantic Coast Line.

What Brandeis wrote had a striking resemblance to what Clark had been saying two decades earlier, but Brandeis succeeded in publicizing the greed of the bankers and marking such practices for ultimate death.

"Bankers," said Brandeis, "were not content merely to deal in securities; they desired to manufacture them also. . . . J. P. Morgan and Company formed the steel trust, the harvester trust and the shipping trust . . . . the investment bankers became, in times of corporate disaster, members of security-holders' 'protective committees' [and] reorganization managers."

The gross abuses which arose from the Federal court's appointment and control of railroads through receiverships became so notorious that in 1894 the legislature of South Carolina presented to Congress a memorial of grievances in the matter of equity receiverships for railroads. In the course of the memorial it was said, "Had all Federal judges been like Mr. Justice Miller, Mr. Circuit Judge Dillon, or Mr. Circuit Judge Caldwell, the courts of equity of the United States would never have been degraded to their present position of being feared by the patriotic and avoided by the honest; nor would they have opened the door to the mismanagement, corruption and nepotism which have marked, and still mark, the administration of railroads by the courts."

The situation became so intolerable that the experienced editors of *The American Law Review* declared, "This subject of Federal railway receiverships is loaded down with abuses which seriously demand the investigation of Congress."

Injury was added to insult by the railroad companies' giving free passes to judges, frequently hauling Federal judges in private cars, without cost, to hold their courts, before whom litigations between citizens and the railroads were to be tried. The free-pass abuse, in vogue at this time, extending to high places, is graphically illustrated by Judge Robert W. Winston in his book, *It's a Far Cry*. He recounts an incident which occurred in a court over which he was presiding at Smithfield. James and Edward W. Pou were prosecuting an action before him for damages against the railroad. A witness for the railroad was asked by the Pous, "Didn't you come here on a railroad pass?" "We object," interrupted Busbee. "What is the object of the question?" the Court asked. "Why, if Your Honor please, we are attacking the witness' character." "Do you think having a pass would affect his character?" "Undoubtedly, Your Honor. What is a pass but a bribe?" "Objection overruled. Proceed, sir," said the Court, "reflecting that in his pocket, at that moment, he had no less than twenty-five free passes, over every railroad and every steamboat in the state!"

The Southern Railway, upon its organization, took a commanding position in the political life of the state. Although it was organized under the laws of Virginia, its seat of government was actually in Raleigh.

Its vice president and general manager was Colonel A. B. Andrews, an experienced and able railroad executive. His background was all that could be desired; he was well-born, an ex-Confederate soldier, handsome, commanding in appearance, plausible, a shrewd judge of men. Andrews and Clark had been lifelong friends, had served in the army together, and Clark had been invited to act as groomsman and his fiancée, Sudie Graham, to act as bridesmaid at Andrews' marriage. Both had been employees of the Raleigh and Gaston Railroad—Clark as general counsel and Andrews as its superintendent. A cordial friendship had existed between the families for years, but now a clash of philosophies and of wills was in the making.

Colonel Andrews had spent his life operating railroads, and his point of view was that of the great railroad magnates of the nation. The Southern Railroad was under the financial domination and control of the House of Morgan, which was dictating policies and practices in North Carolina and throughout the South similar to those which it was employing through control of railroads in New England and portions of the West. William H. Vanderbilt had brutally declared such policy to be "The public be damned." Colonel Andrews was softer spoken, but the iron hand was always concealed in the glove. The propaganda of the railroads at that time was that the railroads had built up the nation and not the nation the railroads; that the bigger the system the better; that it was none of the public's business how a road was operated, what it charged to carry freight or passengers, where or when it built stations, what kind of defective appliances it used in its operations, how many employees it negligently killed, what it paid its operatives, or how many hours they worked; and that the employment of minors was entirely a matter concerning the company. The strategy from the outset on the part of the railroads was to resist all control by the public of any of its instrumentalities and to use the methods and means which had been so successfully employed by other railroads in the West to control legislatures and dominate political parties so as to perpetuate this vicious and unregulated monopoly.

By reason of Colonel Andrews' ability and success, the other railroads in the state constituted him their political generalissimo, and as a result he became the most powerful political factor in the state. Populists might uprise, Republicans might register ignorant Negro voters, and Democrats might put on a white supremacy campaign, but Colonel Andrews continued to do business with them all. Free passes were to be found in the pockets of influential delegates to all nominating conventions, and the winning candidate in most cases was an attorney for one of the railroads, usually the Southern, with a free pass in his pocket.

Clark later satirized the situation by quoting the remark of Astor, "When I am in a Republican state I am a Republican, when in a Democratic state, a Democrat,—but always a railroad man."

This situation fitted perfectly into the organization of political machinery. The managers of these machines knew that to win elections they must have money; that the place to get money was where money is. The masses were prostrate in poverty and the only real money in the country was under the control of the railroads, their allies the trusts, and the bankers, while smaller corporations deemed it an honor to be allowed to trail along behind the big ones.

Clark was particular to catalog the evil practices of the railroads which had aroused the people and to marshal, in a number of addresses, his arguments as to why and how they should be suppressed. He became convinced that the most potent factor for evil in their power was in the unlimited use of free passes given to lawmakers and other public officials, including some judges.

In November, 1896, following his declination of the nomination for governor, he wrote an article for *The Arena* attacking free passes and excessive passenger and freight charges. "There is no influence more debasing in legislation," said he, "than that of the lobby and its employment of free passes." He boldly asserted that, pending the election of members to the legislature, this matter should be called to the attention of all voters, since these favors were sent to members solely to induce them to vote for railroad measures, and that this fact alone should prevent their acceptance by any member. He emphasized that the excuse for their acceptance was, "They all do it."

In 1894, at the request of a member of the General Assembly, he had prepared a bill forbidding free passes, and embodying provisions similar to those in the constitutions of New York and several other states. In his *Arena* article he said that this bill was "favorably reported by the committee, but was not allowed to pass, being stolen from the files no less than three times by some railroad lobbyist. A well known railroad official called on me in person to secure the withdrawal of the bill. On being told that the bill had not only been prepared by request but that it was in the interest of honesty and honest legislation, he used the following language which may be pondered over by all honest men outside of North Carolina as well as within its bounds. Said he, 'It might as well be withdrawn. It can never pass. The fellows who come here to the Legislature are always anxious to be raped with a pass. Why, only yesterday a member asked me for a pass for himself, his wife, his sister, his two children and his aunt, and do you suppose such damned cattle as that will vote against free passes?' "

Clark had become convinced that publicity was the best weapon which the public had to remedy the evils flowing from domination of politics by the railroads and the trusts.

Brandeis later commended this method. "Publicity," wrote he, "is justly commended as a remedy for social and industrial diseases. Sunlight is said to be the best disinfectant; electric light the most efficient policeman, and publicity has already played an important part in the struggle against the money trusts."

One of Clark's first comprehensive addresses dealing with this subject has already been mentioned—the one delivered before the University College of Medicine at Richmond, Virginia, in 1897, entitled "Where Shall the Governing Power Reside?"

"The vital question," declared he, "which this country is called upon to determine and towards the determination of which we are groping our way is, 'Where shall the actual governing power reside? Shall it be in men or money?' It is not a new question, but in a Republic it is the inevitable question whose determination settles all others. . . . The nature of a government is not determined by its forms and titles. . . . What boots it if on parchment we shall continue to read, 'All political power is vested in and derived from the people; all government of right originates from the people, is founded upon their will only, and is instituted solely for the good of the whole,' if it is not a living, potential, actual truth? If, as a matter of fact, great corporations through their agents, whether lobbyists or members of the legislature itself, . . . can elect or control majorities in State Legislatures and in Congress, so as to shape legislation, if they can be potent in the nomination of Federal or State officials, then the real governing power vests in money, not in men; then the parchment declaration is a flaunting lie, and your boasted republic is but a once beauteous form from which the spirit has already departed. . . .

"There is no hatred of corporations as such. . . . The opposition is not to them as servants of the public, but as would-be masters of the people. . . . At Cooper Institute Mr. Lincoln truly declared to a startled generation that the Union could not remain half bond and half free. It is equally true now that this Government cannot be governed partly by free men and partly by an oligarchy of wealth."

The high mark of Clark's crusade, particularly against the railroad combines and their practices, was reached in an address delivered before the eleventh annual convention of Railroad Commissioners held at Denver, Colorado, in 1899, and published by the Interstate Commerce Commission. He opened this address by saying that he had been invited to speak for the forgotten man, "the Joneses who pay the freight." He pointed out that the forgotten man elects no president, superintendent, or board of directors, but that he has to bear whatever burden they see fit to place upon him. He fixes no salaries; many of theirs are higher than that of the President of the United States; he rides in no palace car nor upon a free pass, but he pays the fare of those who do; he has no hearing as to the tax which shall be levied for the movement of himself, his produce or his purchases; he does not desire the government ownership of railroads, but wishes government control, and is willing to give it a fair trial; he has no hostility to railroads as such but only to their abuses; it will be small advantage to the public if the railroads develop the country merely to own its profit themselves.

He then declared: "The sovereign people have decided once for all that these iron horses shall be bitted and bridled" and not allowed to "resort to injunctions (often issued by their former attorneys promoted to the bench) to set aside rates, regulations, and tax assessments made by your Commissions."

In this address he charged that the contributions of railroad and other combines to presidential campaign funds and lesser political subdivisions are a national scandal, but that worse than all this is the influence they exert in the appointment of the life judiciary in the Federal Government.

"The greatest of evils attendant upon the present system, viewed from a financial standpoint, . . . is discrimination in rates. By this means individuals and even cities can be destroyed and others built up by their destruction. The Standard Oil Company, which forced the railroads to carry its products at 30 cents per barrel, while compelling them not only to charge all others 80 cents per barrel but even to pay the extra 50 cents paid by its rivals into the Standard Oil treasury, is a sample of the methods of these modern highwaymen, the trusts. The Standard Oil Company is shown to have received from the railroads a ten million dollar bonus by this means in eighteen months. Other corporations have followed the same method until small manufacturers have been crushed out and equality of opportunity, which was the boast of our institutions, has been nonexistent. The hope of America lies in the very fact that our people will not submit to such abuses much longer."

Clark next attacked the freight rate structure which had been arbitrarily established and maintained by the railroads grossly discriminating against the southern states. He pointed out that the freight rates in the greater part of the northern and western states were more reasonable than formerly, while those south of the Potomac and Ohio were so arranged and continued that their effects were ruinous to the southern states. He pointed out that no one denied that these rates were exorbitant; yet still the railroads maintained them. "In fact, the embargo laid on the development of the southern states by the extortionate charges for transportation is the chief factor in retarding their growth. . . . In some sections of the South the charges are so high, especially in trucking business, that the real owners of the soil are the London and New York bankers, who own the principal railway systems of the South. Their transportation charges take all the profits, leaving the nominal owners of the soil a mere pittance. . . . One large railroad system in North Carolina last year paid its stockholders (by sundry devices) 156 per cent dividends, which is over 400 per cent of the price at which the syndicate bought out the State's stock in the road. Though they thus got back in one year's profit more than four times their investment, they obtained from a Federal Judge an injunction against the Railroad Commission reducing their passenger fares to two and one-half cents per mile, or assessing their property for taxation at one-third of the market value of their stocks and bonds."

Still speaking for "the forgotten man," he took up the subject of free passes: "The evils of the free pass system and the immoral purposes to which it has been put have met wide public condemnation. Eight great states have put in their constitutions provisions against it, making it a forfeiture of office for any officeholder to take a free pass." He pointed out that "it is unlawful in North Carolina to give free passes," but that the railroads ignored the statute and were then issuing, according to the report of the State Railroad Commission, 100,000 free passes annually. "Aside from the injustice of making one portion of the community (and those least able to pay for themselves) pay for the free riding of others, there is the leprosy of the free pass system being the most shameless and most widely spread system of bribery of public officials and others having, or supposed to have, influence with the public."

Clark referred to a number of reforms which were needed in the system, such as the installation of safety appliances by the railroad, electric headlights and other measures which would save thousands of lives of railroad employees killed each year on account of the lack of them.

This address immediately attracted national attention. The public realized that a new voice was speaking. That a judge sitting upon a high court should dare to make such a speech and to recognize publicly the rights and existence of "the forgotten man" was startling. The staid conservatives were unaccustomed to hearing the vicious practices of railroads and big business exposed by a judge, but a long-suffering public received it gladly. Letters of congratulation came to Clark from many parts of the nation—from governors, judges, lawyers, and national leaders. The tenor of their comments was similar to that contained in a letter from John H. Ragan, chairman of the Railroad Commission of Texas, who wrote, "It is a truthful, very able and courageous presentation of the problems connected with the ownership and regulation of the railroads. It is refreshing and encouraging to see that a citizen of your ability and one occupying so high a judicial position has the courage to meet and expose the existing evils of railroad management as you have done. Your countrymen should thank you, and God will bless you for it."

Ex-Governor Altgeld of Illinois wrote: "It was a masterpiece. I never read anything from your pen but what I feel that you should speak more often than you do."

2

It was an ironical fact that the same year, 1890, in which the Congress enacted the Sherman Antitrust Act condemning all monopolies and combines as criminal and providing fines or imprisonment for offenders, the Dukes should have organized in Durham, North Carolina, a monopoly in the manufacture and sale of tobacco. Of course, the Dukes knew of the passage of the Sherman Act and were doubtless advised of the risk they were taking. It was rumored that J. B. Duke, president of the forming monopoly, had stated openly that if the courts would let him alone for ten years he would make a barrel of money. Justice, which Clark once observed, "is lame in its feet," did not overtake him until 1911 when the Supreme Court of the United States dissolved the Tobacco Trust, but in the meantime, he was reported to have accumulated a hundred million dollars.

The Supreme Court pointed out a number of the unlawful means which the Dukes and their associates had employed in order to establish a monopoly in its business and to accumulate these fabulous profits at the expense of the public, such as destroying the small competitors in the manufacture of tobacco whose business it could not buy; underselling them in the sections where they had built up a business, and by various means (such as free gifts of their products to the distributors) making it impossible for the small manufacturer to compete. The monopoly thus constituted enabled the American Tobacco Company to control the price of leaf tobacco grown by the farmers, because there were few competitive bidders for the raw product; and the prices thus fixed were so low that starvation and ruin threatened an entire section of Virginia and North Carolina engaged in the cultivation of tobacco.

By 1911, when the Supreme Court finally dissolved the Standard Oil and Tobacco trusts, it was estimated that, between the time of the passage of the Sherman Antitrust Act and this decision, more than 150 trusts and monopolies had been established in defiance of law and were successfully operating throughout the United States, accumulating profits of untold millions. Clark, with his penetrating mind, saw at the outset that this supposed prosperity and industrial development were not for the benefit of the public, but formed a one-way road where traffic was so arranged that the few were daily growing richer and the producing and consuming public, through exploitation, was rapidly becoming impoverished. The situation in North Carolina was particularly acute in the late nineties, for the combined operations of the railroad monopoly and the Tobacco Trust, acting in concert, formed a double-barreled menace.

Summarizing his conclusions upon the facts and arguments presented in numerous addresses, Clark added this final cracker: "Our people are being robbed by wholesale. They do not receive the just rewards of their labor. They are being pauperized and kept in want, while a few men by trick and combinations are gathering to themselves the earnings of a continent. Search all history, and you will find no age when the robbery of the just earnings of the masses was more systematic, more shameless and less resisted than today. There was never a time when the worship of great riches, however badly acquired, was more open than now."

Justice Clark fully realized that his philosophy ran squarely counter to the aims, purposes, and practices of railroad combines and trusts, which were openly violating the Sherman Antitrust Act and the statute law of his state, and prostituting their duties to the public as servants of the people. In entering the fight as a citizen on behalf of the oppressed public he also recognized that he would be criticized as a judge for not keeping the judicial veil tightly drawn so that as a high law enforcement officer he should be comparable to the three monkeys "who saw no evil, heard no evil, spoke no evil."

On the contrary, he anticipated these criticisms in his Virginia address, boldly declaring: "Be it understood that I come not before you to express or to advocate any views of my own, or of any party, or of any section. It would be an insult to you and unworthy of myself to use this occasion for such a purpose, but I accept the great thought of Terence, the Latin poet, which St. Augustine tells us was received with thunders of applause by a Roman audience: 'I am a man, and whatever concerns the welfare of my fellowmen can never be without interest to me.'" And in less than a month in an address before the law class of Wake Forest College he threw down the gauntlet of war to his critics and detractors: "I know that in all history whenever any man has dared to tell the people their rights, and to tell them that they are oppressed, and that they have the legal right to stop the oppression, it makes him a mark for every hired arrow, and every mercenary bowman. But in the language of Martin Luther, at the Diet of Worms, 'Here I stand—God help me—I can do no other.' . . . And so I say now in your hearing that 'God forbid that the freedom of North Carolina from unjust exactions, and the welfare of her people, should depend upon the grace and mercy of Pierpont Morgan, and such as he.'"

During these turbulent days Clark was wont to say that God made him a man before the people made him judge, and that in accepting judicial office he surrendered none of his obligations and duties as a citizen to the state, the nation, and the public.

CHAPTER IX

KILGO-GATTIS TRAVESTY TRIALS

*"I'm armed with more than complete steel,—
The justice of my quarrel."*—Christopher Marlowe

WHEN THE Reverend John C. Kilgo, President of Trinity College, induced its trustees, in 1898, to pass a resolution condemning Judge Clark, a fellow trustee, without a hearing, for criticizing him, and requesting Clark's resignation from the Board, he opened a Pandora's box of plagues that embroiled his college, his church, and his state in an unseemly and unprofitable wrangle finally ending in a travesty and a tragedy. The prominence of the parties and the far-reaching effect of the controversy provided a paradise for the press, so that the affair became a state sensation, and editors, politicians, ministers of the gospel, and finally the courts, all took a part. The hounds of hell were loosed—bitterness, hate, and revenge dominated the scene, with charges of slander, libel, hypocrisy, and cowardice playing the major roles, until the curtain went down in court upon a verdict stained with two convictions for embracery.

It has been said that there is a reason for everything if you know what it is. The record is complete that behind this remarkable performance, which extended over a period of several years, were a number of reasons far more important than the personal controversy between Kilgo and Clark. These two men, at the time, symbolized opposing forces that were contending for mastery in the educational, economic, and political life of the state. There is no other single engagement in Clark's career which so completely reveals his convictions and courage and so thoroughly shows his determination to fight to the death those evil influences of combined corporate wealth which sought to control educational institutions and to dominate the government. The background of what came to be known as the "Kilgo-Gattis Controversy" had its elements of romance, drama, and melodrama, accompanied here and there by some high thinking and low acting.

Kilgo was a native of South Carolina who came to the state in 1894 when he was elected president of Trinity College. At his inauguration, Clark, speaking for the trustees, said, "We have earnestly sought a worthy successor to our two presidents. We hope—aye more than that, we believe—that in the providence of God we have found him."

The trustees had wanted Clark to be president of the college. Dr. Crowell, the retiring president, in June, 1894, wrote him, "No name mentioned in connection with the presidency of Trinity College receives half so much approval as yours. I write to know whether you are in any sense a possibility, that is, whether you would accept, if elected, on any terms or conditions. If so I want to know so that I may have the assurance of the college being in the safest hands. I would like exceedingly to put your name in nomination next Tuesday." Clark expressed appreciation of the compliment but declined to permit his name to be used.

Kilgo's previous political affiliations as a Tillman South Carolina Democrat fitted well with the views of the North Carolina Methodists, who were overwhelmingly Jeffersonian democrats. He soon justified the expectations of the trustees by issuing a pamphlet on *Christian Education, Its Aims and Superiority,* in which his democratic views were expressed in Tillmanesque fashion.

Speaking of college presidents, he wrote: "The low and material value that is set on scholarships and human success is simply devilish. Too many college presidents have defended education upon the superior advantages it gives in the markets. As a result, too many college men are only big tricksters. The man of wealth has been presented as a successful man. College presidents have pointed to him as the hero of American life. Such doctrines will multiply thieves, but never make men or a nation." He then asked this question: "Is the church unpatriotic because it builds colleges at its own expense to educate the youth of the land? . . . Society must be made more democratic; it must find deeper and warmer sympathies. Character and not money must be enthroned." He declared, "The common public schools will never amount to more than a farce until the church takes the work out of the hands of the politicians and develops it." He concluded, "One cause of antagonism between labor and capital is the supposed, or real, degraded estimate that capital puts on labor. Our colleges must stand for a better type of patriotism or America will yet, like Rome, be sold to the highest bidder. Already too much trading has gone on."

Auspicious as was Kilgo's beginning, he was soon confronted with an increasing college deficit, since many of the supporting Methodists were tobacco farmers whose crops were being taken by the Tobacco Trust at starvation prices. In the meantime the student enrollment of the College during Kilgo's first year of administration decreased from 154 to 126. The Dukes, who were Methodists and Republicans, aided the College by generous contributions to its financial support, while the farmer Methodists grew poorer and the Dukes, through the Tobacco Trust, grew richer. Kilgo undertook to solve his financial problems by more and more turning to get the money "where the money was." In this enterprise he was a supreme success, but a metamorphosis in his philosophy and political thinking took place. From one end of the state to the other, from pulpit and platform, Kilgo denounced Thomas Jefferson as an infidel who wanted to destroy the foundations of society, ridiculed Bryan and the advocates of free silver, espoused the gold standard, boldly defended trusts and monopolies, denounced the political leaders of the state, and joined the fight which was then on, headed by the Baptists, to induce the legislature to cut off all appropriations for higher education.

A single quotation from one of his utterances will illustrate his completely changed attitude; "Trusts and monopolies," he declared, "are not the awful curse of society that we are led to believe by demagogs. Great wealth can and does make happiness. I do not hesitate to espouse the cause of commercialism and to congratulate our nation on being the mother of such a vigorous offspring." This and other similar expressions invited the charge against him of apostasy. The Dukes and monopoly apologists naturally applauded Kilgo's change, but at the same time a large section of the public was shocked to see a minister of the gospel making himself the apostle of money and the detractor of all who dared to disagree with him.

Clark and Kilgo, as we have seen, had met as democratic friends, interested in a common cause, but they had arrived from opposite poles. Their background, equipment, education, and temperament were utterly different. Dr. Garber, professor of church history at Duke University, in his recently published biography of Kilgo, speaking of his learning and educational qualifications, said: "Because of the weakness of his eyes Kilgo was forced to leave Wofford College at the end of his sophomore year. It has been pointed out that in addition to this trouble, 'uninterrupted application to books did not agree with his constitution or meet the requirements of his type of mind. He was too intensely active to remain apart from the world of practical work long.' . . . He often spoke of Snyder [a professor at Wofford College] as his 'real university, the only university I ever attended.'"

In temperament Kilgo was emotional, sensational, and dramatic. He belonged to a school of evangelists which at this period was very popular in the South and in the West. The Reverend Sam Jones, of Georgia, was perhaps the most gifted in this field and exerted a great influence over young Methodist ministers like Kilgo. His method of approach was to dress up old truths in a sensational fashion, interspersed with daring criticism of the old methods. Great crowds attended his highly advertised meetings, and what the divine said or would say spurred the imagination and the curiosity of the multitude. For instance, before Sam Jones would arrive to hold an evangelistic meeting it would be reported of him that when he began his ministry he declared, "By God, I was called to preach and I'll be damned if I don't preach"; that when brought to trial before the church court for such a statement he answered, "Yes, I made the statement but the reporter did not properly punctuate my remarks. It should have read, "By God I was called to preach, and I'll be damned if I don't preach."

Kilgo early became an apt student of this kind of sensational evangelism. His brother wrote of him, "From the very beginning of his ministry he attracted large congregations and great revivals resulted wherever he conducted a meeting. I doubt if my brother during his entire ministry ever preached a sermon or delivered an educational address that did not result in dividing the crowd." Soon after coming to North Carolina he began canvassing the state, preaching and lecturing, and finally divided the people of the state into two factions. He astonished the old-line Democrats by denouncing Jefferson as a "religious monster." He was reported in the daily press as ridiculing the free silver plan and declaring that all who believed in sixteen-to-one should be given sixteen lashes on the back. In an address at Roxboro the press reported: "Kilgo referred to the love of women for fine things, and in a jocular vein suggested that a man could take a diamond ring and lead the average woman anywhere." The Raleigh *News & Observer* reported a sermon he delivered at Goldsboro: "I am bigger than North Carolina."

Over the advice of many prominent Methodists in the state, he joined in the fight that was being waged, primarily by the Baptists, against state aid to higher education. Foreseeing the trouble that such a course would result in, a number of the most distinguished members of his church advised against his taking such a position. The Reverend R. S. Webb wrote him: "As a patron of Trinity, a friend of education, and your friend, allow me to express the hope that you will not be drawn into the discussion of state aid to higher education, which is now agitating the state. It originated with the Baptists. There is room enough for all and work enough for all and therefore let state and church do all they can to expel ignorance from the land."

Josephus Daniels, editor and publisher of the Raleigh *News & Observer,* concluded a letter to him: "I cannot believe that any good would come to Trinity by joining with the other opponents to state appropriations to the University and I do see much harm that might possibly come to it. . . . I am so anxious for your success in the state and the growth of Trinity College, and likewise for the success and prosperity of our State University, which belongs to all of us, that I run the risk of expressing to you my conviction of what is best for you, the church and the state."

Kilgo ignored such advice and in a bold and unequivocal manner took the position that it was unconstitutional and wrong for a state to tax all the people to support higher public education for either men or women. He thus early stated his position: "The state may assume to educate, but its inability to deal with the profound truths and principles of Christian character and its undetermined system of morals unfit it for the work of true education. We cannot afford to hazard the destiny of our youths by turning them over to the liberalism of state morals."

Kilgo's biographer, Dr. Garber, interpreting his thinking upon this subject, wrote: "Another principle which Kilgo championed was that a college or university should not be hampered by any forces that might block academic freedom. He felt that this principle could not receive too much emphasis in the southern states, for the tendency was for educational institutions to become the wards either of political leaders or religious groups. He pointed out that in order to secure financial appropriations the state schools had to cater to political parties, while the church colleges, because of their poverty, were slaves to their constituency. Such intimidated institutions could not educate, for men had to have open fields if they were to find truth; they had to breathe an atmosphere of freedom if the love of truth was to be inculcated."

The press and the public generally construed this process of reasoning to mean that since the state could not properly educate its people on account of political parties, and the churches could not properly educate them on account of poverty, the only avenue left open was to deliver the college to the Duke millionaires, who were both willing and able to endow and support it. This was Clark's estimate of the situation as later expressed by him.

During the years 1896 and 1897, a large section of the press of the state began denouncing Kilgo in the bitterest terms, charging him with selling out the Methodist college to the Dukes and changing his politics from a South Carolina Democrat to a Republican mugwump. The climax of this phase of the controversy was reached when the *Durham Daily Sun* reported a serenade to Washington Duke one evening, by the faculty and student body of the College, led by Kilgo, to express their appreciation of a large donation that Duke had made to the institution. Kilgo was quoted as saying on this occasion: "The first white child was born in North Carolina; the Declaration of Independence was signed in North Carolina; the first bloodshed of the Civil War and present war was shed by a North Carolinian; but greater than these, the greatest philanthropist of the South is a North Carolinian."

A number of the state papers demanded that Kilgo resign as president of Trinity College. A typical editorial appeared in the *Kinston Free Press:* "It would be better for North Carolina, for Christianity, and for Trinity College, in the long run, if a different sort of man was at the head of the leadership of the leading Methodist school in North Carolina, even though the school was less prosperous from a worldly point of view."

2

Clark was brought directly into the controversy in June, 1897, when Kilgo requested the Board of Trustees to change the law requiring the election of the faculty every year so that they might hold office for four years or even longer. The matter was referred to a committee of the Trustees, composed of Judges Clark and Montgomery, and Dr. Swindell. This committee unanimously reported against the change. Promptly after its report was filed, Kilgo wrote Clark saying he had heard that Clark's objection to the change was that it really was an effort to maintain him (Kilgo) in the presidency. Several letters passed between them in which Clark clearly sought to avoid any controversy with Kilgo, but Kilgo continued to press the matter aggressively until Clark finally replied to his last letter, saying: "Its tone impliedly asserts that it is a very grave misdemeanor not to entertain for you the same good opinion which you hold of yourself. In conversation with another Trustee I told him of your growing unpopularity, and I expressed my thankfulness that the Trustees had defeated your recommendation which would have made you irremovable for four years. Your recommendation that the faculty should be elected for four years, was unheard of and unnecessary. You made no exception of yourself from its provisions. I inferred that your motive was to do exactly what your recommendation would have done (if we had adopted it) i. e., give you, as well as the professors, protection from removal for four years. The growing opposition to you, which has become intense with many, in the tobacco section especially; your reported speeches attacking the honesty of silver men (who constitute nine-tenths of the white men of North Carolina); the attacks you have made on the State University; the quarrels you have managed to get up and keep up with Dr. Kingsbury, Rev. Mr. Page, Mr. Webster, and others, have created antagonism which must shorten your stay, unless you are protected by a four-years' term or some influence not based on public esteem. I am sorry that your energies are so little occupied that you are even now seeking to add a controversy with myself to your amusement.

"The attempts of northern multimillionaires to capture by gifts and endowments the control of the education of the children of the people has created a sensitiveness on that subject in the public mind. . . .

"I regret to write you this. Your administration promised success, and you ought to have won it with less ability than your friends credit you with possessing.

"I do not understand your threat to lay my views before the Trustees, but as you somehow seem to think that the Board has jurisdiction of the offense, my views are herein plainly expressed, that there may be no controversy as to what they are."

This ended the correspondence, but it was the beginning of Kilgo's effort and determination to get rid of Clark as a trustee of the College and to discredit him. Kilgo and his friends were active at the various district conferences held during the summer and fall of 1897, and secured the passage of resolutions endorsing him as president and commending the Dukes for their generous contributions to the College.

At the meeting of the Trustees of the College on June 6, 1898, at which Clark was not present, Kilgo submitted the correspondence between him and Clark and stated that if Clark's position was sustained his resignation would be forthcoming. The Trustees exonerated Kilgo, holding that Clark's charges were uncharitable and unfair and resolved that it was the sense of the Board that he ought to resign as trustee of the College.

On June 25 following, a statement appeared in the *Charlotte Observer* that the Trustees had exonerated Kilgo, condemned Clark, and asked for his resignation as a member of the Board.

Having learned from military experience that an offense is the best defense, on the same day Clark addressed a letter to James H. Southgate, president of the Board of Trustees, in which he opened up both barrels: "If any portion of the Board of Trustees had stated to me in a Christian spirit that it was unpleasant to have a difference between Dr. Kilgo and myself and that it would smooth matters if I would resign, I would cheerfully and promptly have done so. I had no intimation of such a wish from anyone; on the contrary, at Dr. Kilgo's instigation, a committee is appointed, I am given no notice, no chance to put in evidence nor to present an argument, I am tried, found guilty and requested to resign. When I even then asked for the names of the witnesses and the nature of evidence and the names of the Trustees who voted against me, so that I might see what weight is to be given to their wishes and if there was a majority present, I am abruptly told I am entitled to know nothing but the verdict. Then in addition to that, this information is given to the public through the Charlotte Observer that I have been asked to resign."

Clark asserted that the motive which activated such proceedings was too plain to need comment; that the public would at once divine who "ran" the proceedings; and that the motive was not the good of the College nor the vindication of justice, but the desire to gratify the wounded vanity of Dr. Kilgo and wreak vengeance on the man who had ruffled it; and that as there were expressions in his letter not gratifying to those who made their millions by illegal trusts at the expense of the toiling masses, there were doubtless some who felt it necessary to propitiate them by condemning, unheard, the man who had been bold enough to let it be seen that he did not fear "injustice" though wrapped in gold. Continuing, he said, "For eleven months I heard not a whisper about that letter, and then on the 15th of June, 1898, I am suddenly informed I have been tried, found guilty, and asked to resign for having written it. . . ." He concluded, "This proceeding, Mr. Southgate, was not instituted for the benefit of the college; it was palpably done to soothe Dr. Kilgo's vanity and to placate the trust that more money might be obtained from it. . . . Recently, Dr. Kilgo, in an affluence of sycophancy, led a procession to the house of Mr. Duke and in a public speech extolled him as the greatest man the state had ever produced and as superior to all the sacrifices of blood and treasure the state had ever made. . . . In substance, he said, 'My Lord Duke, give us money and your name shall be exalted above all names.' This deification of wealth, no matter how obtained, is not Christian education. This is not the language, these are not the thoughts which a college president should teach his pupils."

In a subsequent letter, June 30, to Southgate, Clark wrote that he could account for the Board's conduct only upon the ground that "Dr. Kilgo satisfied the Board that he is the only man who can get big donations from the cigarette trust, that he is the only man who can 'milk the cow' and that when the awful threat was made that if he was not 'sustained' they would lose their milker, he was 'sustained.' "

This correspondence was published in the press and added fuel to the flames. Kilgo found himself in a hot spot and Clark was turning on the heat. Then followed a most remarkable proceeding called a trial. The Trustees had already condemned Clark, had asked him to resign from the Board, and had exonerated Kilgo, but Kilgo conceived the idea that it would help the situation to have a special meeting of the Trustees called and have himself tried before the same jury which had already acquitted him on the same charges. Accordingly, the committee was called and met on July 8. The Reverend G. A. Oglesby, pastor of Duke's church in Durham, was named prosecutor, and they framed a bill of indictment containing five counts, four covering Kilgo's reputation in South Carolina and in Tennessee, and the fifth "Dr. Kilgo's record in North Carolina."

Clark was invited to attend the hearing, which was held behind closed doors with newspaper reporters excluded. The hearing lasted, counting adjournments, several weeks. At the outset the question arose as to who was the prosecutor. Kilgo admitted that he was the defendant and "wished to deny in toto the accusations." The minutes of the proceedings disclosed that Clark announced: "I am not the prosecutor here. This Board instituted the proceedings and I have come before you, and if you want the information you shall have it." Southgate, the presiding officer, said: "I think your point is well taken. Judge Clark is not the prosecutor here." But since the sole question at issue was the truthfulness of the accusations, Clark maintained that the matter should be inquired into by an impartial jury. He then challenged the entire Panel upon the ground that they had previously formed and expressed the opinion that the charges were not true and that Kilgo was innocent. The chairman overruled his objection. He then made the point that since B. N. Duke was a member of the Board he should not sit, as he was a member of the Tobacco Trust and personally interested in the outcome. The chairman overruled this objection. Clark then suggested that Reverend N. M. Jurney, a member of the Board, should not sit on account of prejudiced statements he had formerly made. As the minutes show, Jurney replied: "I did not make the statement as Judge Clark quotes it. What I said was I would stand by Dr. Kilgo and Trinity College and fight for them until they knocked my teeth out, and then I would chew for them with my gums."

When Kilgo's private secretary was suggested as the reporter to take the testimony, Clark objected upon the ground that a disinterested person should be selected; this objection was overruled. He then requested that the reporter be sworn; this request was also denied.

Kilgo then made the point that the fifth count in the indictment as to his reputation in North Carolina should be excluded from consideration and that no testimony ought to be taken on that count. Clark replied that so far as the College was concerned that was the milk in the cocoanut. Chairman Southgate sustained Clark's position, from which Kilgo appealed to the Board and they sustained his contention.

The Board excluded all of the evidence which Clark offered

bearing upon the fifth issue as to Kilgo's reputation in North Carolina. Among the pertinent items of evidence excluded was an affidavit of John R. Webster, a former speaker of the House of Representatives and a prominent Methodist, in which it was stated that he heard Kilgo in a lecture at Madison in 1897 say "that the kindergarten or primary departments of the graded schools were public ranches into which people who could not or would not control their children pitched them to be rid of the responsibility of their care and restraint, and that if he was hunting for vice and immorality he would not go into dark sections of the state commonly called 'dark corners,' but he would go into the graded schools and the other Christless institutions of learning."

When the evidence was concluded, Clark asked the privilege of making his argument, which he had written out. Kilgo objected to this unless he would agree not to publish it. The Board sustained the objection and Clark was not allowed to make the argument.

Kilgo by this time realized that instead of trying to damn Clark he had better compliment him out of the controversy and look elsewhere for a scapegoat. Pursuing this strategy, he said, according to the minutes of the proceedings: "So, then, Judge Clark is not the original accuser, and, I have it in my mind to say, I believe it is the honest truth that Judge Clark has been most falsely dealt with by some common gossiper in whom he thought he had a right to have confidence. You cannot make the defendant believe, you never will do it, though Judge Clark himself testified to it, he will never believe that Judge Clark, born and raised in the home from which he comes, cultivated as he is, with the high social environments of his life, would have made a charge like that without believing that he had just grounds upon which to make it."

Kilgo then turned upon Thomas Jefferson Gattis, a superannuated Methodist preacher who had been a witness in the case.

Gattis had spent the best years of his life in the ministry of the Methodist Church and was universally regarded as a man of irreproachable piety and character. He had been subpoenaed by the prosecution and examined in the case. In the course of his testimony he said that Kilgo's reputation in South Carolina was that of a wire-puller and that he had mentioned this fact to Judge Clark. "Here, gentlemen," said Kilgo, "if you will take in the whole situation and connect it with the testimony of Mr. Gattis, you will likely find the original slanderer. . . . Behind a pious smile, a religious walk and a solemn twitch of the coat tail, many men carry a spirit unworthy of them. He has been occasionally to South Carolina and evidently gossiped too much for a preacher about the defendant. You remember quite well how he in his testimony dodged the issues and would look so solemn and say, 'I cannot answer.'" Continuing, "Mr. Gattis is the only other witness for the prosecution on this charge and his knowledge antedates the judge's charge, and hence Mr. Gattis is the original gossiper." To this he added: "Between the man hiding himself by the highway and making a victim of an innocent traveler and the man who in the dark assassinates the character which the man has tried to build for himself, send me to the woods with a revolver and let me murder every passerby rather than malign my fellow man."

A wag afterwards remarked that the fact that Gattis had the name of Thomas Jefferson aggravated Kilgo's hostility toward him.

3

The Board promptly voted again to exonerate Kilgo of the accusations and rendered a signed verdict in which B. N. Duke joined. Clark thereupon gave to the press the speech which he had been denied the privilege of making to the Board. Its opening paragraphs contained this statement: "No duty more unpleasant has ever devolved upon any man than this has been to me. It pains me to be at variance with anybody and especially with those whom I have deemed my friends for years. I cannot but believe that some influence back of Dr. Kilgo has planned this as an adroit scheme to create a division between me and some that have heretofore been my friends, but I have been driven, pulled, dragooned into this controversy, which is so opposed to all of my feelings. In Kilgo's speech he boasted that he had reopened the fight while he was building up sentiment for the trial. I observed the propriety of keeping quiet. The papers owned in part or controlled by the Dukes and the entire monopoly press assailed me. In coming here today to lay these facts before you I have simply done my duty. I desire no harm to Dr. Kilgo. I have no personal animosity to him, but I am antagonistic to the view he has expressed in the matters I have referred to. I earnestly desire the best good of this College."

Clark quoted with approval from an address delivered by Professor William James before the American Bar Association in 1890, in which he stated that beyond all question in this country the great merchant prince, the railroad president, the great manufacturer and banker have succeeded to the place of power once held by the great orator, statesman, lawyer, or clergyman. The professional class, he said, is losing ground, the business world gaining it. Whether for weal or woe, the control of government, of society, of education, of the press, yes, even of the church, is slipping more and more rapidly into the hands of the business classes, and it is this class which to an ever-increasing extent will dominate our political and social life. Clark's comment upon this was, "Down with manhood, up with the dollar. The proposition is at least clearly stated."

Clark had stated to a fellow trustee at the trial that in his opinion the purpose behind this agitation was ultimately to take the College away from the Methodist Church, which through long years of sacrifice and labor had built it, and turn it over to the Dukes; that a similar result had occurred at Vanderbilt University, which had been taken over by millionaires and lost to the Methodists as a denominational institution; and that Rockefeller had accomplished the same result with Chicago University, a Baptist institution.

Clark believed that a number of his enemies were encouraging Kilgo to single him out and use this incident to embarrass and discredit him, but he did not know the far-reaching extent to which prominent personages, big business, and political influence had combined to accomplish his undoing.

Among the correspondence of Kilgo now on file in the archives at Duke University are letters from Josiah Bailey which shed light upon the extent, aim, and purpose of Clark's enemies in this controversy. Bailey (now United States Senator from North Carolina) at that time was editor of the *Biblical Recorder,* an organ of the Baptist Church in the state. He tendered the editorial page of his paper in which to carry on the campaign against state appropriations for higher education. On July 16, 1897, he actively entered the Clark controversy *sub rosa* in a personal letter to "Dear Brother Kilgo" as follows: "I must tell you in absolute confidence that I was at Judge Clark's yesterday afternoon and perceived beyond a peradventure that he carries a knife under his shirt for you. . . . If he shows his hand I will drive him back; else he isn't the demagog he is said by some to be."

On November 8, 1897, he again wrote Kilgo of the activities of his enemies: "As for Abernethy and Holt—what a pair to draw to—blatherskite and a skunk; a nice match for Sissy; after McIver's own heart and twin sisters to Joe Daniels and Thompson; a million of them against a fairly decent cause would only help it. Three—dollar popguns! But we must look out for Clark and for Jarvis and our benignant and beautiful Julian Carr—I could almost write a poem on him. If they can destroy you, they will; they shall not do it unless it be at the cost of their own lives. And there is not one of them who knows the impulse of unselfishness. What a marvelous gang of demagogs old North Carolina has bred. Keep me informed. If I don't say what you want said, send a line. We are bound together, and the man who strikes you strikes me; and we must together withstand the sissies, the skunks, the demagogs and conspirators. Ours is a holy cause, but it has to fire mighty low to hit its enemies." He adds a postscript with respect to Crawford, who was editor of the Methodist *Christian Advocate* and opposing their program: "Ain't Crawford a 'daisy'? Such an ass editing a paper. Joe Daniels must be his ideal and model." It is understood that "Sissy" referred to Edwin A. Alderman, later president of the University of North Carolina, Tulane University, and the University of Virginia.

Daniels, in his recently published volume *Editor in Politics,* speaking of Bailey's connection with this affair, wrote: "At that time Bailey and Kilgo were singing a duet of adoration of trusts when not opposing decent appropriations to the University and other state educational institutions."

In this same volume Daniels reports that Bailey and Kilgo decided to do some trading with the Democratic machine, headed by F. M. Simmons, and concluded a treaty with him providing that if he would see to it that the legislature elected in the following fall would not increase appropriations to the University or any state-controlled colleges, they would join in the Democratic movement then on to rid the state of Negro domination, and fight for white supremacy.

Simmons, in his memoirs, writing of this incident, said, "I promised the various denominational colleges, which were then rather hostile to state institutions, that I would not increase the appropriations for the latter during the session of 1899. Through Jarvis I also promised the large corporations that their taxes would not be increased during the biennium." "The Editor in Politics," commenting, says that the defense by Simmons does not justify his secret agreements: "It convicted railroad executives and church leaders of taking advantage of politics to obtain ends that people would not grant after open discussion. How much money the railroads contributed to the campaign chest was not disclosed."

Considering its exalted source, this statement deliberately made years afterwards by Senator Simmons constitutes one of the most astounding confessions ever made in American politics. It not only shows the close combination of Clark's enemies but it evidences a paucity of principle and a code of conduct which were to govern the Simmons machine in North Carolina for a quarter of a century. It is a perfect example of the evil forces with which Clark had to contend and consistently fight, without compromise, to the very end. It is a significant fact that Bailey performed so well his part in the setup that he soon became the amanuensis of the Simmons machine.

4

After the trial, Kilgo's speech was published in the Raleigh *Morning Post* and other papers of the state, and later Kilgo and his friends published and circulated a Blue Book purporting to contain a stenographic report of the hearings before the Board of Trustees, including Kilgo's speech. When it became publicly known that Kilgo had abandoned his fight on Clark and had selected Gattis as his victim, upon whom he poured out his vial of wrath, Gattis' many friends throughout the state were outraged and insisted that he should vindicate his character by instituting an action in court for slander and libel against Kilgo for what they regarded as a cowardly assault upon a blameless brother minister. This he promptly did by instituting an action in the superior court of Granville County, charging Kilgo, B. N. Duke, W. H. Branson, and W. R. Odell with libeling him in the speech referred to, and demanding $100,000 as compensatory and punitive damages. (Before the litigation ended, Branson died and Odell was let out of the case.)

A number of highly distinguished counsel were engaged in this trial, which resulted in one of the most sensational actions ever occurring in the judicial history of the state. Cyrus B. Watson was the leading counsel in the case for Gattis, and ex-Judge Robert W. Winston, for Kilgo and Duke. At the trial Kilgo's attorneys deemed it advisable not to undertake to justify the truthfulness of the statements made about Gattis, but pled that the occasion under which they were made was a privileged one and therefore Gattis was not entitled to recover even if the statements were untrue. At the first trial the jury rendered a verdict finding that Kilgo and his associates had libeled Gattis, that the words were maliciously uttered and that he and the other defendants should pay the plaintiff $20,000 damages. Judge Hoke, who presided at the trial, declined to set the verdict aside. Upon appeal to the Supreme Court a new trial was ordered, at which a second jury answered similar issues submitted to them in favor of the plaintiff and assessed the damages at $15,000. Judge Shaw, who presided at that trial, declined to set the verdict aside. The Supreme Court again remanded the case for a new trial. The case was then removed to Raleigh, and upon a final hearing the trial judge held that there was no evidence of express malice on the part of Kilgo and his associates to overcome the quasi-privileged character of the statements, and accordingly dismissed the action. Upon appeal to the Supreme Court (Judge Clark not sitting on any of the appeals), the Court divided two and two, which under the rule of the Supreme Court resulted in an affirmance of the decision below. The opinion of the Court stated: "Upon the question, whether there is any evidence that the defendant Kilgo was activated by malice in publishing the pamphlet, the justices are equally divided in opinion, two of the judges holding that there is evidence in the case, certainly when coupled with what was improperly excluded, which requires that the cause be submitted to the jury...."

So ended a controversy and a series of trials, which during its course aroused the people of the state, engendered many bitter enmities, and decided nothing. Gattis had become the unhappy victim in a conflict between giant forces which resulted in the impairment of his health, in the wasting of the little substance which he had, and in his death, which occurred a few months later.

One of the founders of Trinity College was the gifted and consecrated Dr. Braxton Craven, who became its first president and shaped its high mission. Clark was sustained in the trying ordeal through which he passed by a vast host of his fellow churchmen, who wanted the college, as did he, to follow the spiritual pathway marked out by Dr. Craven.

Notwithstanding the many years that have since passed, there remains the memory of two things connected with the litigation, one a scandal and the other a witticism.

At one of the jury trials R. N. King made an affidavit that he was approached by ex-Sheriff Rowan Rogers to help out Kilgo, and a regular juror, S. P. Markham, testified that J. P. Sorrell asked him to work for the defendant and suggested that they would pay him. Because of these activities the presiding judge ordered Rogers and Sorrell attached for contempt of court. They were found guilty and sentenced to thirty days in jail for jury tampering. At the next term of criminal court these men were both found guilty of embracery and sentenced to six months in jail. *The News & Observer* gave flaming publicity to this stink and demanded: "Go higher up; if Kilgo and Duke had nothing to do with it, the question is who was responsible? ... It is a serious matter, Rogers and Sorrell must squeak or they must suffer." The implication of this demand was clear, but the matter ended without anybody's "squeaking".

The witticism referred to was a declaration made by the great trial lawyer, Cyrus B. Watson, in his closing argument to the jury, for Gattis. Said he, "Over the gateway to the entrance of Trinity College there is this inscription, 'Eruditio et Religio.' It should be now changed so as to read, 'Eruditio et Religio et Cigaretto et Duko.'"

Chapter X

IMPEACHMENT OF THE JUDGES

In North Carolina's long history there had never been an impeachment trial of a member of its Supreme Court. When the General Assembly, at its session in 1901, adopted articles of impeachment against Chief Justice Daniel M. Furches and Associate Justice Robert M. Douglas, charging them with high crimes and misdemeanors in office, it created a sensation of the first magnitude.

The state was already afire with political strife, and this act on the part of a Democratic legislature against two Fusion justices of its highest court added fuel to the flames.

The impeachment apparently involved the acts of the judges in only a single case, but its repercussions were all-embracing. The merits or demerits involved were that the Fusion legislature of 1897 had created the office of Shell-Fish Commissioner, to which one White was appointed for four years; the succeeding legislature, controlled by the Democrats, passed an act abolishing the office and directed the state treasurer not to make payments of salary to him. White instituted an action in the superior court for a mandamus to require the state treasurer to pay him a back salary of less than $1,000; three of the Fusion judges, constituting a bare majority of the court, affirmed the decision of the lower court, holding the legislature had acted unconstitutionally in abolishing the office and forbidding payment. From this decision Justice Clark dissented, as did also Justice Montgomery, one of the Fusionist members. Counsel for the plaintiff in that case, at the next session of the Supreme Court, applied for a writ of peremptory mandamus commanding the treasurer to make payment to White. Members of the court consulted among themselves as to the authority and propriety of issuing such a writ, and over the vigorous protest of Justice Clark ordered the clerk of the Supreme Court to issue the writ, to which order Justice Clark prepared, and asked leave to file, his dissent, setting forth his reasons therefor. But the majority of the judges declined to allow him to file it. Furches in the meantime was appointed chief justice, succeeding Faircloth, who died between the date of the filing of the original opinion and the impeachment proceedings—which accounts for his not being included among the justices placed upon trial.

By Specification 5, Article 4, of the impeachment, Clark was brought directly into the proceedings:

"That, well knowing that two of the Associate Justices of the Supreme Court of North Carolina did not concur with the aforesaid majority of the court in directing the aforesaid mandamus to be issued, one of the dissenting Associate Justices (now Clark) claiming the right to do so was refused and prevented by the aforesaid majority of said Supreme Court, including said David M. Furches, Associate Justice (now Chief Justice) and the said Robert M. Douglas, Associate Justice, from entering his protest against the issuing of the said mandamus writ upon the minutes of the said Supreme Court, and was also denied the right to file his opinion giving his reasons and grounds for dissenting from the action of said Supreme Court in directing the aforesaid mandamus writ to issue whereby the aforesaid David M. Furches, Associate Justice (now Chief Justice) and the said Robert M. Douglas, Associate Justice, did then and there commit and were guilty of high crimes and misdemeanor in office."

The offending judges alleged in their answer that the substance of the articles of impeachment was that they were guilty only of having followed a doctrine laid down more than half a century before by North Carolina's famous Chief Justice Ruffin in the celebrated case of *Hoke* v. *Henderson,* which had never been overruled by any succeeding court—that an office was property which belonged to the office-holder and that the legislature could not disturb it.

The managers for the impeachment denied this and contended that for partisan and unworthy reasons these judges had undertaken to extend the Ruffin doctrine, making it applicable to the court's authority to issue a peremptory writ of mandamus compelling the state treasurer to pay money to a defunct officer after the General Assembly had abolished the office and positively directed that no further payment should be made.

The majority judges in the White case declared this doctrine to mean that a public office to which there is attached a salary has a vested interest—a property in the holder—and as such property-holder he is protected by the law and the Constitution of the state and of the United States, and no legislature has authority to deprive him of the emoluments of his office by abolishing it or withholding compensation. Clark had been the first jurist in North Carolina to challenge this doctrine, and as stated by Justice Montgomery, one of the Fusion justices, in his dissenting opinion in the White case, "Justice Clark has rendered numerous dissenting opinions (which are a part of the history of this court) in which he has with marked ability attacked the doctrine so long and so firmly established in the decisions of this court, that an office is property and that it exists by contract between the state and the office-holder."

The substance of Justice Clark's dissenting opinions in these so-called "office-holding cases" involving what is known as the Ruffin doctrine was: The legislature is the great and chief department of government; it alone is created to express the will of the people; the emoluments of office-holders cannot be more sacred than the right of the people to control their own government and to change the management of their own property whenever they think proper; the legislature has all the power the people themselves have except where restricted by the Constitution; the executive and judiciary have none except what is given them by the Constitution; and the supreme power in every government of every kind is the law-making power wherever it may be vested.

In the light of the issues raised upon the impeachment trial, it was inevitable that Justice Clark's name and his opinions would play an important part in the trial. In Justice Clark's opinions referred to by Justice Montgomery, and in other cases, he had completely demolished the reasoning advanced in *Hoke* v. *Henderson,* pointing out that every state in the Union, as well as the Supreme Court of the United States, had repudiated the doctrine, the latter court having held: "The legislative power of a state, except so far as restrained by its own Constitution, is at all times absolute with respect to all offices within its reach. It may add, issue, create, or abolish their duties. It may also shorten or lengthen the term of office. And it may increase or diminish the salaries or change the mode of compensation."

He took occasion also in these decisions to declare and emphasize his objection to judicial supremacy over the legislative department of government. Said he, "Whatever tends to increase the power of the judiciary over the legislature diminishes the control of the people over their government, negatives the free expression of their will, is in conflict with the spirit and express letter of the organic law and opposed to the manifest movement of the age."

He concluded with the declaration: "This is our government. In it there is no room for judicial hegemony."

Upon the trial Clark's dissenting opinions and would-be dissent, which the judges would not allow him to file, constituted the backbone of the evidence offered against the judges. But his suppressed dissent which the managers introduced also showed that he had earnestly sought to avoid a conflict between the Court and the legislature.

"In view of the action of the General Assembly," he wrote, "by the resolution above referred to passed since the opinion of this court, there is a conflict of jurisdiction between this and the legislative department of the government, it will be both courtesy and wisdom not to make a further conflict inevitable by permitting the Clerk to issue a peremptory and absolute order to pay the state's money to the plaintiff. It would be more seemly to give the legislature soon to assemble an opportunity at least to withdraw their inhibition upon the treasurer and auditor against paying plaintiff. For the first time in the history of this state these writs, if they shall issue, will direct the public treasurer and the state auditor to pay public funds entrusted to their care to parties to whom, by an act of the legislature, they are forbidden to pay them."

And in a memorandum to the clerk of the Supreme Court, which was also made a part of the record, Clark wrote: "I hereby instruct you not to issue the said writ because (1) it is not authorized by the former opinions of this court; (2) its issuance at this juncture is contrary to the course and practice of the court; (3) the court is without any jurisdiction to issue the writ; (4) the court has not ordered you to issue it, and you are without any authority until so ordered."

Notwithstanding this warning and admonition a majority of the Court individually directed the clerk to issue the writ, since they did not seriously regard Clark's views. Indeed the controversy over his filing a dissent took a humorous turn, as testified by Clark upon the trial. Said he, "Justice Douglas remarked 'let it go in the obituary column.' I said it might suit the obituary column, but it is not my funeral."

While the impeachment proceedings were in progress Clark's enemies were busy circulating the suggestion that he would have to be a witness in the case, and that when he took the stand the fireworks would begin. Clark expressed to the managers of the impeachment his willingness to be examined as a witness, and when he took the stand a deathly silence pervaded the packed Senate chamber. On direct examination he was questioned only about his dissenting opinions in the White case, other like dissenting opinions, and the conversations which he and the judges privately had about the propriety of issuing the writ. To the great surprise of all, only a few unimportant questions were asked him upon cross-examination. As he left the stand, someone associated with the defense stated in an audible voice, "He should be further cross-examined." Whereupon Clark calmly returned to the witness chair and said, "I understand there is someone who wishes to further question me." But no further questions were asked.

As a result of the trial and acquittal by a Democratic Senate the entire proceedings took on the aspect of having been unwarranted and consequently a serious mistake. The principal advocates and leaders in the impeachment proceedings were William A. Allen, who later became a justice of the Supreme Court, Locke Craig, afterwards elected governor, and George Rountree, a distinguished lawyer from Wilmington. They were all important cogs in the Democratic political machine which Senator Simmons had efficiently organized. Neither Simmons, who later became United States senator, nor any of the Democratic "warhorses" of the party ever cared for Clark. They used his opinions from the bench, which were very damaging to the impeached judges on trial, and the fact that his associates would not allow him to file his dissenting opinion in protest against the issuing of a peremptory mandamus, and no doubt conferred with him about the circumstances connected with the disagreement among members of the court.

But lurking behind the impeachment proceeding were two matters of far more importance in the minds of the Democratic leaders than the salary of the little Shell-Fish Commissioner. The first was the fear that this Fusion court would declare unconstitutional the recently adopted amendment to the Constitution of the state providing the "grandfather clause" as a test of the right to vote, which meant the total elimination of all illiterate Negroes from voting. This was quite literally the proverbial "nigger in the woodpile." There was also the fear that the court might hold the state liable to the holders of many millions of the fraudulently issued bonds of the state under carpetbag rule during Reconstruction days. Neither of these weighty matters came out in the open during the proceedings, so that the trial took on the appearance of a puny political performance.

Following the acquittal of the judges, an effort at face-saving began among some of the Democratic party leaders who had instituted the impeachment proceedings. A large number of Democrats in the house had voted against the impeachment, led by the wise and able H. G. Connor, who later became a member of the Supreme Court. Joining with the friends of the impeached judges in avowing that Clark was responsible for the whole affair, and acting as chief mouthpiece of this propaganda, was the *Raleigh Post*. This daily organ, established and financed by the special interests in the state, was supported by the enemies of Clark and of *The News & Observer,* and it was striving to discredit both and put them out of business.

Certainly Clark resented his associates' improperly declining to allow him to file his dissent in the White case, and it was true that he had repeatedly, in former dissenting opinions, tried his best to discredit and have overruled the doctrine of *Hoke* v. *Henderson*. But to assert that he had caused the Democratic political machine, headed by Senator Simmons and his able lieutenants, to institute the proceedings, is beyond belief. What seemingly happened was that they used Clark's ammunition on this occasion to try to convict and remove from office two obnoxious political judges, and having used him, later turned on him, as we shall see in the succeeding chapter. The Democratic machine was already preparing to retire Clark from the bench at the next election, and during the course of the impeachment trial F. H. Busbee, one of the counsel for the judges and Colonel Andrews' trusted legal adviser, was gathering evidence against Clark from the discredited Fusion governor, Russell, to throw into Clark's campaign for chief justice like a singed cat by the tail.

CHAPTER XI

CONTEST FOR CHIEF JUSTICE

As THE 1902 election approached, it became evident that the Democrats would carry the state and retire Furches, the Republican Chief Justice of the Supreme Court, whose term of office was expiring. Clark's term of eight years, for which he had been elected associate justice, was also expiring the same year, and he chose to stand for the nomination for chief justice. This action on his part at once precipitated a fight which for bitterness has never been surpassed in the political annals of the state.

As there was no Governor to elect that year, all eyes were turned to the office of Chief Justice and Clark became the central figure of the state campaign. He was now universally regarded as the ablest man on the Court, and his critics charged that he dominated it. In dissenting opinions, public addresses, and articles in magazines of nation-wide interest, Clark had established himself as an irreconcilable liberal and had wielded a pen which dripped with denunciation of the many evils which he asserted were sapping the life-blood of democracy.

It was startling for a Supreme Court judge to call names and give the people facts which, if true, branded men in high places and powerful institutions as exploiters and public enemies. Of course, such an attitude invited a fight to the death, a fight in which no favors would be asked and no quarter shown—and this is precisely what happened.

In looking back at the contest it is amazing that a lone judge without money and without political organization should have had the courage to tackle a combination representing a force in politics that knew no master. In this fight Clark was fortunate, however, in knowing in advance who his chief enemies were; he knew, because he had made them.

The most powerful influence he had to deal with was the combined force of all the railroads in the state—the Southern, Coastline, Seaboard, and Page's Road. He had denounced their practices of issuing illegal free passes, charging exorbitant passenger and freight rates, obtaining unfair tax valuations, and interfering in the politics of both parties.

The next in importance of his enemies was the American Tobacco Company, which was hand and glove with the railroads in a determination to get rid of this dangerous judge. This alliance was what is called a "natural," for Clark had also condemned the Tobacco Trust as a violator of the Sherman Antitrust Act and had declared that it should be criminally prosecuted under the Antitrust Act for destroying innocent competitors and robbing the farmers of their tobacco.

These companies had at their command a number of newspapers whose editors carried in their pockets free passes on all the railroads.

Topping the list of papers was the Raleigh *Morning Post,* a daily newspaper established and supported, it was openly said, by these interests and their affiliates for the purpose of retiring Clark to private life and counteracting the influence of *The News & Observer,* which was standing back of Clark like a brick wall in all of his fights against monopolies, trusts, combines, and railroad domination, and was also with him in the Kilgo controversy.

Clark's quarrel with Kilgo had alienated a number of Methodists in the state, and Josiah Bailey, editor of the *Biblical Recorder,* chief organ of the Baptist denomination, had already shown his animosity to Clark. The Democratic political machine, then headed by Senator Simmons, had no liking for a free lance like Clark, who had the temerity to criticize the big interests who supplied most of the funds for the party's biennial campaign. The nomination for chief justice was to be made by a state convention of delegates gathered from all the counties in the state, comprising a territory of five hundred miles in length, extending from the sea to the mountains. Necessarily these delegates came by train to the convention, and free passes were freely furnished. Then, too, there were active lawyers in most counties who were local counsel for the railroads and who were expected to do their duty in seeing to it that this arch enemy of the railroads did not control the delegations from their respective counties.

In addition to all these forces, it was known that the Democratic political machine wished to see a conservative member of the Old Guard elected chief justice and would use its influence against Clark. This machine was so thoroughly organized and ably managed that it was destined to control the political affairs of the state for more than a quarter of a century. Most of the men who had joined the Populist party and fused with the Republicans in 1894 had now come back to the Democratic party and were as loud in their denunciation of Governor Russell and the Republican party as were the Democrats. Realizing Clark's hold upon the masses, his enemies shrewdly introduced another element into the contest by starting a whispering campaign that Clark had been responsible for the unpopular impeachment proceedings instituted by the legislature of 1901 against Judges Furches and Douglas, which had resulted in their acquittal.

As the campaign opened, these opposing forces fired a broadside at Clark. They declared that he was unfit to be chief justice; that he was smeared with Populism, that he was a Bryanite and an enemy to the property interest of the state. They also charged him with stirring up class hatred by advocating the cause of labor and writing dissenting opinions calling attention to radical social reforms which would abolish child labor and deny the right of employers to plead assumption of risk in actions brought on behalf of infants who were injured while working at dangerous machinery; that he had an overweening ambition and wanted to make himself dictator.

An amiable and harmless Democratic lawyer, Judge T. J. Hill, whose home was in Halifax, Clark's native county, was brought out as a candidate against him. While keeping up his work as a member of the Court, Clark communicated by letter with friends throughout the state, asking them to look after his interests in their several counties, but he had no political organization. Every outward appearance indicated that the combination against Clark was so powerful that defeat was certain.

As the campaign progressed his enemies grew bolder and more reckless with their charges of unfitness. About sixty days before the convention was to meet, there occurred one of those miraculous things that so often happen in a political contest, which suddenly changed the current of the campaign. For some time a whispering campaign against Clark, of a most discreditable character, had been going on, and as the nominating convention approached, it grew more audible. This whispered charge was that he had secretly conspired with former Republican Governor Russell to betray the state and party; that he had written the Governor notes which showed that he had prostituted the high office of Supreme Court Judge; and that at the proper time these notes would be published, when the people of the state would be shocked at the vile conduct of their idol.

Clark's friends became greatly alarmed when they learned that he had written Governor Russell several notes, of which unfortunately he had not kept copies and the exact contents of which he did not remember. But he assured them that when revealed, the notes would not reflect upon his character as a judge or as a man. The excitement in the state over this matter became intense, for everyone realized that the situation contained dynamite and plenty of it.

The peril of Clark's position was aggravated because Governor Russell had gone out of office in 1901 without friends, bitterly hated by the Democrats and even the Populists as well. Russell had been elected governor by a fusion of the Republicans and Populists on a reform platform, pledged to regulate and control the all-powerful railroads of the state. He ended his term of office by abjectly surrendering to the railroads, while in the meantime he had appointed many Negroes to public office and in numerous other ways had offended the sentiment of the white people of the state. All that was necessary in those days to destroy the chances of a candidate for nomination by the Democrats was to tie him up with the hated Russell administration.

The forces that were on the cry for Clark's blood appreciated this fact and sent their two trusted and most able representatives to make the kill—Captain W. H. Day and Fabius H. Busbee. Day was division counsel for the Seaboard Air Line Railroad, a lifelong Democrat and one of the ablest lawyers in the state. Busbee held a like position with the Southern Railroad, and both were neighbors to Clark in Raleigh. Busbee was among the most prominent Democratic lawyers in the state and had the deserved reputation of being resourceful, brilliant in debate, and possessed of a vitriolic tongue.

Clark's enemies regarded it as a shrewd political move to select Day and Busbee to lead the vicious assault against him. It was generally known in the state that Day and Busbee had served with Clark as officers in the Confederate Army; that they were lifelong Democrats and had theretofore been his personal and social friends. It will be recalled that Captain Day, referred to affectionately by Clark in his early diaries as "Billy Day," acted as his second when he challenged Pugh to a duel.

But, alas, politics and business had made strange bed-fellows, and the members of many families were arrayed against each other in what was then recognized as a deadly combat.

It developed that Day and Busbee had obtained the Clark notes from Russell, and their publication was anxiously awaited by the public. Here again Clark showed his Napoleonic daring by demanding of Russell that he be allowed to see the original notes and take copies of them. Russell directed Day and Busbee to let a friend of Clark's, Ben Lacy, see the notes and take copies of them. On Tuesday, May 6, 1902, Clark received these copies, and to the amazement of the railroad lawyers, Clark fired first by publishing them the following Sunday morning in every daily paper in the state, in an open letter, giving the public an exact copy of each and every note with explanations as to why and under what circumstances each was written. In opening this public letter, which was addressed to a fellow Confederate veteran, Colonel E. J. Holt, Clark stated that Russell had been elected governor as a reformer and as a pretended friend of the people; that he had appealed to Clark to advise him as to his duties and powers and that Clark had tried to help him.

Clark pointed out in this letter that in order for the correspondence to be understood, it was necessary to review some of the important facts which led up to his writing of the letters. He emphasized that Russell, after his inauguration as governor and his then-declared purpose to enforce the law against offending railroads, had come to him for advice as to how the law could best be enforced. In his letter to Russell demanding to see a copy of the notes is this declaration:

> "When as Chief Executive you were endeavoring to enforce the law against the great railroad corporations, who were openly violating it, you sought me and asked my judgment and advice. Believing that all violations of the law should be repressed, no matter how powerful were those committing those violations, I thought it my duty to give you whatever proper aid I could. If in so doing I made any communications which were official, they should still be in the executive files. If they were personal and confidential, received and accepted by you as such, why are they now in the possession of the attorneys of the corporations whom you were then proceeding against for violating the laws of the State?"

Clark concludes:

"This was the advice of a law officer, a Judge, to the chief executive as to the execution of the laws which were being openly and notoriously violated by powerful and wealthy criminals."

Clark then detailed a number of flagrant violations of the law which the railroads were engaged in and which the Governor was condemning and proposed to stop. He declared that among such instances was the violation of a statute of the state forbidding the issuing of free passes under a penalty of five thousand dollars, which was openly and flagrantly done; that "this influence bought by these 'pasteboard favors' was a most powerful weapon in the hands of the corporation; that the Governor found that railroad fares and freight rates in the state were sixty per cent higher than the average in the Union, and that taxes paid by the railroads were over a half million dollars less in proportion to mileage than in Tennessee and were the lowest in the Union." And said Clark, "The Governor found that two members of the railroad commission (which had been created to reduce fares and rates to a fair basis and see that the railroads paid fair taxation) were partners of the railroad in running a railroad eating house."

The severest criticism leveled at Clark on account of his notes to Governor Russell was a penciled correction of a summons which the Governor had prepared to be served upon these two unfaithful commissioners, citing them to appear before him to show cause why they should not be removed from office. Clark answered this criticism by saying that it was proper for any law officers, from a justice of the peace who wrote out his warrant to a justice of the Supreme Court who prepared and issued a bench warrant, personally to prepare the indictment even though the case was to be ultimately heard before the officer issuing the indictment. In this case the hearing to which the notice to the railroad commissioners applied was to be had before the Governor, who under a legislative act was solely authorized to hear complaints against these commissioners, and if sufficient cause were shown upon the hearing to suspend them from office.

In this connection Clark revealed a partnership between these two railroad commissioners and Colonel Andrews, the vice president of the Southern Railroad, which was so startling that the public's attention was diverted from Clark to their shameful course of dealings. Here Clark became the aggressor, asserting:

> "It had been charged in the press that Col. A. B. Andrews owning one-fourth interest in a hotel at Round Knob, and J. W. Wilson, Railroad Commissioner, owning the other three-fourths interest, had rented it to S. Otho Wilson, another Railroad Commissioner, that Otho refused to rent unless it was agreed by the railroad that Round Knob should be made the eating house and stopping place for the trains (and he could not pay rent unless this was done) that in open defiance of the law which these commissioners were sworn to administer, the supplies both by freight and express were carried free, Otho's family were also carried free in defiance of the law against free passes, and his furniture was carried at one-half rates, and that one-half not paid. With such a scandal before him Governor Russell was forced to issue a notice to the two commissioners to appear before him to show cause why they should not be suspended till the Legislature met. They appeared, the witnesses proved substantially the above facts, he suspended them. Upon the face of the statute, his action could not be reviewed by the Supreme Court, but by the Legislature alone. The Wilsons were tried by the Legislature, and notwithstanding the Legislature was Democratic, Governor Russell's action was sustained, for J. W. Wilson, whose term expired, was not elected, and Otho resigned."

Clark then asserted:

> "When the Southern Railroad received Governor Russell's submission they seemed to have gone through his pockets and got all he had that they could misrepresent and use

against me. It is all printed above. Having destroyed Russell by the aid of the odium against him, they then sought to destroy me by printing and insinuating that I was his ally, his friend, his intimate."

Turning to his personal defense:

"My highest aspirations have been for the good of my native State. I wish to see every boy and girl given a better chance in life. I wish to see the corporations treated fairly and justly, but to pay a fair share of taxation and to charge the public reasonable rates in return for the franchises the public has given them without charge.

"I have made mistakes, I have committed errors, but God knows I have nèver done a dishonorable act. The charge that I have done so, made by corporation agents, has surprised the public only less than it has myself."

Clark concluded his letter by quoting the following note which he said he received from a mountaineer who lived among the coves in Yancey County:

"Judg Clark, I have hearn tell of you, but never seen you. Mr. Wilson sent me one of his pamflets about you and I red it. If all he and them other railrode fellers ses about you was so, I ses the railroades would have had you for ther man long ago, sure pop, so I ses its all a string of lies.
Yours till death."

When this correspondence was published, the campaign for delegates to the State Convention had a month to go, and Clark's letter overshadowed all other issues. Impartial observers pronounced it a devastating political document, and the general public construed the correspondence with Russell as evidence that Clark was trying to protect the people of the state from the continuing injustice of the railroads. Dr. Charles D. McIver, President of the Woman's College, at Greensboro, expressed the opinion that it was the most brilliant and unanswerable political document that had appeared in the state in his lifetime. Some who were not partisans thought that Clark had acted imprudently in his dealings with Russell, but they acquitted him of any selfish or corrupt aims. The friends of the railroads fought back, and Busbee wrote a letter to the press in reply, but the die was cast, and county after county unanimously instructed their delegates to the convention to cast their votes for Clark for chief justice. As a desperate last hour move, Clark's enemies threatened to bolt the convention if he were nominated, but this effort gained no headway.

2

Amid intense excitement the convention met in Greensboro on July 16. There were two nominations to be made by the convention for associate justices of the Supreme Court, and a lively contest was on for these positions, but as to them there was no rancor or bitterness.

Clark selected, to nominate him, Claude Kitchin, the brilliant congressman whose home was in Halifax County, where Clark was born and reared and where his opponent, Judge Hill, then lived. The Kitchin family was illustrious in North Carolina; two brothers, Will and Claude, were then members of Congress, and their father, Captain W. H. Kitchin, had previously served as congressman from the Halifax district.

The fact that Clark was a native of Halifax County and that his opponent, Judge Hill, was then a resident of that county, and the further fact that Halifax was the home county of Kitchin, added to the drama of the situation.

When the chairman of the convention announced that nominations for chief justice were in order, a deadly silence pervaded the great hall, which was filled to overflowing with delegates and spectators. Kitchin, then in his early thirties, tall, erect, and strikingly handsome, advanced to the speaker's platform, and in a matchless voice proclaimed:

"Halifax County, on whose soil he was born, in whose midst he was reared, whose people have known him from childhood and have watched with abounding pride his career from manhood's moment until this triumphant hour, commissions me to propose for Chief Justice of the Supreme Court of North Carolina a nomination full worthy, without apology or defense, of the unanimous endorsement, of Judge Walter Clark.

"His integrity, his ability, his courage, his scholarship attainments, his pride and love of state, his long and faithful services, his Christian character, eminent in all, unquestioned in all, these, Sirs, are the offerings which his native county brings here and presents to the state."

Addressing himself to the criticism that Clark was not a Democrat, he declared:

"In county, state and nation, he has ever stood by the principles and candidates of the party, in word, in act, in hope and in heart. But Judge Clark, they say, stands accused. Would that I had voice loud enough for every man, woman and child in North Carolina to hear when I assert that with all the wrongs and blunders alleged against him by his enemies, no one has yet been reckless enough to charge to him one wrong, one blunder, against the people's cause or in disobedience of the people's will. He has encouraged and advised the enforcement of the law against the strong as well as against the weak. His offense is that he did not countenance and would not tolerate its evasion by the strong. His offense is that he did not bandage his eyes and seal his lips. He has upheld and defended the Constitution. His high crime is that he could not be controlled by men. He was accused, the evidence produced, and man was never given to behold a sublimer spectacle than the people of a whole state rising—not in the passion of indignation, not in the heat of excitement—but in the majesty of a calm sense of fairness and right gathering together in township and county to do simple justice to this one fellow-man. They heard, they weighed, they vindicated. In this vindication the people have written for honest manhood in North Carolina a deep and indelible assurance that calumny cannot rob truth of its victory or duty of its reward."

The effect of this speech was devastating to Clark's enemies, and although his opponent's name was presented to the convention it received little attention and Clark was nominated by an overwhelming majority.

The aftermath of this contest revealed a number of interesting things—some tragic, some painful, and some humorous. Clark's crushing victory ended all opposition to his being Chief Justice, but unhappily it also ended a lifelong friendship with Day and Busbee. It was a cruel fate that separated these old friends, but the issue was so acute and the result so important that the bitter contest had to run its course. By the very nature of the conflict it grew personal. Busbee, who was high-spirited and sensitive, resented very deeply the thrust which Clark had made at him as the tool of the railroads. Tradition has it that smarting under these blows he took up with his friend and coadjutor, Day, the advisability of challenging Clark to a duel. Day is reported to have said to him, "Before you challenge Clark you should count the cost. I know Walter Clark; he is a crack shot, utterly fearless, and I can tell you what will happen. If you challenge him he will promptly accept, and when you two meet on the dueling field he will deliberately shoot to kill you." Busbee decided for once that discretion was the better part of valor.

Another story went the rounds that Busbee was asked by a non-partisan friend why he was so bitterly opposed to Clark; that he understood Clark was in every way a decent citizen, had been a brave Confederate soldier, was a consistent member of the church, devoted to his family, and that his personal habits were irreproachable, to which Busbee replied, "Yes, that is so, but the trouble with him is that he hasn't the virtue of a single damned vice."

The magnitude of Clark's personal and political triumph over the open opposition of the combined railroads left a few permanent bitternesses. It has been repeatedly told that a prominent railroad official, suitably attired, attended Clark's funeral nearly a quarter of a century later and a friend of both men expressed surprise at seeing him present. He replied, "I have come to be sure that Walter Clark is dead. I never attended a funeral with more pleasure."

Chapter XII

ATTEMPTED LARCENY OF A RAILROAD

In politics nothing is contemptible.—Beaconsfield

WHEN THE governor of a sovereign state causes his attorney general to apply to the chief justice of the state for a bench warrant charging a prominent railway official with the attempted larceny of a whole railroad, aided by the the machinations of a Federal judge, it is notice to the world that a sensational trial of the first magnitude is in the making.

The background and sequel of this legal struggle is an interesting chapter in the state's history, while the chief justice's connection with it is significant.

The state, in conjunction with a few private individuals, had built the Atlantic & North Carolina line of railroad from Goldsboro east to Morehead City, a seaport on the Atlantic coast. This road had long served a public purpose, but the sparsely settled territory through which it ran did not afford enough traffic to make its operation profitable. It came to be regarded as an "orphan railroad." The state, owning a two-thirds majority of the stock and therefore in control, selected its operating officials from party supporters of the administration which happened to be in power at the moment.

On account of the large shipments of fish from Morehead City over the line, it came to be popularly known as "The Mullet Road."

When Aycock became governor of the state, succeeding the Republican, Russell, a suggestion was made to lease the road to some responsible operator who would guarantee the state against a loss and, if possible, return some dividends to the stockholders. V. E. McBee, who previously had been connected with the Southern and Seaboard roads, submitted to Governor Aycock a proposed lease for the road, but its terms were unsatisfactory and, pending further negotiations, Finch, a nonresident henchman of McBee, applied to Judge Thomas R. Purnell, district judge of Eastern North Carolina, for the appointment of a receiver for the road to take over its management and control. The application for the receivership was made to Judge Purnell while he was in Norfolk, Virginia, outside of his district; and without notice to the state he appointed McBee temporary receiver of the road until August 4, 1904, when the state would be given an opportunity to show cause why the receivership should not be made permanent. This high-handed and peremptory action outraged Governor Aycock, who promptly directed his attorney general to apply to Chief Justice Walter Clark for a bench warrent against McBee and his man Friday, Finch, charging them with fraud and conspiracy in an effort to acquire the road by unlawful means, which, if permitted, amounted practically to a theft of the road. A significant circumstance in this extra-legal proceedings was that the application for a bench warrant should have been made to Chief Justice Clark. It was generally known that Governor Aycock, before his election, had been an attorney for the Southern Railway and that he and most of his political associates then in charge of the state disliked Clark and resented the criticisms in his prepared addresses and magazine articles condemning the railroad monopoly in the state, its practices, and its interference in politics. There were two other able Democratic justices on the Supreme Court, friends of Governor Aycock, to whom this application for a bench warrant might have been made, but everyone realized that this action meant a war to the death with a bold and brazen adversary, involving also a direct conflict with the Federal judge, Purnell. It was a shrewd move on Governor Aycock's part to select Chief Justice Clark, because the situation required an able and fearless judge whose reputation was that he would apply the axe wherever needed and let the chips fall where they might. Another reason which actuated his selection was that after Clark's recent triumphant nomination and election as chief justice by the people, he possessed their unqualified confidence; and if the testimony which the state offered at the hearing satisfied him that a crime was being committed, and he so found, the people of the state would support the administration in this unusual and daring move. But, above all, the public welfare was involved, and Clark's known philosophy "that the public welfare is the supreme law" appealed mightily to the governing powers.

The Chief Justice held the hearing in the Supreme Court room, which was packed to overflowing by as intense and excited a crowd as ever attended a trial. Present as counsel for the defendants were W. H. Day (the same Day who, with Busbee, had led the corporation cohorts in an effort to prevent Clark's nomination for chief justice), and J. W. Hinsdale, both able lawyers, while the attorney general was chief counsel for the state. Unlike most criminal hearings, those in attendance had come from the elite of the city of Raleigh and the surrounding territory. The defendant McBee was prominently connected socially and had many friends among the leading business men in that section of the state. The Raleigh *Morning Post* had taken sides with McBee and was lending its influence to the defendants. Present also in court was Josephus Daniels, pencil in hand, to give an account of the proceedings for his *News & Observer,* which had been supporting the Aycock administration by repeated broadsides against the unusual conduct of Federal Judge Purnell and the manifest effort to swindle the state out of this road. This paper had announced editorially that the honor of the state was involved. When the Chief Justice inquired if both sides were ready for the hearing, they replied in the affirmative, but, as a surprise move, counsel for the defense arose and stated to the court that they would waive for their clients a preliminary hearing and consent that the court might bind them over for trial before the superior court without further ado. Such a course was permissible in preliminary hearings of criminal charges, and it was assumed that the court would simply enter an order finding probable cause and transfer the case for further hearings to the grand jury of the superior court. But to the surprise and astonishment of everyone, the Chief Justice announced that the matter before him involved a charge of conspiracy and fraud brought by the state against prominent citizens concerning the control of one of the state's railroads; that it was of great public concern; and that he felt that in justice to both sides the facts should be developed before him so that the truth of the transaction might be known. He then directed the attorney general to present his testimony upon which the state relied to support the charges in the bench warrant.

The evidence disclosed that after McBee had failed to induce the Governor to agree to a lease of the road which he had proposed, he secured his co-defendant Finch, a native of New York, to purchase from Ed Chambers Smith of Raleigh forty-seven shares of stock in the Atlantic & North Carolina Railroad, agreeing to pay therefor $100 per share, although the market price of the stock was not more than $25 per share. To close this phony purchase Finch paid Smith a nominal amount in cash, giving his note for the balance of the purchase price, with the stock attached as security, which by agreement remained in the possession of Smith. Finch then instituted suit in the United States District Court at Raleigh, alleging that he was a bona fide stockholder of the railroad, and applied to Judge Purnell for a receivership of the road, requesting that his co-defendant McBee be made receiver; thereafter, without any further evidence before the court and without an opportunity for a hearing by the state, Judge Purnell appointed McBee receiver with authority to take over the immediate possession and control of the entire road and its equipment, which McBee at once did. From this and other evidence offered at the hearing, Chief Justice Clark reached the inescapable conclusion that the receivership proceedings were a scheme by McBee and Finch to get charge of a road that McBee could not lease; that Finch had made the pretended purchase of stock to enable McBee to carry out this scheme; and above all was the fact, which was known to every trained lawyer, that Judge Purnell had no authority while out of his district and out of the state, to hear an application for receivership and to appoint a receiver in so important a matter without even giving the state an opportunity to be heard.

Chief Justice Clark's ruling that the state should put on its testimony and develop its case paralyzed the defense, while *The News & Observer's* full report of the proceedings acquainted the public with a scandal in high places which sounded the death knell of the attempted conspiracy. *The News & Observer* heaped its praises upon the Chief Justice for his able and fearless handling of the case, accompanied with little-concealed contempt for Judge Purnell's action in the matter, strongly intimating that he was a party to the conspiracy. These editorials so irritated Judge Purnell that he cited Daniels for contempt of his court, convicted him, denied him the right of an appeal, and ordered him to jail. Editor Daniels was never actually sent to jail, but to the Yarborough House, a comfortable hotel, where he held receptions for his many friends who called to assure him of their support of him and their condemnation of Judge Purnell. Daniels' counsel applied to United States Circuit Judge Pritchard for a writ of habeas corpus, alleging, primarily, that he was not guilty of contempt, because the remarks were not made in the presence of the court, but written in his office which was about four blocks removed from the court building. Judge Pritchard ordered his release, and so ended the legal and illegal drama in which Daniels became the hero for having been sentenced for contempt, while the railroad crowd and the conspirators added a few more oaths to their denunciation of Clark for having exposed their infamy.

Chapter XIII
PROPHET OF A NEW ORDER

"What is essential and actually new in the world is social democracy." —Vandervelde

BY THE END of the nineteenth century students of government and society began to realize that changed conditions had brought new problems never dreamed of by the founding fathers. Clark the historian realized that the chief problem of three million people in the beginning was how to establish liberty, while the problem of one hundred million people in his own day was how to use that liberty so as to promote peace and prosperity and secure happiness for all. Political democracy had done its work, but a socialized democracy was now needed. Just as equity two centuries earlier had been introduced to make the law more just, socialized democracy was now needed to make political democracy responsive to human needs.

Clark's triumphant nomination for chief justice in June, 1902, had left him free to expound his philosophy of law and government, to dream dreams for the future of the common man in America. It was the beginning of the fulfillment of his career and it emboldened him to prophesy a new order for the public welfare. His address, as president of the State Literary and Historical Association, in the following month of July at Roanoke Island, reflects his happy state of mind and his confidence in the future. He opened this address with the declaration, "Well do we come here to visit the spot where the shackles of the ages were broken, precedent forgotten and where man first began to stand upright in the likeness in which God had made him." Satisfied that the old order had passed, he asserted, "The change started here, when a new race began, without feudal burdens and amid the breadth and freedom of untrammeled nature. With new paths to tread, new roads to make, new rivers to travel, new cities to build, men began to think new thoughts and to add, to the freedom of nature the liberty of speech and of action." Upon this sacred spot, on a historic occasion, he summarized his creed, that in this day of wider intelligence and general education, "let us hope and believe that there is a third way, hitherto unknown in practice, and that by the operation of just and wiser laws enacted by the sovereignty of the people a more just and equal distribution of wealth will follow and the enjoyment of material well-being will be more generally diffused among the masses." All power, he asserted, "is derived from and belongs to the people and should be used solely for their good"; this he regarded as the fundamental teachings of the Declaration of Independence and the Bill of Rights. Translated it means, "Put money in the service of production, production in the service of humanity, and humanity itself in the service of an ideal which gives meaning to life." His complete trust in the ultimate wisdom of the people led him to visualize a state fulfilling the dreams of the reformer and satisfying the demands of the realist. Clark concluded this notable address with a prophecy—one hundred years hence—"that every village will be connected with its neighbor by electric roads, for steam will have ceased to be a motive power; that education will be universal and poverty unknown; that every swamp will have been drained to become the seat of happy homes; that every river will be deepened and straightened; that public works operated for the benefit of the people and not for the enrichment of a few, will bring comforts and conveniences, now unknown, to the most distant fireside; that the hours of labor will be shortened; that the toil of agriculture will be done by machinery and that irrigation will have banished droughts; that the advance of medicine, already the most progressive science among us, will have practically abolished all diseases save that of old age; that simpler laws and an elevated and all-powerful public opinion will have minimized crime and reduced the volume of litigation; that religion less sectarian and disputatious about creeds and forms will be a practical exemplification of that love of fellow man which was typified by its divine founder; that every toiler with brains or with hand will prosper; and that under juster laws the only inequality in wealth or condition will be that due to the difference in the energy, efforts and natural gifts of each possessor."

The cynic said this was an iridescent dream; the hardened industrialist declared it was pure socialism and impossible of accomplishment. Yet, "time—God's mighty right arm of recompense," within a third of Clark's century mark, amazingly fulfilled much of his dream.

Clark understood that behind all reforms lay the means of getting them, and to this end he placed his trust, not in forms of government, but in the untrammelled will of the people. With this vision he was irresistibly led to struggle to make men free— free from ignorance, free from injustice, free from arbitrary legal discrimination, free from exploitation by the strong of the weak, and finally, to make women free and safeguard the health and bodies of their children.

At Hot Springs, Virginia, the following August, Clark delivered an address before the State Bar Association entitled, "Old Foes with New Faces," which ranks among his ablest deliverances. It embodies an astonishing graph of the best that has found expression in the New Deal. In this address Clark referred to Goldsmith's couplet, so hackneyed by political orators of the time:

> "Ill fares the land, to hastening ills a prey,
> Where wealth accumulates, and men decay."

"But," said he, "it has never been the accumulation of wealth that has brought ills to any people, nor caused men to decay. The increase of wealth should bring progress and development—a better fed, a better housed, a betted educated, a more leisured, and a nobler race. But the unequal distribution of that wealth, its accumulation in a few hands, leaving the mass of wealth producers in poverty and neglect—it is this that has always brought down great empires and destroyed great nations."

Supporting this thesis, Clark asserted that owing to the use of machinery we surpass all preceding ages in the creation of wealth —"but in the just *distribution* of this increase our methods are defective to the last degree." Declared he, "We are suffering from *Economic Indigestion* in its most aggravated form. In all history, wherever the body politic has suffered from such ills, if relief did not come, political convulsions and revolution have followed."

He pointed out that again and again through the ages, the subject masses have moved uneasily beneath their overlords. Then, "In one blinding flash of light there came the French Revolution" as retribution for a thousand years of oppression and wrongs uncounted, that revolution which he quoted Carlyle as saying was "truth clad in hell-fire." He asserted that mankind would still be on a far lower level if the French Revolution had not occurred, and that all the executions by the guillotine added together did not equal half the number of people put to death unjustly, or starved to death by oppression in any one year of the two preceding centuries. He declared that history has been a long economic struggle by the wealth producers to have a larger share of the wealth created by their labor, and that civilization has been exactly measured by the successive rise of the different strata of society to power.

"First the king was absolute; then the nobility forced him to admit them to a share in the enjoyment of the wealth created by the toilers; then the upper middle class, and then the lower middle class forced admission, and then nominally the whole people were admitted to a partnership in government.... Nominally," said he, "for nowhere have the real wealth producers, the toilers, actually asserted their full weight, for had they done so they would have been the government, being more numerous than all other classes."

Opposed to this philosophy and world movement, he declared, was a powerful reactionary group determined to perpetuate the old order and keep all wealth in the hands and under the control of a favored few. He posed the question: "Which force will win? These 'old foes with new faces,' these new claimants to appropriate the wealth of the nation to their own uses; these successors of those who have been repudiated by every nation in turn—or the new forces of organized labor?" He asserted, "The conflict is on, and is irrepressible." With rare insight he declared: "The vast mass of the nation outside of the two opposing lines look with doubt and distrust upon the labor organizations, for they do not know yet how far they will go. This intermediate mass of the nation is opposed to the trusts, and to all rule by corporations. If convinced that organized labor meditates no attack upon the rights of private property and no control of Government in their own special interests, but that each man shall be free to own and enjoy that which he has honestly earned, then labor and the great bulk of the people, the farmers, the merchants, the professions, may unite and terminate the predominance which is given in practice, though not in our form of government, to aggregated, consolidated wealth. Napoleon said that an 'army went on its belly,' meaning that the first problem in war was the feeding of the fighters. So whatever power controls the distribution of wealth, and decides the comfort, the sustenance, the material welfare to be allotted to the masses, is the real government. That power is not at Washington, nor at the State capitals. All legislation against the power of trusts has proved nugatory. The real government of this country today in this respect is in the hands of these last, who have shown themselves stronger than the law. So in Rome, the standards and the coins bore the superscription 'The Senate and the Roman People' and there were Consuls and a Senate and other republican forms, unimpaired, long centuries after all government had been centered in the Pretorian Cohort and its chief."

He boldly declared that skilled labor is entitled to a fair share of the increased production resulting from the use of improved machinery; that as a rule the skilled laborer is not getting it; the consumer, too, is entitled to a fair share in the reduction of the cost of production, but he is not getting it. He then issued the warning that this condition "only exists now till the public can be satisfied as to the best way to destroy the system without injury to the established rights of property and to our other constitutional guarantees."

Clark's uncanny ability to foresee and prophesy the future was strikingly shown in this same address when he concerned himself with the problems of monopoly and agriculture. His familiarity with the abuses of the American Tobacco Company induced him repeatedly to use its record as an example. He declared that the Government had done nothing to enforce the Sherman Antitrust-Act, and in this discussion will be found the germ of *crop control,* with which the nation under the New Deal is now so familiar. He recalled that the Tobacco Trust could not enter France, Austria, or Italy because in those countries all tobacco was sold by the government. "Our former system of free manufacture and sale by everyone is preferable, of course, but if the tobacco trust will reduce all manufacture and sale to possibly only one party, it is better that this one party should be the Government rather than the tobacco trust. The Government would restore fair prices to the farmer, *based upon the size of the crop,* reserving to the Government, as in France and other countries, only a fair profit for revenue and even that profit will go to reduce the weight of taxation and not to swell the estates of a few multimillionaires, as now."

Clark as a boy had fought to preserve states' rights in the South. He was now fighting to preserve human rights in the nation. He believed with Lincoln that God made man before he made money and that wealth created by the daily toil of men should not, under the guise of law, be devoured by the avarice and greed of business tycoons through trusts, monopolies, and combines for the benefit of a favored few. Illustrating, he asserted that countless thousands in our republic are growing restless. "When they look upon a million-dollars-a-year salary to a steel trust president and hundred-thousand-dollar salaries to many others; when they see the palaces, the steel yachts, the appliances and luxuries of countless wealth, which are daily flaunted before those who created but do not enjoy that wealth, and then turn to their own squalid surroundings, they are debating the justice of the present distribution of wealth. . . . Whatever is unjust must perish. These men are not Egyptian fellaheen, and when they demand they will not be denied. There is no higher power in this land than the will of the people when they make up their mind. It is wisdom, the highest wisdom, to discuss, not put out of sight, these social problems and aid if we can toward a just solution; for solved they will be, in some way. The present arrangement cannot and will not abide." He approved Henry George's declaration, "To educate men who must be condemned to poverty is but to make them restive; to base on a state of most glaring social inequality, political institutions, under which men are theoretically equal, is to stand a pyramid on its apex." He followed this with a warning, "A million bayonets cannot support such a pyramid upon their points."

His remedy was as orthodox as Jefferson's interpretation of the Declaration of Independence: "Equal rights to all, special privileges to none." Clark did not advocate giving a quart of milk a day to every child on earth, but with an insight given to few men of his day he predicted that the forgotten man would eventually demand and must receive a just share of the wealth created by him, and live by divine right a free citizen in a world which respects the code of laws given by Him who created it.

CHAPTER XIV

THE NEW COURT

> "*Four things belong to a judge: to hear courteously, to answer wisely, to consider soberly, and to decide impartially.*" —Socrates

THE PEOPLE of North Carolina have always held in high esteem their courts of justice. Their regard has been reflected in the character and legal learning of the lawyers who have been selected to sit upon their Supreme Court. The names of former Chief Justices Gaston, Ruffin, and Pearson are still recalled among the leading jurists of America. Dean Pound and Justice Frankfurter have both declared that Ruffin is one of the three greatest jurists this country has produced. The superior and supreme court judges, since the adoption of the Constitution in 1868, have been nominated by party conventions and elected by the people. It is the proud boast of North Carolina that notwithstanding the vicissitudes of politics and the changes of party control, history does not record the election of a single corrupt justice. They have not always been learned, they have not always been wise, but they have never been corrupt. And those who question the capacity of a democracy to govern, may profitably ponder the judicial history of North Carolina. From its earliest days a custom has grown up in the state which has acquired the sanctity of unwritten law, that justices of the Supreme Court should be selected from different parts of the state and that they should be men familiar with the habits, business, and social life of the people.

In the election of 1902, Clark became chief justice and Connor and Walker, associate justices. In the election of 1904 the two remaining Fusion justices of the Supreme Court, Douglas and Montgomery, were retired, and W. A. Hoke and George H. Brown became their successors. The reputation of this new Court for learning, ability, and prompt dispatch of business reached perhaps the zenith of renown in the judicial history of the state. Its membership was to continue unchanged until 1909, when Connor was appointed by President Taft to be Federal judge of the eastern district of North Carolina.

This Court constituted a judicial mosaic of the best that the profession had to offer. Analyzing this composite picture, we see the Chief Justice standing at the left, an extreme liberal; Brown at the right, a confirmed conservative; between these two stood Hoke, the ideal exponent of democracy; Walker, the devotee of precedent; and Connor, the natural chancellor. This combination, when in unison, produced opinions that attracted wide attention and gave to the bench an honored position among the courts of last resort throughout the nation. It was frequently remarked during the latter years of this Court that any member of it would adorn the bench of the Supreme Court of the United States. The different background, equipment, and philosophy of these justices gave to the Court a power born of a diversity reflecting every shade of thought, and contributed to forming a well balanced court.

Connor, prior to his election in 1902, had served a number of years as superior court judge, and under the rotating system prevailing in North Carolina was acquainted with most of the practicing lawyers and understood the hopes and ambitions of the people. In personal appearance he was tall and slender, dignified in dress and bearing, and looked the part of an accomplished jurist. In conduct he was gentle as a woman, while by temperament he was singularly free from passion and prejudice. He preferred to follow the trodden paths of precedent, rather than the newly blazed trail of the reformer. His bent of mind was distinctly that of the chancellor, always orthodox, entertaining a reverence for the Constitution. A significant insight concerning his judicial qualities is found in the cause of his retirement from the Supreme Court bench. In 1909 a vacancy occurred in the eastern Federal district of North Carolina, and a bitter political internecine war arose among the Republicans of the state for the appointment. President Taft became disgusted with the unseemly scramble over the judgeship and turned to the Supreme Court of the state, selecting Judge Connor, a lifelong Democrat, for the vacancy.

The other four members of the Court, except Walker, had each enjoyed a similar experience of being superior court judge, their terms of office in this capacity ranging respectively from four to fifteen years.

Walker by birth was an aristocrat. His ancestors had possessed ample wealth and he was reared in the famous Cape Fear section, where much attention and pride was attached to noble breeding and good manners. He came to the bench from a firm whose clientele was principally big business interests. He was experienced in corporate law and preferred the counsels of the office to the rough and tumble contests of the courtroom. His frequent long opinions were devoted to following precedents and interpreting the Constitution and statutes in a purely legalistic fashion. He was not an idealist or a reformer, but his sense of justice and high regard for the relative value of things made him a distinguished and honored member of this Court.

Brown was self-made, without the benefit of a college education. For fifteen years he had continuously served as superior court judge and had held court in every county of the state. As a trial judge he had earned a state-wide reputation for ability, prompt dispatch of business, and clarity of judgments. He had a brilliant legal mind, and without reference to textbooks or previous decisions of the court seemed intuitively to know the law and how to apply it. Conscious of this power, he relied upon it and never burned midnight oil or wasted energy for a search in musty law books to find what some other judge had declared the law to be. Brown had a fine physique and a Websterian head; he was reserved and austere in personal demeanor and had few intimate friends; still he was capable of the sincerest affection for those whom he admitted to this circle. He possessed a rare quality—seldom found among lawyers—of being a good financier and business man, and accumulated a handsome estate, which, incidentally, he never lost. Schooled in the teachings of Coke and Blackstone, he came to be regarded as the finest example of what is known to the profession as a "common law judge." Naturally, such a judge was not a reformer; yet reformers admired him because they knew he was honest, able, and fearless, and they also knew just where to place him. With this background and equipment he went to the Supreme Court bench carrying the established conviction that a judge's duty was to interpret and construe the law wherever possible so as to foster and encourage business, and the bigger the business the better he liked it. He quite honestly believed that, in the main, business should be let alone; that competition and the law of supply and demand would automatically afford the necessary restraints and remedies. He was content with the existing order, had little patience—a fact not always concealed—with the so-called moral uplifters—social, political, and judicial reformers. Thus panoplied, he stood like the Rock of Gibraltar as the judicial conservative of the Supreme Court.

Hoke, with an experience of fourteen years as superior court judge, had likewise held the courts of every county in the state. As a presiding judge on the circuit he made an impression by his personality and judicial ability unsurpassed in the annals of the state. He looked, spoke, and acted like a man born to command; he possessed a keen sense of justice, which was happily attuned to the needs and the will of the best thought of the state. He understood, espoused, and reflected the democratic hopes and aspirations of the people. He was one of those rare characters who are powerful yet gentle; intellectual but not dogmatic; imperious but not oppressive; a born aristocrat, he lived the life of a democrat. He came of a long line of political democrats, who had rendered conspicuous service to the state in both war and peace. He rarely dissented from the opinions of Clark, whose liberal spirit and great learning he admired. Upon the death of Clark, Hoke naturally succeeded him as chief justice. History has enshrined him as an exemplar of the best type of judge that a democracy can produce.

Clark was proud of and devoted to this Court, over which he was to preside as chief justice the remainder of his life. The members were companionable and intellectually congenial, notwithstanding their differences of opinion, which were never personal. The chief justiceship suited Clark and he suited it. He loved the work and appreciated the public acclaim which was accorded what is now affectionately referred to by the profession as the "old court." Clark brought to the Court as chief justice an aptitude for the dispatch of business, which is rare among judges and lawyers. The Supreme Court of North Carolina, like nearly all of the courts in the United States, was far behind with its calendar of cases. The litigants were impatient with the law's delay, and congested dockets had grown to be a matter of deep concern. As chief justice, Clark at once organized the bench and in a short time disposed of all accumulated cases and brought the work of the Court up to date.

This single fact invited favorable attention of the profession throughout the country. In his correspondence are numerous letters from chief justices and presidents of bar associations in various states, from Massachusetts to Florida, and as far west as the State of Washington, inquiring how he had succeeded in clearing his docket and keeping up with the business of the Court. The chief reason for this was that he worked almost incessantly day and night and stimulated his associates to do their part. He wrote a system of rules for the procedure of the Court, which are still in use. His encyclopedic mind and familiarity with all the decided cases in the Court's long history gave him a power and influence enjoyed by none of his associates on the bench. Judge

Devin, at present an associate justice of the Court, recalls an incident that illustrates this fact. One day he was present in Court when an attorney arguing a case stated that he had the names of four cases in the North Carolina Reports which he wished to call to the Court's attention, but that unfortunately he was not prepared to cite the number of the Reports in which they appeared. The Chief Justice suggested that he repeat the names of the cases and as he did so Clark, from memory, gave him the book numbers and pages of the reports.

It is a significant fact that among the numerous associates of Clark, during his thirty-five years on the Supreme Court, all bore witness to his uniform courtesy, amiable temper in conferences, and willingness to help with the writing of their opinions in cases where they encountered difficulties. The story was repeated among the lawyers that when the Court decided a hard case and found it difficult to write a satisfactory opinion they would ask the Chief Justice to write it, and he would, stating the losing party out of court on the facts.

The Chief Justice took great pride in the tradition, good name, and fame of his Court. In 1892, soon after he became a member of the Court, he wrote a history of it which was published in *The Green Bag,* a national law magazine, and Judge Seymour Thompson, editor of *The American Law Review,* wrote him that it was the best history he had seen written of a Supreme Court. Clark was very active in encouraging the building of a new and more commodious home for the Supreme Court. When the structure was finished he personally solicited, from the members of the bar and from the family and friends of Chief Justice Ruffin, five thousand dollars with which to erect a life-size bronze statue of him to be placed in the rotunda. The North Carolina Bar Association sponsored the unveiling of this statue and the ceremonies were held in the hall of the House of Representatives, the Chief Justice delivering the address on Ruffin's life and character.

His interest primarily in securing the erection of a new Court building was to house a growing law library which the Court was collecting. Among the first things he did after becoming an associate member of the Court, in 1889, was to encourage the collecting of an efficient modern library, and through his continuing efforts and personal selections he built a library which today is the pride of the state and the profession. Wishing to perpetuate the name and fame of those who had preceded him on the bench, he persuaded the families and kinspeople of former justices of his Court to present portraits of them to be hung upon the walls of the courtroom. When these portraits were presented to the Court from time to time, suitable ceremonies were held and the record of the proceedings was duly published in the bound volumes of the Court's reports. A similar course was pursued with respect to the portraits of a number of the state's most distinguished deceased attorneys, whose portraits were hung upon the walls of the library.

Strangely, the state up to this time had never adopted a motto. The Chief Justice composed one which he considered expressive of the North Carolina character—*Esse quam videri*—(To be rather than to seem). Incidentally, this motto embodied something of Clark's philosophy. He prepared the legislative bill adopting the motto, which his friend, Senator Jacob Battle, a member of the General Assembly, presented for adoption.

When the new Supreme Court Law Building was dedicated, Clark accepted it on behalf of the Court with this statement:

"Welcome within these walls; in this calm atmosphere shall ever be the debate of minds intent on the search for truth and justice, but the people of this State shall demand that in the discussion and decision of matters in this their highest court and their ultimate tribunal to pass upon matters touching their lives, their liberties and their property, passion shall have no power, party rage no place, and their prejudice shall die at the door."

Chapter XV

WOMEN, CHILDREN, AND MINORITIES

"The man makes history; the woman is history."—Spengler

THERE IS nothing in Clark's long and strenuous career which more clearly reveals the character of the man and jurist than does his attitude toward women and children.

A discerning woman in Raleigh once said of him that he completely trusted only women and children. Their weakness, dependence, and helplessness in a man-made society, whose laws denied them protection, equality, and justice, made him their champion in every relation of life, and inspired him to write in their behalf opinions that will never die. In one of his early opinions he wrote: "We cannot envy any may who deems that his mother, his wife and his daughters are inferior to himself. History shows few great or good men who do not greatly owe their success to their mothers or their wives."

When Clark went upon the bench he found the law with respect to women cruel and in many instances revolting. Little had been done, either in North Carolina or elsewhere in the nation, to free them from what he regarded as the injustices of the common law. Both on and off the bench he waged a relentless war to free married women from the bondage of the old common law, which still obtained in North Carolina. After twenty years he completely won this fight. In 1911 he wrote the opinion in *Rea v. Rea*, which *The News & Observer* hailed as, "Married Women are Emancipated." The editor of this paper commenting upon the opinion said: "The decision gave women absolute control over their property as before marriage . . . and was widely commented on and highly commended all over the country. It was hailed as insuring a broader and more enlightened policy."

To win this fight Clark carried on a crusade for two decades, calling the public's attention to the barbaric history of the past which had kept women in subjection and pointing out the absurdities of many previous rulings of his own Court. He showed the history of the law as related to married women and their rights. Here again he was employing the technique of pitiless publicity as the only hope of correcting such evils. He pointed out that under the common law a woman could own no property, make no contracts, "not even for necessaries and not even with the consent of her husband"; that she could not will or devise her property, and upon marriage the husband and wife became one—and that one was the husband; that the moment she married, the husband became entitled to all of her personal property and the rents and profits from her real estate; if she died, he was still entitled to all of the rents and profits, while at his death she received only a child's part of his personalty and a life right, called a dower, in only one-third of his realty; that in North Carolina the husband was even permitted to sell all of his realty without her consent and deprive her of dower, and she could not appoint a guardian for her children, even when she outlived her husband. As to her personal rights, the married woman came under the absolute control of her husband, who could chastise her if he saw fit, provided he did not use a switch larger than his thumb and inflicted no permanent injury. "Once, in England," Clark observed, "when a judge held thus, the ladies sent to get the measurement of His Honor's thumb."

He recalled that Pearson, Chief Justice of North Carolina, as late as 1868, supported this doctrine in an opinion, upon the ground that it was the husband's duty "to make the wife behave herself," and that if he beat her without good cause, it was held the courts would not punish him because it was too small a matter to take notice of, unless she was permanently injured. Declared Clark, "The reason seems to be worse than the decision."

In colonial days the husband had the right to imprison his wife, and if, in her terror, she was driven to take his life, she was guilty of petty treason, as was a slave who took the life of his master, and the penalty as to both was to be burned alive at the stake. The people reversed this law in North Carolina in 1793, but not until after a widow in Iredell County, in 1787, was thus "drawn and burned at the stake" for the murder of her husband.

Clark emphasized that this condition of married women was not created by any legislative body, but was made entirely by judicial decisions, that is, by the common law taken from England, which was simply judge-made law, and this was implicitly followed by the courts of North Carolina until 1848, when it was slightly modified so that a wife's real estate could not be sold by the husband for his debts without her consent. Up to the Constitution of 1868 the property and personal rights of married women in North Carolina had remained substantially as Shakespeare stated the law of England to be in his day, when he made Petruchio say of his wife, "I will be master of what is mine own. She is my goods, my chattels; she is my house, my household stuff, my field, my barn, my horse, my ox, my ass, my anything."

Clark argued that it was the intention of the Constitution of 1868 to emancipate women fully as to their property rights, "but unfortunately it had to be construed by judges who had been raised up in the old belief as to the total incapacity of married women.... Judges raised up in that idea construed the Constitu- as nearly as possible into the likeness of that which had been." He boldly asserted: "Lay it down as a rule that judge-made law has, owing to the training and age of our judges, tended at any given moment to represent the convictions of an earlier era rather than the ideas represented by Parliamentary legislation."

It very naturally followed that when legislators, imbued with his conviction that the only hope of reform was through legislation, assembled in Raleigh, they turned to him to prepare suitable bills to accomplish this result. He prepared many such bills at the request of members of the General Assembly, and nearly every reform in the law freeing woman from judicial slavery in North Carolina is the result of Clark's influence.

Clark was specific and direct in his demands for the rights of women. This is how he catalogued them: "Equal pay for equal services; equality of property rights so that a wife may have the same control over her property as a single sister or her husband; the repeal of all judicial decisions that give to the husband the right to chastise or imprison her, which give to him more control over her than she has over him; equality of right in the custody of children and in the appointment of guardians; the same grounds of divorce for wife as for husband; and finally, an equal share in the conduct of the government by an equal right to the ballot in the selection of officers or in the taxing of her property, and equality of right to hold office."

In one of his dissenting opinions he wrote, "As late as 1899, in at least two sections of our Code, 'married women, infants, idiots, lunatics and convicts' were placed in the same category. Practically they had more or less been deemed in that category, in all respects, by the decisions of the Courts until these have been overruled by the Constitution or by legislative enactment."

Clark's effort to wipe out these injustices and to recognize women as human beings of equal status with men, constitutes a romance in the liberalizing of the law. "Women and children are the great heart of the world," he wrote in an opinion; "without them there can be no future. Helpless they may seem, but the very continuance and existence of all humanity hang upon them. Justice should have no sword sharper, more sudden or surer, than that which should be drawn in their defense."

When a majority of the Court still insisted that the common law forbade a woman's holding public office, even that of a notary public, only one of the justices—Hoke—concurred with him in his dissenting opinion. A petition to re-hear was filed, pending which Clark wrote Sir John Simon, Attorney General of England, to know if the common law of England forbade a woman's holding such an office. He replied that the common law had never been so construed. Clark called this letter to the attention of his associates, but they still adhered to the majority opinion. They were joined to their idols, but Clark did not let them alone. In a dissenting opinion he assembled a number of historical facts regarding the capacity of women to hold office: "From the time of William the Norman, the founder of the dynasty which still reigns in England, there have been forty executive heads of the Government, and seven of these have been women. Among these, the two ablest executives, certainly the two more illustrious and successful, the first of whom reigned for forty-five years and the latter for sixty-four, were Elizabeth and Victoria. In that country women have held many other high positions, and among them, as all lawyers know, the highest legal position in England, that of Lord Chancellor, was held by a woman, Eleanor of Provence, nearly a century before any man was trusted in that high office, other than an ecclesiastic. Women have held many other positions in England of every kind (among them that of sheriff, who there is a judicial officer and sits on the bench with the judges), though they were not voters until thirty years ago when they were granted municipal suffrage. . . . We know that in other countries the greatest executives have been, in Russia, Catherine the Great; in Austria, Maria Theresa; in Spain, Isabella."

Running through all his opinions is the conviction that in a modern democratic society, the courts should not perpetuate by their decisions the injustices of the law against the rights of women and children, which were exclusively judge-made and developed under a feudal system which knew not the democratic spirit. As cases came before him involving the rights of women, he never failed to accord them the same quality of justice that men received. One of the first opinions delivered by him after going on the bench was in the case involving the slander of a married woman. The defense was that prior to her marriage she had had illicit intercourse, and that although since her marriage she had been constant, still she was not an innocent woman within the purview of the statute. It was a case of first impression in the state, but Clark took the position that the defendant was guilty of slander.

Soon afterward another case arose, brought by a daughter in her own name for seduction. The defense was that under the common law the father alone could maintain such an action. Clark regarded such a defense as legal quibbling, and disposed of it in short order by sustaining the action.

In a case holding that a woman was not a freeholder in the sense that she could sign a petition calling for a school levy election, he wrote: "To construe a statute of the legislature, passed now, with reference to long-antiquated holdings of former judges in regard to women, is illogical and unjust." He asserted that women are gradually being freed by legislation, in the interest of a higher civilization, from "many disabilities and wrongs (and in nearly every instance by courts inventing such disabilities, and rarely, if ever, by legislation)."

In a dissenting opinion he held that a married woman was entitled to maintain an action for her earnings and damages for injuries to her person. As a result of this opinion, the following year the General Assembly provided that a married woman could maintain such a suit without the joinder of her husband.

By this time Clark realized the sad fact that very little assistance could be expected from judges in reforming either the procedural or the substantive law. Said he, "The contention that a wife has no more intelligence or responsibility than a child is now out of date. No one believes it. It was as to this very presumption of the wife being under the direction of the husband that in *Oliver Twist,* Bumble the Beadle said: 'If the law presumes that, the law is an ass, an idiot.'"

Much of the opposition to Clark's liberal views, with respect to the rights of women, grew out of the fact that the old timers thought women already had enough if not too many rights. Significant of the thinking of the times was the remark by a member of the Supreme Court, in an address before a class of law students at the University of North Carolina: "Young gentlemen," he said, "women have already been granted by the courts and the legislature so many privileges that the only right left a husband in North Carolina is to sit on his back porch and smoke a pipe—provided he behaves himself."

Many distinguished gentlemen of the old school were greatly shocked by what they termed "Clark's radical views" in insisting that the female of the species should have the same privileges and rights which the law accorded to the male. Reviewing this struggle by Clark to emancipate married women from the rigors of the law, one is amazed at the continued resistance to his efforts by so many intelligent and well-meaning people, including judges.

Candor compels the statement that it can be accounted only for on the ground that his critics and opponents were simply ignorant of the trend of legislation in other states, and particularly by the Parliament of England from which those laws were inherited. By almost continuous study and research Clark had acquired an accurate knowledge of these judicial and legislative reforms. This broad information gave him a power not equalled by any of his contemporaries. Added to this was what might be termed "a sixth sense," his early realization that it was impossible to perpetuate in a republic a legal system half democratic and half feudal.

Clark believed, as few other judges did in his day and generation, that a free people did not at heart entertain any such views with respect to their women and children as were embodied in much of the law. It turned out to be the irony of fate that those who opposed his views were finally confronted with the historical fact that he was not insisting upon any more rights and privileges for women in North Carolina than the Parliament of England had already granted to the women of that country. In other words, there existed the strange paradox of American judges relying upon the teachings of English common law long after the English themselves had repudiated it as being unsound and unsuited to a democratic state. To be more specific, England's married women's property acts, beginning with 1870 and continuing to 1893, had swept away the restrictions of the common law and given to women freedom to contract. Said the English jurist, Albert V. Dicey: "Her private property she could control, and her husband could not touch it. If she wished to sell it or give it away, she need not ask his consent. The act gave to every married woman more complete and independent control of her property than was possessed by the married women of France or of Scotland."

And what was still more significant, the courts of equity in England, instead of denying such liberal interpretation of the law as Clark had contended for, actually extended its liberality wherever possible. Dicey concluded his observation on this subject with the striking phrase: "The rules of equity, framed for the daughters of the rich, have at last been extended to the daughters of the poor."

2

Having written the last chapter in the law emancipating woman as to her property rights, Clark enlisted the same year in her "battle for ballots." In June, 1911, the Chief Justice delivered the first prepared address favoring woman suffrage that was made by any leader in the state. From then on he was recognized as its most distinguished advocate, and became the legal adviser to the State League of Women Voters, and by invitation one of the counsellors of the National League. Mrs. Carrie Chapman Catt, its president, consulted him about the best means of amending the constitutions of several states of the South and West so as to give to women the right of equal suffrage. During the following years until the fight was won, Clark was on the firing line with pen and tongue, speaking throughout the state and in Virginia. He declared, "We have heard much of the 'submerged tenth.' I now have the honor of speaking to you in behalf of the disfranchised half." Clark's critics, he said, had, of course, lined him up with the "long haired men and short haired women," even though by this time he had little hair left. From the very nature of the contest it was inevitable that he should aid in writing the last chapter in the book of Freedom for Women. For them he had from the first advocated four freedoms—freedom of person, freedom of property rights, freedom of ballot, and freedom to hold office. He had lived to see accomplished, largely by his own efforts on the bench and through legislation inspired by him, the total emancipation of married women with respect to their property rights—the amelioration of the harshness of the common law affecting woman's right of person. He now seized upon the opportunity to complete a program to assure her equal rights with men under the law and participation in the administration of government. Clark fought for the cause of equal suffrage because he believed that woman's freedom would greatly strengthen the foundations of democracy. Here again was exemplified his philosophy that a republic should guarantee freedom to all its citizens, men and women, white and black, alike, subject only to such restrictions as society found necessary to protect itself against the ignorant and vicious. In an address before the Equal Suffrage League of Virginia, at Richmond, he declared, "In every land civilization has been measured by the status of the women." He prophesied that, since women were being educated and given freedom to contract, it was no longer possible to deny them equal right to vote and to hold office.

The most powerful weapon of the great Napoleon, said Clark, was not his artillery but his declaration that his government stood for the principle of "an avenue open to merit without distinction of birth." This kept the Bourbons out for twenty-five years. In our country, certainly, we should call to the aid of the government and of our civilization every power of the intellect and proclaim "an avenue open to merit without distinction of sex."

The cause of women's rights appealed to Clark emotionally as well as intellectually. Associate Justice Seawell of the Supreme Court of North Carolina tells of a striking scene which occurred when Mrs. Catt was addressing a joint session of the North Carolina General Assembly, over which he was presiding. During her able and eloquent appeal to the men of North Carolina to make their women free, tears ran down the cheeks of the Chief Justice. In more than one of his addresses he expressed for his own nation Curran's burning hope for Ireland—that she should be "redeemed, regenerated, and disenthralled by the inevitable might of universal emancipation."

3

"The sob of the child in its helplessness 'curses deeper than the strong man in his wrath'." So wrote Justice Clark in one of his most important opinions for the Court, denying the right of an employer to plead that a child engaged at work at dangerous machinery assumed the risk incident to the employment, and when injured was barred from recovery.

Clark endeared himself to the mother heart by assuming the guardianship of the legal rights of her children, but here again he ran head on into violent conflict with those pseudo-economists who maintained that the way to build the South was to encourage capital from outside to invest in various manufacturing enterprises in a state where they could secure cheap labor and where there was no law against employing children at minimum wages, thus reducing the cost of manufactured articles. Such a practice was abhorrent to Clark not only because it would result in injustices to the children, but also because it would impoverish the plant-bed of a democratic society.

He therefore took time by the forelock and in numerous cases that came before him after he went on the Supreme Court he proceeded, in dissenting opinions, to express his condemnation of the prevailing law with respect to the employment of infants in industry. The happy hunting ground of the industrialist who was looking for technical defenses in actions brought against him to recover damages for injuries suffered by infants while working at dangerous machinery, was what is denominated in the law books as "Pleas of Contributory Negligence" and "Assumption of Risk." These hoary pleas to defeat infants' rights were, Clark asserted, a hangover from the common law, invented by judges to protect property rights as against human rights. In the first case coming before him involving these questions, he took his stand in favor of what he declared were the humanities of the law. In that case (*Ward* v. *Odell*), the defendants had put a child of eight or nine years of age to work in a factory filled with dangerous machinery. The child's eye was put out, and the company, when sued for damages, pleaded that the child was guilty of contributory negligence. The judges were divided, but Clark wrote the opinion of the Court affirming a recovery for damages: "The humanity of the age," said he, "has in very many of the States placed on the statute books laws forbidding the employment of children under 14 years of age in factories. So far as these statutes are based upon the inhumanity of shutting up these little prisoners eleven and one-half to twelve hours a day (the ordinary factory hours in this State according to the State's official publications) in the stifling atmosphere of such buildings, or depriving them of opportunity for education, or using the competition of their cheap wages to reduce those of maturer age, these are arguments on matters of public policy which must be addressed solely to the legislative department. But there is an aspect in which the matter is for the courts, that is, whether it is negligence *per se* for a great factory to take children of such immature development of mind and body and expose them for twelve hours per day to the dangers incident to a great building filled with machinery constantly whirring at high speed. The children without opportunity of education, without rest, their strength overtaxed, their perceptions blunted by fatigue, their intelligence dwarfed by their tread-mill existence, are overliable to accidents. Can it be said that such little creatures, exposed to such dangers against their wills, are guilty of contributory negligence, the defense here set up? Does the law, justly interpreted, visit such liability upon little children.... Whether they are thus imprisoned at work too early by the necessities of their parents or not, it is not the consent of the children. It is not law, as the appellant's counsel insists, that the factory is not liable because the father hired the child to the company. It is the child's eye which was put out, not the father's. The father could not sell his child, nor give the company the right to expose him to danger."

Years later the Pettit case came before the Court, in which the trial judge had denied a mother the right to recover damages against the railroad for the death of her infant child while at work for the railroad in a dangerous place. The Chief Justice dissented in one of his most notable opinions. He recited that the child was under twelve, small for his age, and had not taken off knee pants; that he was employed by the railroad to carry messages across the yard filled with eighteen or twenty tracks with engines and trains moving backward and forward every few minutes. Among these were through trains and also the shifting-engine moving freight and passenger cars to make up trains. His duties required him to carry messages over and across this yard, and while doing so one night he was killed. On a Sunday morning he was found dead on the tracks, with his leg cut off. Declared the Chief Justice: "It may be asked, and it will be asked by future ages as well as by the present, why an innocent child of this immature age should have been subjected to such perils, so far beyond his comprehension. This record gives the answer. His mother had seven other children to support. He had a stepfather. And in this combination of circumstances, the mother testifying that she did not know the dangerous nature nor the character of the employment, and indeed did not consent to his being employed, the defendant was able to procure this child's services for the munificent sum of

$12.50 per month. This was truly 'the price of innocent blood.' Had the defendant employed a man or a boy of mature years it would have had to pay a sum for his services more in proportion to the peril. Such a person would have known the dangers and would have charged for the risk. By employing these little children the defendant is able to cheapen to that extent, by the competition, the price of other labor."

Among the last and one of the best dissenting opinions that Judge Clark wrote was one concerning a case in which the Court held that since the common-law rule was that a minor child could not sue its parent, on the theory that domestic matters should not be publicly aired, the child therefore could not sue the parent's insurer for injuries sustained in an automobile collision caused by the parent's negligence. Clark contended that this was not the common-law rule but that even if it were, its "crudeness, not to say the brutality, was being modified to make the law more humane and open the door of justice more widely to all, without discrimination of race, color, age, or sex." To the suggestion that domestic affairs should not be brought into the public eye, he applied a phase of his philosophy: "The plea that publicity should be avoided by silencing the cries and ignoring the suffering of the helpless is not one that commends itself to humanity. Publicity and the arm of the law are what is needed for the protection of those who are otherwise in the absolute and irresponsible power of those who inflict injuries."

4

Akin to Clark's insistence upon the freedom of women and the protection of children from exploitation in industry was his sympathy for the rights of helpless minorities. Today, when Hitler compels the wholesale murder of Jews in Germany and carries on his program of systematic extermination of the race throughout Europe, it is significant and refreshing to read one of Clark's noted opinions relating to this race. An inconspicuous little Jew named Munick went into the office of the Durham Water Company to settle his bill for water rent, paying a portion of it with fifty pennies wrapped together in one package. He had received his receipt from the clerk when the superintendent of the water company came upon the scene, brushed the pennies off from the receiving counter to the floor, berated Munick for bringing in so many pennies, struck him in the face, called him a goddam Jew, and made him pick up the pennies. Munick brought suit against the water company for damages on account of assault, but the lower court dismissed the action for want of sufficient evidence. Upon appeal to the Supreme Court, Chief Justice Clark reversed the action of the court below, declaring:

"There is no explanation of the conduct of the company's superintendent, and the only provocation which we can infer from the language used by the superintendent is the fact that the plaintiff was a Jew. He made no other charge. The treatment which the plaintiff received is paralleled by that which is portrayed by Scott in *Ivanhoe,* in the treatment of Isaac of York seven centuries ago, and by Shakespeare as meted out to Jews in the *Merchant of Venice,* also centuries ago. The world has long outlived this treatment of an historical race, except perhaps in darkest Russia when under the Czars. When Disraeli, later Prime Minister of the British Empire, was reproached in Parliament for being a Jew he made a memorable reply: 'When the ancestors of the right honorable gentleman were painted savages roaming naked in the forests of Germany, my ancestors were princes in Israel and high priests in the Temple of Solomon.' Every voter, every witness, and every official takes an oath upon a sacred book, every sentence and word in which was written by a Jew. When the Savior was incarnated after the flesh He was of the Tribe of Judah and his mother, whom a great church holds immaculate if not divine, has her name borne by millions throughout the civilized world. Whatever the shortcomings of an individual, it is strange that in this day of enlightenment such prejudices as are shown in this case should survive against the race to which the plaintiff belongs."

5

Born in a slave-owning home, Clark was taught always to treat the Negroes kindly and to care for them rather than abuse them, as unfortunately some masters did. This attitude he consistently maintained through life. When, in the army, Neverson, the Negro boy who faithfully attended him as a bodyguard, went with him to the line of battle, he would send the boy back with their horses so that he would be personally out of danger; together they shared their scanty meals, and together they endured war's hardships as true companions. For thirty-five years, after Clark became a Supreme Court Judge, Alston, a former slave, attended him daily in and out of the courtroom and his home, carrying books, papers, and opinions back and forth like a secretary and, bowed with sorrow, finally followed his remains to the grave.

As late as 1919, Dr. James E. Shepard, a prominent Negro educator and president of the North Carolina College for Negroes at Durham, wrote Clark a letter of appreciation for the services he had rendered the Negroes and for his consistent justice in dealing with them. In reply Clark wrote:

"I have been the employer of colored labor ever since I became of age. I know them well and I have never received anything but kindness at their hands. I have the kindest feeling for the race and have seen the difficulties which surround their efforts to rise to better things. In my judgment, the best remedy for the situation in which the colored people find themselves is that which your race has been observing; i.e., extend the education as far as possible to all your people, impress upon them sobriety, self-control under what at times may be aggravating circumstances, the acquirement of property by industry and thrift, and the attainment, by their personal conduct, of the respect of white people. These things your people have been doing for many years. You have risen steadily in the scale as to those things which command respect, and a steadily increasing number of white men everywhere are appreciating the change. Avoid giving this a setback by the intemperate utterances, especially by the young men of your race who are impatient at what they deem continued injustice. Most often this matter is due to the language used by office-seekers, who appeal to and excite race prejudice for their personal ends. I am sure that the vast majority of the white people of North Carolina wish to do equal and exact justice to the colored race, and their number is increasing with the proofs which the colored people are giving that they are better educated and are attaining a higher standard of morality and right living."

Chapter XVI
THE POLITICAL MACHINE CLICKS

"A politician thinks of the next election; a statesman of the next generation." —James Freeman Clarke

"Society is divided into two classes—the shearers and the shorn. We should always be with the former against the latter." —Talleyrand

WHEN Governor W. W. Kitchin, Chief Justice Walter Clark, and ex-Governor Charles B. Aycock entered the political arena in 1912, determined to unhorse Furnifold M. Simmons and retire him from the United States Senate, a fierce conflict was staged. These contestants comprised the four ablest and most popular leaders in the state. Each had made for himself a reputation extending beyond the bounds of the state and none of them had ever tasted political defeat. No campaign in the state's long history had ever engaged so many powerful personalities in a contest for one office.

Simmons for twelve years had represented North Carolina as its senior senator; Aycock was a former governor; Kitchin, the incumbent governor, had twelve years' experience as congressman to his credit, and Clark was chief justice. These men embodied a complete graph of the political thinking of the people. Simmons, by nature and environment, was a stand-pat conservative and stood at the extreme right, supported by the railroads, big business, and the most efficient political machine that the state had ever known. Aycock, a very kind and humane man, a great orator, was a natural middle-of-the-roader, but in the cause of education he was liberal-minded and earned the title of North Carolina's educational governor. Aycock, in announcing his candidacy for the Senate, stated his political principles to be: "I am a Democrat; I am not a conservative, or a reactionary Democrat; I am not a progressive Democrat, for the word Democrat with me is a noun

[177]

substantive of so fine and large import that it admits of no addition, or diminution or any qualifying word or phrase." To the minds of fighting liberals this statement placed Aycock in the contest squarely astride the political fence.

Kitchin, young, handsome, and matchless in debate, was liberal but cautious. He stood to the left of the center, not far enough to satisfy the pronounced liberals, but too far to please the conservatives. Unfortunately for Kitchin, he had failed as governor to dramatize his position as a liberal leader. One of his friends thus criticized his failure: "When accepting the nomination for governor, Kitchin replied to the charge of his critics that he had dynamite in his pockets, by denying it. He should, instead, have answered that he had his pockets filled with dynamite and proposed to use it."

It was generally understood that Governor Kitchin would be a candidate to succeed Senator Simmons, but the surprise to the Simmons machine came when ex-Governor Aycock, who had been Simmons' lifelong friend and political intimate, turned on him and announced his purpose to succeed him in the Senate. In an opening statement of his candidacy for the Senate, ex-Governor Aycock did not mention Simmons by name, but did declare, "I am in favor of the election of United States senators by the people, and when I say by the people I mean *by the people* and not by money, not by organization, not by machinery. . . . I would not wish to be elected to the United States Senate by money, by machinery, by organization—if I were elected by this means I should glorify and honor the means which elected me." The public accepted this statement as applying solely to Simmons, since neither Kitchin nor Clark had any money to speak of and the political machinery of the party was solely in the control of Simmons. Aycock quoted in his speech an editorial from the *Charlotte Observer,* which was supporting Senator Simmons, saying that while Aycock was popular with the people he would not win the senatorship because he had no money, no organization, and no machinery back of him. Aycock resented this statement as it necessarily implied that since Simmons had the organization, money, and machinery there was no use for anybody to try to defeat him.

Aycock also put Simmons' record of voting with Republicans for high tariff measures, on the spot by declaring, "I agree with Governor Woodrow Wilson. 'The tariff is the one central issue of the coming campaign; it is at the head of every other economic question we have to deal with, and until we have adjusted that properly we can settle nothing in a way that will be lasting and satisfactory.'"

Aycock's declaration against monopolies and trusts harked back to Clark's thesis upon this subject, which he had been expounding for twenty years. Said Aycock, "Rockefeller and Carnegie and Morgan and Duke, and thousands of others, leading men, great financiers, known throughout the world, parading as representative Americans, envied of us—today occupy the position of being and belonging to the class of men who violate law and are subject to wear prison stripes."

In the face of this political setup, Chief Justice Clark's friends, both in and out of the state, regarded it as the appointed time for him, the nationally known and recognized liberal leader in North Carolina, to succeed Simmons in the Senate. Bryan had said editorially in his *Commoner* in 1904 and again in 1908 that Chief Justice Clark of North Carolina would be a proper man for the Democrats to nominate and elect president of the United States. In 1911 Bryan wrote Clark that he would like to see him in the Senate, where he would have a larger sphere of influence and could be of greater national service at a time when such a man as he was needed there.

Democracy had won a sweeping victory on the tariff issue in the congressional election in 1910, and a wave of liberalism was sweeping the nation. Theodore Roosevelt had sensed the growing demand for reform in government and control of big business, had capitalized on it, and was charged with purloining Bryan's political clothes and Senator La Follette's thunder in order to get himself elected president on the Republican ticket. Brandeis was soon to make his contribution with a sensational series of articles on *Other People's Money*.

All of this was an old story to Clark. For two decades, he had, like John the Baptist, been crying in the wilderness to make ready a people, until his voice was now heard and his teachings at last respected throughout the nation. Liberal leaders everywhere felt that Clark's deep learning, resourcefulness, and devotion to the progressive cause would at once give him a commanding position in the Senate and afford him the opportunity of serving the nation in a more effective way than he could as chief justice of the Supreme Court of North Carolina.

This contest was both dramatic and fateful. The actors engaged, the issues involved, and the result, all combined to change the political fate of many. The Democrats with the help of the Populists had redeemed the state from Fusion misrule, but the control of the party had been taken over by the reactionaries. The existence of such a situation was the result of a combination of events, beginning in 1898, which must be considered in order to understand the incredible state of affairs in 1912.

When the white people of the state united in 1898, resolved to free the state of Fusion misrule and Negro political domination, F. M. Simmons was chosen chairman of the Democratic State Executive Committee to lead the fight. The political contest of that year and of 1900 was characterized by bitterness, hatred, and sometimes ruthlessness. For the success that followed, much credit was due and was accorded the political organization which Simmons and his associates built up. This organization extended all the way down to the smallest precinct and functioned with deadly efficiency and daring. With derision and fear the Fusionists referred to it as the Simmons machine, while the Democrats regarded it at the time with pride as the people's organization to restore good government to the state. In order to win, the Democrats had used the organization to induce the Populists to return to the party fold, telling them that the national organization under William Jennings Bryan was the true exponent of a democracy's ideal. As a reward for his matchless party service in these two campaigns, Simmons was elected in 1900 to the United States Senate, to succeed Marion Butler.

The liberal forces in the state were exultant. A great educational renaissance, led by Governor Charles B. Aycock, was under way. Clark was made chief justice and the General Assemblies were enacting progressive measures—even the returned Populists were pleased with the program. But as time passed, the liberals became disturbed over the fact that Senator Simmons was not co-operating in Washington with the liberal leaders of his party in support of progressive measures, and was opposing Bryan's leadership. What was even more apparent, he was controlling the party machinery of the state to promote the interest of reactionary men, many of whom were known to be in sympathy with the Tobacco Trust, the railroads, and other big business interests. The growing discontent against Simmons' domination of the party and his record in Congress came to a climax in 1908, when W. W. Kitchin, then a member of Congress, announced his candidacy for governor. After a knock-down and drag-out fight with Simmons and his machine-picked candidate, Locke Craig, Kitchin was nominated and elected governor. At the convention which nominated him, Simmons tried, unsuccessfully, to prevent the endorsement of Bryan for the presidency, and from then on made no pretense of being a liberal or having any sympathy for the national leadership of the party.

The Progressives of the state, encouraged by Kitchin's victory over the Simmons machine, began to lay down a barrage against Simmons' reactionary and Republican leanings, evidenced by his votes and speeches in the Senate.

A tower of strength in this movement was *The News & Ob-*

server. By 1911 this paper, by its consistent fight for liberal men and measures, had attained its zenith in political influence in the state. Josephus Daniels, its editor, had fearlessly supported Clark for two decades in his crusades against monopolies, trusts, railroad abuses, Kilgo, and the activities of the Simmons machine. The news columns of this paper and its editorial page were giving Simmons and his alter ego, political generalissimo A. D. Watts, pluperfect hell. It charged the Simmons machine in 1911 with preventing the legislature from passing a legalized primary law, with opposing antitrust legislation and other similar progressive demands. Senator Simmons by now had become *persona non grata* with the liberals, in both the state and the nation, and was being openly charged with deserting the Democratic causes and politically affiliating with Republican leaders like Aldrich, Lorimer, and Penrose. *The News & Observer* editorially specified the charges of political apostasy against Simmons: "Senator Simmons not only voted wrong but made a protection speech in favor of the tariff on lumber, as bad a protection speech as Quay made for iron when the Wilson Bill was under consideration. During the consideration of the Payne-Aldrich Tariff Bill, Mr. Simmons voted so often with Mr. Aldrich for protection schedules that the northern Democrats and independent papers referred to him as a protectionist. The great sin Mr. Simmons has committed against the Democratic doctrine has been his support of the ship subsidy steal, the most undemocratic measure that ever crossed the threshold of the senate."

Another severe indictment which *The News & Observer* leveled against the Senator was that to the astonishment of the people of North Carolina he had voted for the seating of the corrupt Lorimer, who should have been driven out of the Senate in disgrace. It declared that "the Senator who voted to put a white mark on Lorimer at the same time put a black mark on himself."

Simmons' conservatism, his reactionary course in the Senate, his intimacy with Aldrich and Penrose invited William Jennings

Charles Farrell

The law office built by Clark at Halifax when he was twenty-two. In it are two beautifully carved Italian marble mantelpieces. For many years Claude Kitchin and Edward Travis used it as their office. It is still in service as a law office.

"This court constituted a judicial mosaic of the best that the profession had to offer. Analyzing this composite picture, we see the Chief Justice . . . an extreme liberal; Brown . . . a confirmed conservative; . . . Hoke, the ideal exponent of democracy; Walker, the devotee of precedent; and Connor, the natural chancellor."

Bryan's condemnation. Bryan wrote editorially: "The Commoner does not take part in a contest between Democrats except where a principle is involved. In North Carolina, where Senator Simmons is one of the candidates for re-election, a principle is involved. He is not a progressive and it is a mystery to the outside world how a state like North Carolina has tolerated him so long."

The candidacy of Governor Wilson for the Democratic nomination for president was now looming upon the horizon, with his new freedom, tariff for revenue only, and his approval of the Bryan leadership of the party nationally. In this state of affairs the liberal Democrats of North Carolina felt that it was both incongruous and unseemly to re-elect the senior senator, who had always opposed Bryan, was now against the nomination of Woodrow Wilson, and had an undemocratic record on the tariff.

Friends of Aycock felt that he had made a mistake in not making more specific his platform of principles. Kitchin's friends thought he had made the mistake of devoting most of his time to criticizing Senator Simmons' record in the Senate and his failure to support democratic measures. Neither friend nor foe ever suggested that Clark had fallen into either of these errors, or that he had failed to let the public know what he stood for and the measures which he proposed to support if elected to the Senate.

Clark's platform was liberal and progressive through and through, and in complete accord with the national policies of the party as espoused by Bryan, Wilson, and other liberal leaders. He advocated unequivocal legislation to destroy the trusts, election by the people of senators, federal judges, and postmasters, and a tariff for revenue only. He advocated the initiative, referendum, and recall, except for the judges. With respect to labor laws he demanded "the enforcement of laws regulating the hours of labor, and prohibiting child labor and requiring approved safety appliances in factories and on railroads." Further commenting upon the practices of the railroads and their failure to adopt safety appliances for the sake of economy, he asked: "Shall we always be subjected not only to robbery but to the loss of life and limb by the wealth creators of our country in order that the privileged few may grow still more inordinately rich?" He also advocated a general parcel post, the operation of the telegraph and telephone by the post-office department, the extension of public schools and good roads. His platform concluded with this bold declaration: "The highest tax that the American people pay except that which we pay to the great trusts and monopolies which control our government, is the tax which we pay to ignorance, and the 'mud tax.'"

With this line-up, the apparently irresistible logic of the situation was that Simmons would be defeated for re-election and that the real contest was between the other three candidates. The political cloud overhanging Simmons' candidacy at the time has been graphically described by Josephus Daniels in his book, *Editor in Politics:* "It was believed that the Southern Railway and the American Tobacco Company, the two big rich corporations in the state not averse to taking a hand politically, and the rich tariff beneficiaries were supporting Simmons. Friends of Clark, Aycock, and Kitchin believed that the chief trouble they would have in the campaign would be because the big corporations, including the big lumber concerns, having urged Simmons to vote for high tariff on lumber, would spend more money for Simmons than all of the rest of them combined could raise, *as they did.*"

In the face of this shocking state of affairs, Clark had every reason to believe that the people would nominate him. In his campaign for chief justice in 1902 he had fought the combination of the Simmons machine and the vigorous opposition of the railroads, monopolies, trusts, and combines, but in that fight he had the unalloyed support of Daniels and *The News & Observer*.

As the campaign opened, a tragedy occurred in the sudden death of Aycock. Simmons knew that Kitchin had only a skeleton organization and no money with which to build one. He also knew that Daniels disliked Kitchin and that *The News & Observer* had been very critical of his administration as governor. In this state of affairs he leveled his machine guns at Clark and, as we shall see, he shot him both in the face and in the back. Simmons had as his secretary, A. D. Watts, who was one of the most astute and daring political manipulators that the state has ever known. He was the man on the ground directing the operations of the Simmons machine, and after the contest was over boasted of one trick that he worked on Clark. He had Simmons men in several counties of the state write Clark, telling him that since he had no organization in his particular county the writer would be glad to take charge of his campaign in that county and look after his interests. Clark, innocently, walked into the trap, and when the votes were counted they turned out to be for Simmons.

Another and a more important catastrophe happened to Clark when *The News & Observer* went out of politics and its editor, Josephus Daniels, went into politics. The Simmons machine, which, as has been stated, always opposed Bryan and was against the nomination of Wilson, at the Democratic State Convention held in the spring of 1912 undertook to prevent an endorsement of Wilson's candidacy. A majority of the delegates to the Baltimore Convention, which later nominated Wilson, was for him, but the personnel of the delegation was composed largely of Senator Simmons' friends. Daniels was Democratic national committeeman from his state and wished very much to be re-elected; but to gratify this ambition it was necessary that he have the endorsement of the delegates who attended the Baltimore convention. Simmons and his machine naturally resented *The News & Observer's* violent criticism of Simmons' course in the Senate, and as a counter-irritant his friends announced that he would be a candidate to succeed Daniels as national committeeman.

Clark was greatly encouraged at first over the trend of affairs at the Baltimore convention. His friend Bryan was master of the convention, and it was becoming more and more certain that the liberals would write the platform, which Clark knew would be in line with his platform for the Senate, and name the candidate for president. This enthusiasm was short-lived, as the unexpected announcement came from Baltimore that the Simmons delegates had unanimously joined to re-elect Daniels national committeeman and that Daniels was going on to New York to join the Wilson headquarters. Promptly it was announced that E. E. Brittain, a friend of Senator Simmons, would act as editor of *The News & Observer* through the campaign. It soon developed that *The News & Observer* had adopted a policy of not taking any further part in the senatorial contest and that for the first time it would require all senatorial candidates to pay advertising rates for all messages they wished to address to the public through the press. This policy, of course, was highly pleasing to the Simmons forces, because they had plenty of money, but at the same time it put Clark's campaign for the senate in the dog house.

The election returns gave Simmons a majority of the total votes with Clark running a poor third, but in the meantime *The News & Observer* had collected as pay for political advertisements from the three candidates the sum of $2,865.84. Clark chipped into this jack-pot $112.

The tragic ending of the campaign, so far as Clark was concerned, did not come as a surprise to him. After the happenings at Baltimore he realized that he would be defeated, and he communicated this opinion to his family and a few intimates. Among those who knew Clark, there was never any question of his courage to criticize either friend or foe when he thought a principle was involved and the occasion demanded it. Clark attributed his defeat mainly to Daniels' and *The News & Observer's* desertion of him, and he did not hesitate to say so. He asserted that Daniels, in order to be re-elected national committeeman, surrendered to the Simmons machine, quit the fight against Simmons, left the state, and turned over his paper to a subordinate, whom he knew to be a friend of Simmons, and this stopped any further criticism of Simmons and his record in the Senate. Clark likewise expressed the opinion that Daniels had used his influence with the National

Committee to have it keep hands off in the fight over the senatorship.

This left in politics only two newspapers of state-wide circulation, the *Charlotte Observer,* a stand-pat, anti-Wilson, Simmons supporter, and the *Greensboro News,* an independent paper.

In his publication *Editor in Politics* Daniels tells the story thus: "The Charlotte *Observer* and Greensboro *News* both came out in October in support of Simmons, and the newspaper support was pretty well divided in the State, but Simmons had the best of it. *The News & Observer* did not take sides. As head of the Literary Bureau of the National Democratic Committee, I spent the summer and fall in New York at Democratic Headquarters, helping direct the campaign for Wilson's election. An attempt was made to draw Wilson into the senatorial fight, but Tumulty wired that Wilson was 'hands off.' I had explained to Wilson the situation in North Carolina and suggested that he remain detached."

The breach of friendship between Clark and Daniels, who like brothers had smote hip and thigh the enemies of liberalism and reform for a quarter of a century, soon came to light.

On May 7, 1913, Clark in a letter to Clarence Poe, approving an editorial which Poe had written in *The Progressive Farmer* upon the reactionary status of the South and the cause of it, asked Poe what else he could expect when men who have an opportunity to elect liberals vote for conservatives. "I am not complaining that any man did not support me; that is a matter for each man to decide for himself, but the point I make is far broader and that is that the real cause of the reactionary condition of the South is that men like yourself and Mr. Daniels who earnestly advocate these measures do not support progressive candidates. I know that the heaviest drawback I had was that you two did not give me your support, though you had been publicly advocating the very measures that I stood for. Men who proposed reactionary views stood for the candidate of that element, openly and earnestly. The progressive leaders did not 'vote as they shot.' . . .

It is certain that the State will remain reactionary as long as those who preach progressive doctrines do not support the candidates of that way of thinking.... I am writing this letter to you because I wish to see progressive measures win in this State, which they can never do if those who preach progressive needs shall turn against those candidates who have always stood for these measures."

Poe's defection from Clark at the outset of the campaign may be explained as a result of his affection for one of Aycock's daughters, whom he later married.

The breaking up of this alliance, which for so many years had done perfect teamwork for liberalism and reform in North Carolina, proved discouraging to those other liberals who had for so long borne the heat and burden of the day.

An immediate sequel to Wilson's inauguration as president was the distribution of patronage in North Carolina to the members of Simmons' machine.

Overman, the junior senator, was a lovable man, but, like Clark, had neither organization, money, nor machine, and this placed him politically at the mercy of Simmons. As a result, Simmons and Watts took charge of the administration of patronage in the state and even appropriated to their intimates the best offices in the western part of the state, to which Senator Overman was entitled.

When it became public that the President had been asked to appoint A. D. Watts to the office of collector of internal revenue for the Western District of North Carolina, Clark, on April 19, 1913, wrote Daniels: "I hope you can see your way to prevent the appointment of Mr. Watts. You know the baseness of his personal and private character, and that no decent woman would be seen with him. Surely the democracy of North Carolina can at least furnish enough men of good character for the offices." Watts was appointed without opposition.

Watts, while secretary to Senator Simmons and before his

appointment to office, was very diligent in Washington to see that only the thick-and-thin Simmons men should be politically rewarded. A reputed incident went the rounds: Dr. George T. Winston met Watts on the street in Washington and was asked his business there. Winston replied that he had just called on the President. Watts then inquired what they talked about and he replied they discussed Marcus Aurelius, whereupon Watts hurried back to the Capitol, told Senator Simmons of the conversation, and asked him, "Who in hell is this fellow Marcus Aurelius?"

2

The results of this senatorial contest were far-reaching. Aycock's elimination by death, Kitchin's defeat, which contributed to wrecking his health, and Clark's running a poor third, made Simmons and his machine the undisputed master of the Democratic party in North Carolina. However, as time was to show, Clark's reputation was unimpaired by his sad adventure into this sordid political scramble. Above all, he had maintained his integrity both as a man and as a sincere liberal. He had resorted to no political tricks and had made no deals to promote his personal or political interest. He kept faith with the national leaders and the progressive causes which he and they had so consistently, over the years, espoused; and he went down to defeat fighting for these causes. Virtue in this case had its own reward. The Simmons machine, in order to sidetrack his candidacy, openly declared that Clark was so great a chief justice that the state could not afford to lose him as head of its judicial system. Strangely enough, this ingenious flattery had its effect upon many voters, even though, as Clark said, the same crowd in 1902 had declared that he was unfit to be chief justice and exerted their every effort to retire him from public life.

That the Chief Justice had become nationally known and recognized as a liberal and a great legal scholar is illustrated by an editorial note preceding his article, "Judicial Supremacy," in *The*

Arena for February, 1908. In this note the editor, Benjamin O. Flower, said:

"Late in November the distinguished Chief-Justice of North Carolina, Hon. Walter Clark LL.D., delivered an address before the Economic Club of Boston which was received with marked approval. Justice Clark is one of the strongest, clearest, and most fundamental thinkers and advocates of pure democracy in public life in America today and is one of the ablest of our leading judges. He served for 14 years as associate justice of the Supreme Court of North Carolina, and then was nominated for the most honorable position in the state—that of Chief Justice. He was opposed by the railroad corporations and the tobacco trust, but he was elected by the largest majority ever given to a candidate in the state.

"The address delivered in Boston was so timely, and so clearly did it present a very serious question that affects in a vital way the life of democratic government that we requested Justice Clark to put the substance of this address into a paper for THE ARENA that the many thousands of serious-minded men and women all over the nation might be brought face to face with a situation the gravity of which it would be difficult to overestimate. This he has done, and we herewith present it, urging all friends of free institutions to give it the careful consideration it so richly deserves."

When a vacancy occurred on the Supreme Court of the United States in 1914, there was a widespread appeal to the President to appoint the Chief Justice to that position. The North Carolina delegation in Congress, headed by Congressman Pou from the Raleigh district, called on the President in a body and urged the appointment of Clark. Pou wrote Clark that the President expressed admiration for his ability and learning and would, he thought, most likely appoint him. In the meantime, a few North Carolina friends of the Chief Justice called on Secretary of State Bryan, asking his endorsement of Clark. Before the request was even finished, Secretary Bryan interrupted with the declaration that he had known Chief Justice Clark for many years and regarded him one of the ablest statesmen and jurists in this country. "If I were president," said he, "I would immediately appoint him to the bench, where a man like him is very much needed."

Pou again wrote Clark that those close to the White House and experienced newspaper correspondents in Washington felt certain that the President would name him. Later, John H. Clarke, of Ohio, was given the appointment. Pou wrote the Chief Justice that he understood the President did not appoint him solely because he felt that on account of his age, sixty-seven, it was inadvisable to do so. When the Chief Justice received this information he remarked that it was the irony of fate—"I was thought too young to be appointed Brigadier General in the Confederate Army and now am regarded as too old to be appointed to the Supreme Court of the United States."

Chief Justice Stone of the Supreme Court of the United States later recalled that he had been Dean of the Columbia Law School at the time, and that when the appointment was made it was observed among members of the law faculty that the President had appointed the wrong Clark.

CHAPTER XVII

GOVERNMENT BY JUDGES

"Let us consider the people at large as the source from which all power is to be derived, and whatever restraints may be imposed upon them, if they have not their happiness as their only aim, are the fetters of tyranny and the badges of slavery."—William Hooper, signer of the Declaration of Independence

"We are under a Constitution, but the Constitution is what the judges say it is, and the judiciary is the safeguard of our liberty and of our property under the Constitution."
—Charles Evans Hughes

AT THE ANNUAL MEETING of the North Carolina Bar Association, held at Wrightsville in August, 1914, the Chief Justice was subjected to one of the most disagreeable experiences in his entire judicial career. One Rome G. Brown, of Minnesota, professing to represent a committee of the American Bar Association which had been appointed to combat the agitation for the recall of judges, delivered a scathing denunciation of the Chief Justice, who was present in the audience. Brown charged, in substance, that Clark was prostituting his high office as chief justice by joining Theodore Roosevelt and others in a demagogic attack on the Federal judiciary. His abuse of the proprieties of the occasion and the falsity of the charges brought an immediate reply from a member of the association, who called attention to the fact that the Chief Justice had not only never approved Roosevelt's position with respect to the recall of judges, but, on the contrary, had repeatedly, in public addresses and in a dissenting opinion of the court, expressed his disapproval. For the first time in the history of the association an address was omitted from the publication of its proceedings, but Brown's display of viciousness did not end with the convention. The Chief Justice's friends learned that Brown proposed to have his address published as a part of the proceedings of the American Bar Association. As a result, Justice Brown of the North Carolina

Supreme Court and Harry Skinner, a prominent member of the North Carolina bar, attended a meeting of the committee of the American Bar Association in Washington and protested the publication of this address upon the ground that the charges against the Chief Justice were false and that by reasonable inquiry Brown should have known this fact. The committee declined to incorporate the address in its proceedings.

The singling out of the Chief Justice for this attack was only part of a program to discredit the effect of a series of addresses that he had delivered, advocating amendments to the Federal Constitution which would abolish life tenure in office for Federal judges and would take away from the courts the assumed authority to declare acts of Congress unconstitutional. Two years before, in 1912, Charles A. Beard, a noted historian, had written a book on *The Supreme Court and the Constitution,* in which he made the Chief Justice's address upon this subject at Philadelphia the starting point of his discussion. Clark's eminent position and the force of his arguments had by now made his utterances of national concern. In the recent debates in Congress over President Franklin D. Roosevelt's Supreme Court bill, the views of the Chief Justice as expressed in these addresses, and Beard's book, were repeatedly referred to. The importance of the subject to the nation, then and since, makes it imperative that Clark's views be correctly stated.

It undoubtedly came as a surprise to many and a shock to some when the Chief Justice of the Supreme Court of the conservative Old North State began a crusade against the life tenure of Federal judges and against the authority assumed by the Federal courts to declare acts of Congress unconstitutional. Jefferson had criticized the Federal judicial system, as had other, subsequent statesmen, but Chief Justice Clark was the first Supreme Court jurist boldly to take such a position and openly make war on it.

Because Clark was convinced that the evils complained of could be cured only by amending the Constitution, his approach to the subject was thoroughly realistic. He had carefully thought out what he regarded as the needed amendments, but he recognized the great difficulty in securing them so long as the public was educated to the belief that the Constitution was a sacred instrument without fault or blemish. In a series of carefully prepared addresses he undertook to expose this fallacy, maintaining that the Constitution was much less democratic than the Declaration of Independence, having been written by men who wished to throttle the democratic processes which the people had ordained in their Declaration of Independence. The thinking of the legal profession was dramatized by the slogan, "Back to the Constitution," while Clark insisted that we go back to the Declaration of Independence. He undertook to establish by historical references that the aims and purposes of the makers of the Constitution were to safeguard property rights, rather than to promote human rights. His treatment of the subject was different from, and more exhaustive than that which had been previously employed by other reformers, while his proposed remedies were specific and understandable.

His first address on the subject was delivered before the Bar Association of Tennessee, at Nashville, in 1897. It was entitled, "Revision of the Constitution; Election of Judges and Senators by the People." This was followed by articles in *The American Law Review, The Arena,* and other similar publications. In 1906 he delivered an address at the University of Pennsylvania upon "Some Defects in the Constitution of the United States," and his last address was at Cooper Union, New York, in 1914, in which the subject was still further elaborated. These addresses attracted national attention and soon after their delivery were reprinted in the *Congressional Record* at the instance of Senators Overman, Owen, and the senior La Follette. From these addresses and articles we are able to learn his precise views and the arguments which he employed in their support.

When the Chief Justice accepted an invitation from the Law Department of the University of Pennsylvania to deliver his address on the defects in the Constitution, in the city of Philadelphia, he realized that the setting was perfect, for it was here that the Declaration of Independence had been proclaimed and the Federal Constitution drafted. He made it the occasion to deliver one of the best prepared addresses of his long career. In it he reviewed the history of both documents, sharply emphasizing that the Declaration was a covenant among free men, openly arrived at to assure a government based solely "upon the consent of the governed," while the Constitution was secretly made by a few prominent business and professional men to protect property rights, ignoring completely any reference to human rights.

Clark reminded his audience that Hamilton had expressed the motives of the delegates when, in a speech to the convention, he stated that the members were agreed that "we need to be rescued from the democracy," and, observed the Chief Justice, "they were rescued." He declared, "The convention which met in 1787 was as reactionary as the other had been revolutionary and democratic; the Declaration of 1776 was concerned with the rights of man. The convention of 1787 entirely ignored them." The soul of the Constitution, the Bill of Rights, was deliberately omitted and later inserted in the first ten amendments because it was the only way to secure ratification of the Constitution by the several states. Clark was here reflecting the views of his own state, since North Carolina had rejected the Constitution in its original form and subsequently ratified it only after Washington had been elected and inaugurated president.

He argued that for seven years the people of this country sacrificed themselves to obtain a government based upon the principles of the great Declaration of Human Rights, and then, when the struggle was over, with "sublime audacity the reactionary party—the champions of government of the many by the few— quietly, unostentatiously, but effectively, took control of the government." He maintained that the method and means employed by the delegates attending the convention were thoroughly undemocratic; that when the delegates met they sat behind closed doors to protect themselves against any influence from public opinion; that the members were sworn not to make copies of any resolution or other action, or to correspond with constituents, or communicate with others as to matters pending before the convention, while a record of yeas and nays was forbidden; that Madison kept a secret copy of the proceedings which, however, was not published until the lapse of forty-nine years when every member of the convention had passed beyond human accountability; that only twelve states were ever represented and one of those withdrew before the final result was reached; that of its sixty-five members only fifty-five ever attended, and so far from being unanimous, only thirty-nine signed the Constitution and some actively opposed its ratification by their own states; that in several states ratification was had by the barest majority and in New York it was ratified by a majority of only one, and this was accomplished by persuading a member of the legislature to absent himself when the vote was taken; and that in no state was there a ratification by the vote of the people.

Beard's able treatise took issue with Clark's conclusion that the makers of the Constitution did not intend to vest the Federal judiciary with the power to declare the acts of Congress unconstitutional. Upon Clark's contention, in his Philadelphia speech, that the makers of the Constitution did not intend to promulgate a democratic document, Beard made a most valuable contribution: "Everywhere in Europe the government was in the hands of a ruling monarch or at best a ruling class; everywhere the mass of the people had been regarded principally as an arms-bearing and tax-paying multitude, uneducated, and with little hope or capacity for advancement. . . . It is small wonder, therefore, that under the circumstances, many of the members of that august body held popular government in slight esteem and took the people into consideration only as far as it was imperative 'to inspire them with the necessary confidence,' as Mr. Gerry frankly put it."

Coming to the point that the Constitution nowhere granted the power to the judges to declare an act of Congress unconstitutional, Clark pointed out that even in such a convention, thus composed and secluded from the influence of public opinion, the persistent effort to grant the judges such power was in different forms repeatedly and overwhelmingly denied. This proposition was made four times, said he, "as we now know from Mr. Madison's journal." The first of these proposals was tendered June 4, receiving the votes of only two states, and was renewed no less than three times, i. e., on June 6, July 21, and finally on August 15. Although it had the powerful support of James Madison, afterwards President of the United States, and James Wilson, afterwards a Justice of the United States Supreme Court, it was defeated; but nevertheless, he declared, in his Cooper Union address in 1914, those who drafted the Constitution did succeed in placing the judges beyond any influence of public opinion by making them appointive for life at fourth hand by the President, who was to be chosen at third hand, subject to confirmation by a Senate chosen at second hand. Nothing could be more absolutely out of accord with a republic than the appointment of officials for life. "Not that the judges, either elective or appointive, either state or federal, have been corrupt; to the credit of the bench it must be said that such instances have been exceedingly rare, but experience has demonstrated the absolute unwisdom of placing irreviewable power in the hands of any man or set of men by life tenure, no matter how wise or pure they may be. It had proved so in the past as to kings, though there had been some good kings, and it proved equally so as to life judges, for state after state had abolished it."

Discussing the appointment of lawyers to the Federal bench for life, Clark asserted that such appointments carried no presumption of divinity and that history taught that the Federal judiciary, from the beginning, had become involved in partisan power politics. Elaborating this phase of the subject, he reviewed the unseemly scramble by the Federalists during Adams' administration to pack the bench with partisan lawyers, after the administration had been repudiated by the people. "Marshall," said he, "was a great judge and rendered many valuable decisions, but as a matter of history we know he had strong bias, and like other men some faults." By way of illustration, he noted that while Marshall was secretary of state, he was appointed chief justice in January, 1801, and took his seat on the bench; "yet he held both offices to the night of March 3, 1801 when his office as secretary of state expired; it was he who, at midnight, signed the commission to Marbury, which he left on the table because unable to deliver it before the clock struck twelve, for Levi Lincoln, the new attorney general, stood by him (as Parton says) with Mr. Jefferson's watch in hand and forbade him to proceed. It was this commission which Marshall attempted to validate as chief justice, when a mandamus was asked to compel Madison, the new secretary of state, to deliver it."

Albert Beveridge, in his life of Marshall, commenting upon this occurrence, states that the only moral excuse offered for it was that since Jefferson had won the presidency he would fill these Federal judgeships with democratic lawyers.

Clark further declared that the Federal judiciary, by reason of its life tenure and its assumption of authority to overrule the acts of Congress, had made itself a citadel, and big business interests had sought to keep this citadel filled with conservative lawyers whose political and economic views were to their liking. "The vested interest," said he, "for ninety years held back the election of United States senators by the people; their remaining sheet anchor now is a selection of judges appointed by the Executive to hold office for life." These appointees as a rule have been men of ability, he continued, "but men who, because of their ability,

Clark at his desk in the library of his home. Immediately above his desk are portraits of his wife and of Thomas Jefferson.

Chief Justice Clark at seventy-two. From a portrait by Clement Strudwick now in the home of Clark's son, John W. Clark, in Greensboro.

have been retained in the service of great corporations. When these men, who have spent their professional life in advocating the decision of causes from the standpoint of their employers, are translated to the bench, they naturally view such questions from the same standpoint. This is not corruption on their part, for the stronger their convictions the more tenaciously they will assert those ultra views in their opinions on the bench. The complaint is not of corruption but of usurpation of control over the lawmaking power, which, under the Constitution, should be in the people." Clark argued that no such power existed in any other country and never had; that the judges not only have never exercised such power in England, where there is no written constitution, but that they have not exercised it in France, Germany, Austria, Denmark, or any other country which, like them, has a written constitution. A specific complaint was against the assumption of authority by Chief Justice Marshall in the famous case of *Marbury* v. *Madison,* in which he held that the court had the implied power under the Constitution to declare an act of Congress unconstitutional; that even this doctrine, when first announced, was qualified by the rule that the act complained of must be unconstitutional beyond all reasonable doubt, whereas subsequent courts had assumed to declare acts unconstitutional where the Supreme Court was divided four to five.

It was in this address, referring to divided courts, that he coined the phrase "five elderly lawyers." "The absurdity of the situation," he argued, "resulted in placing control of the government in the power of a small body of men, not chosen by the people and holding office for life, which in the last analysis empowered 'five elderly lawyers' to ignore the opinion of four of their associates on the bench, the declared opinion of the Congress and the President of the United States." He pointedly attacked the continuing and increasing encroachment by the Supreme Court upon the rights of the people to make their own laws through a co-ordinate department of government.

As a convincing illustration of his thesis, he recalled that the Supreme Court of the United States had held the Federal Income Tax, one of the most just of all taxes, unconstitutional by a five to four decision of the Court. This result, involving hundreds of millions of dollars yearly, was accomplished by the remarkable performance of one of the Justices, Shiras, changing his mind overnight and joining the minority, and thus by one vacillating vote destroying the Income Tax program of the government until the people, through a long process of years, changed the Constitution.

He also alluded to the charge that President Grant had packed the Supreme Court so as to create a majority of Judges who would hold the Legal Tender Act constitutional after it had previously been held unconstitutional by a division of the Judges of the same Court.

He maintained that the crux of the whole matter, involving the welfare of a hundred million people under the present system, lay in the answer to two queries: "What are the beliefs of the majority of the Court on economic questions?" "What happens to be their opinion of a sound public policy?" It is most significant that the Chief Justice here discerned and stated the real evil in this assumed power by the Court—a power so great because it was both arbitrary and irreviewable.

He then took up the shifting devices which the Court had in more recent years employed as excuses for extending this doctrine of review and nullification. He criticized the Court's employment of the phrase "due process of law" as a justification of their opinions in such cases, since historically and as a legal concept it related only to procedure. In support he quoted Professor Corwin of Princeton University: "Due process of law is not a legal concept at all, but merely a roving commission to judges to sink whatever legislative craft may appear to them, from the standpoint of vested interests, to be of a piratical tendency."

Closely akin was the Court's employment of the Fourteenth

Amendment to bolster their holding that acts of Congress were unconstitutional, which Clark asserted was both illegal and unsound. It was passed, said he, "for the protection of the negro but has been construed as useless to him, while it has become a tower of safety to the vested interests." Of the doctrine of judicial supremacy he said: "It is based upon the idea that though a majority of the senators who are sworn to serve the Constitution may either viciously or ignorantly violate it in the passage of an act, and though the majority of the House may do the same thing and though the President may also violate his oath of office by failing to veto an unconstitutional act, and a minority of the court itself may do the same, the 'five elderly lawyers' who constitute a majority are infallible and never do so, not even when they reverse their predecessors, or, as in the income tax case, their own court." Such views were regarded as very radical, but the Chief Justice had an abundance of distinguished support in previous utterances of America's greatest statesmen.

While the arguments for and against the authority or propriety of Federal judges' assuming such far-reaching authority have been beclouded with much legalistic reasoning, the issue at bottom, as the Chief Justice saw it, was a simple one. To put the question in plain language, understandable to the layman, he thus stated it: "Shall our government be controlled by judges or by the people?" For, reasoned he, if the Federal courts are allowed to nullify acts of Congress and state legislation dealing with the economic life and the public policy of the people because they do not approve them, then, sugar-coat it as you will, we have a government in fact controlled by judges. Lawyers and law-writers gave to this assumed power the technical name of "judicial supremacy," but Clark, accustomed to calling a spade a spade, denominated it a "government by judges" and set about to prove it, by showing that Jefferson had declared the Federal judges to be "a corps of sappers and miners steadily undermining the Constitution."

Andrew Jackson had resented the Court's assumed superiority with respect to the Acts of Congress, and in a veto message put himself on record: "The opinion of the judges has no more authority over Congress than the opinion of Congress has over the judges, and on that point the President is independent of both. The authority of the Supreme Court must not, therefore, be permitted to control the Congress or the Executive when acting in their legislative capacities, but to have only such influence as the forces of their reasoning may deserve."

Lincoln was to follow with his daring repudiation of the Court's opinion in the famous Dred Scott case. In one of his debates with Douglas, Lincoln asserted his opposition to that decision "as a political rule which shall be binding on the members of Congress for the President to favor no measure which does not actually concur with the principles of that decision. . ." "We propose so resisting it as to have it reversed if we can, and a new judicial rule established." In his inaugural address as president, in the presence of Chief Justice Taney, who had written the opinion in the Dred Scott case and who had just administered the oath of office to him, Lincoln made this fateful declaration: "The candid citizen must confess that if the policy of the government upon vital questions affecting the whole people is to be irrevocably fixed by the decisions of the Supreme Court the instant they are made, in ordinary litigation between parties in personal actions, the people have ceased to be their own rulers, having to that extent practically resigned their government into the hands of that eminent tribunal." Under Lincoln's leadership the Dred Scott case was overruled in blood and not upon a petition to the Supreme Court for a rehearing.

It is a singular fact that the liberal forces, led by Jefferson, Jackson, and Lincoln, who so vigorously opposed judicial supremacy, never drew a precise line of demarkation between those classes of cases where the Supreme Court might properly declare an act unconstitutional upon purely justiciable grounds and those cases affecting the economic order and public policy of the nation, which, from the very nature of the case, in a democracy should be determined by the people through legislation. Chief Justice Clark apparently came nearer doing so than any other liberal had done. In his Cooper Union address, he, a third time, clearly stated the issue: "Who shall determine the economic questions and the public policy of the nation—the courts or the people?"

The defeat of President Franklin D. Roosevelt's late Supreme Court bill settled nothing, "for nothing is ever settled until it is settled right." It is still in the lap of the gods as to who shall finally determine the economic questions and the public policy of this nation. It is significant that the present Supreme Court has already sensed that these two matters so vital to the public are not justiciable questions to be determined by "five elderly lawyers." In this matter, as in others, with the attitude of the present Court, Chief Justice Clark would have been in complete accord because his polar star was that the "public welfare is the supreme law" and there never was a time in his life when he believed that he or any other judge, state or federal, had the authority to fix by judicial decree the economic order or the public policy of the people. And certainly not in litigation between private individuals to which the government was not a party and had no voice.

His precise view upon this phase of the subject was definitely stated in an opinion from the bench delivered many years before: "I would not be understood as contending that the power which the courts have so long exercised (often for good, sometimes not), by declaring legislative acts unconstitutional, is invalid"—but he denied the authority even by implication where "the statute in question is a public law relating to a public subject within the domain of the general legislation of the state and involving the public rights and public welfare of the entire community."

In one of his addresses he joined with Justice Harlan of the Supreme Court in a warning, which unfortunately was not heeded: "When the American people come to the conclusion that the judiciary of the land is usurping to itself the functions of the legislative department of the government and by judicial construction only is declaring what should be the public policy of the United States, we will find trouble."

Accumulating events had satisfied the Chief Justice that judicial supremacy was growing worse rather than better, and he had seen that a reactionary president, like Taft, had openly boasted of the number of conservative lawyers he had appointed to the Supreme Bench; that when he turned the White House over to the liberal Wilson he told newspaper men that above all other things he was proudest of the fact that six of the nine members of the Supreme Court, including the Chief Justice, bore his commissions, and "I have said to them, 'Damn you, if one of you die, I will disown you.'"

Clark's correspondence reveals that he was in communication with the leading liberals of the nation, in both the Democratic and Republican parties, men like Bryan, the senior La Follette, Brandeis, and Theodore Roosevelt. All of these men were greatly exercised about the assumption of power by the Supreme Court, which was resulting in that Court's holding an increasing number of acts of Congress and state legislatures unconstitutional. This feeling was expressed by Theodore Roosevelt in a letter which he wrote Clark in 1913: "I feel that there is very urgent need that there should be ultimate authority over the executive, legislative and judicial law, and I cannot see where this ultimate authority can be placed, except in the people themselves. I believe there should be an easier method of amending the constitutions, both state and national, and I should like to see it possible to amend or construe the National Constitution *ad hoc* by permitting 'on a vote of Congress' any decision of the Supreme Court declaring a law passed by Congress invalid to be laid before the people at the next election to be voted on in the several states; and if a majority of the votes, including a majority in enough states to make a majority of the electoral college, should be cast for the proposition then it would be part of the supreme law of the land without regard to the decision of the Supreme Court."

The Chief Justice did not agree with Roosevelt about the recall of judges or the recall of judicial decisions. Said he, "The recall as applied to the judges is objectionable, in my opinion, for many reasons, and among them this—that it can be applied to cases of ordinary litigation where the judge is exercising only his legitimate judicial functions. If as to such matters he proves corrupt he can be impeached, and if he proves feeble he can be dropped at the end of his term." He believed that the Constitution should be amended and that a constitutional convention for that purpose should be called. Nearly a century and a score of years had elapsed since the Constitution was written, and times and conditions had so greatly changed that the Constitution should be made, as the constitutions of all the states had been, in keeping with the demands of a new and living generation. Concluding, he said, "By vote of five 'infallible' judges against four 'fallible' judges, the powers of Congress and the State are set aside and their statutes held unconstitutional on the specious theory of 'liberty of contract,' 'due process of law' and 'equal protection of the laws,' meaning simply what the court believes was for the real good of the people."

Forty years ago Chief Justice Clark concluded his address before the Tennessee Bar Association, joining with Judge Seymour Thompson, editor of *The American Law Review,* in a most significant warning: "There is danger that the people will see all this at one sudden glance and that their furies will then break loose, and that Hell will ride on their wings."

CHAPTER XVIII

JUSTICE TO LABOR

> *"Thou shalt not muzzle the ox that treadeth out the corn. And the labourer is worthy of his reward."* —I Timothy 5, 18

FROM EARLY MANHOOD Clark was interested in the problems of labor, particularly, at first, in connection with plantation life and the Negroes, and also in connection with the landless whites, who had little opportunity to better their condition. As industry developed and technology became a dominating factor, he was concerned over the welfare of working people in factories, on the railroads, and in other hazardous employment. He made known his sympathy for the rights of labor, through his dissenting opinions and addresses, which attracted the attention of the American Federation of Labor; Gompers wrote that labor regarded him as one of its ablest and best friends.

Clark himself was such an incessant worker that he sympathized with those who toiled, and expressed a contempt for the idlers in society, "those who do nothing for the support or the comfort of humanity." Among his first decisions after going upon the Supreme Court was one condemning what is known as the Fellow-Servant Law, in accordance with which, if an employee of a railroad or other corporation was killed or injured by the negligence of a fellow-servant, no compensation could be recovered and his family was left destitute. This, he asserted, was another example of judge-made law, depriving the injured employee of any remedy. As early as 1898 he drafted the act which the North Carolina Assembly passed, abolishing the old Fellow-Servant Law as applied by the courts to railroads.

His views upon the labor question were fully stated in an

address before the Trade Council in Wilmington in 1914. In this address he took pains to declare very definitely his convictions with respect to the demands of labor and allied reforms which indirectly affected labor as well as the general public. He avowed his belief in the abolition of involuntary servitude, except as a punishment for crime; in free schools, free text books, and compulsory education; in a rest of one day in seven and an eight-hour work day; in municipal ownership of public utilities; in abolition of the sweat-shop system; in sanitary inspection of factory, workshop, mine, and home; in liability of the employers for injury to body or loss of life; in the nationalization of telegraph and telephone; in anti-child-labor laws, and their enforcement; in woman's suffrage co-equal with man's suffrage; in suitable and sufficient playgrounds for children in all cities; in public bathing facilities in cities; and in the initiative and referendum. He protested the abuse of injunctions in labor disputes.

Clark formulated in his own mind the things which he considered of greatest importance to labor: "The first and greatest need of labor is for freedom—that they shall not be hampered as in the past, by laws fixing a maximum rate for wages; nor by prohibition of their forming organizations among themselves for the promotion of their own interests; and that they should be protected against the more powerful classes by laws restricting the hours of labor, fixing a minimum rate—that is, a living wage—which the employer should pay in such cases, and securing the working classes from injunctions and trial for contempt by judges, without the intervention of a jury."

Years before, the Chief Justice, in an address at Elon College on the Gospel of Progress, displayed a vision with respect to a new order in the world that would make even the progressive of today envious: "The abolition of slavery in this and other countries, and of serfdom in Russia," said he, "are but parts of a world-wide improvement in the condition of the toilers of the world, the working classes, upon whom in the last analysis depend the subsistence, the clothing—indeed, the continued existence of the human race. And the betterment in their condition is only just beginning. With the diffusion of knowledge among them as to the importance of their labors and the power of their numbers, it is certain that farmers and laborers will not remain content with the small share allotted to them out of the results of their toil and their relative unimportance in government." Clark had no illusions about the inevitable conflict between the toiling masses and the privileged few, which such doctrines as his had in the past and would in the future entail. His own experience with trusts, monopolies, combines, and other favor-seeking corporations, had long ago taught him that between these forces there was an eternal conflict.

Is it too much to say that, had the wisdom of the jurist and the admonitions of him and other statesmen of the period been respected, the nation would have been spared the unseemly struggle between ruthless labor leaders on the one hand and certain unyielding employers of labor on the other?

Clark never doubted that future generations would wonder and ask: Why did the able men in control of big business, during his era, so long and bitterly resist the humanities of the age by continuing to employ infants at low wages to work at dangerous machinery until the lawmakers made it a crime? Why did they work men and women for long, debilitating hours until the law fixed a standard of eight hours a day? Why did they employ high-powered lobbyists to influence lawmakers against reform in the law helpful to the laboring classes? And, finally, why did they exercise the right to organize and create monopolies in industry for profit to themselves, and at the same time deny to the laborers who helped create their wealth the right to organize unions for their own self-protection? Clark was convinced that history's answer would be—selfishness and stupidity. Time has proven that Clark's views upon labor were as wise and just as were his demands that capital when invested in public utilities, such as the railroads and electric power companies, should submit to government regulation of their rates and services.

The senseless controversy and wrangle resulting in strikes and lock-outs, which impede America's war effort, has invited the ridicule of our enemies, who point to them as an example of the impotence of democratic government. It is a tragedy that the American public and our allies should suffer from the follies of a few obstinate and selfish spokesmen of both labor and capital who have abandoned the rule of "live and let live" and insist upon "rule or ruin and the nation be damned." All of which is reminiscent of a squib that Joe Reece, of Greensboro, a contemporary of Clark, repeated once a year editorially in his paper: "There are so many ways to be a damned fool it is hard to miss them all."

Two of the most far-reaching movements affecting labor in Clark's lifetime were the agitation leading to the Safety Appliance Act passed by Congress to protect railroad employees, and the demand for an eight-hour labor law. Here, again, Clark was the first jurist to attract the nation's attention and the commendation of organized labor with respect to both of these matters, through his able and sympathetic opinions. The two following quotations will amply illustrate. As early as 1902 the Secretary of the Interstate Commerce Commission, E. A. Moseley, wrote Clark from Washington:

"I certainly trust that you will be made Chief Justice of the State. I cannot forget the great service which you just rendered to the railroad employees of the country by your interpretation of the safety appliances law. It being the first judicial interpretation of the law, it has been of inestimable value to them. It is refreshing to a man occupying the position I do, knowing the condition of affairs, to occasionally find some one on the judiciary who takes the people's view on a public question and who hands down decisions in accordance with that view."

Knowing his sympathetic attitude toward the rights of labor,

President Wilson selected Clark as an umpire for the National War Labor Board and he was assigned to act in a case involving the question of an eight-hour-a-day employment of labor, in which the President was so deeply interested. Clark wrote the opinion in the case. The American Federation of Labor in its publication, *American Federationist,* November, 1918, editorially said:

"There has just been written into the history of the struggle for the eight-hour day a most significant chapter. This chapter is officially entitled, 'Opinion by the Umpire,' and was written to support the Umpire's award in the case of the Molders vs. the Wheeling Mold and Foundry Company, before the National War Labor Board. Judge Walter Clark, of the Supreme Court of North Carolina, widely known for his keen and sympathetic interest in all things that make for a better humankind, wrote the opinion and the award.

"It should be noted carefully that this is not an award for a 'basic eight-hour day', but is a straight, clear-cut award for an actual eight-hour day. Judge Clark goes deeply into the case for a shorter workday and puts the bulk of the weight upon the need of the human organism for rest from toil in order that health and happiness may be preserved. He does not neglect the matter of increased productivity in the shorter day, however. Both points are brought into the argument when he says: 'There is a vast body of experience that a ten-hour day shortens the lives of the employees, injures their health, and that in point of production there is an increase by the substitution of eight hours for a longer period.'

"This opinion by Judge Clark is certain to become one of the vital chapters in the long history of the struggle for a shorter workday. That it should be written with the war as its flaming background is one of the features, that while seemingly strange, is really in keeping with such a great part of the trend of events of today.

"A great part of the industrial directorate appears to feel today that the demand for an eight-hour day has been met when the 'basic' eight-hour day has been installed. That is not the case. As a matter of fact the 'basic' eight-hour day is not necessarily an eight-hour day at all. It may only be a measure for the computation of wages, and in most cases it is little more than that. Under a lessened demand for industrial output the overtime charge may serve as a sufficient deterrent for work beyond the eight-hour limit, but conditions are such today that 'emergencies' are found readily for exacting ten and more hours of work.

"Judge Clark meets this situation ably and thoroughly. He provides that the management and the workers in the shop shall jointly determine when there is an emergency that requires a lengthened workday. This is progress toward industrial democracy, and progress that will be welcomed, not alone by the workers, but by all citizens who understand the trend of the time and who are in sympathy with true democracy.

"It is the opinion of the vast body of American workers that the eight-hour day ought to be a reality. It is the opinion of the workers that, while all are willing to strain every nerve for the national cause in the great war, there must be no advantage of the situation taken to impose a burden upon the workers for any purpose except one definitely having to do with the winning of the war. Gain for employers at the expense of the workers must not be made under the guise of winning the war. All who sincerely wish our war effort to be most effective and who wish to conserve the health and life of American workers will hope that the provision for a shop board to determine when emergencies exist will prove effective.

"With Judge Clark's pleading for an eight-hour law we shall have some difference of opinion. For his admirable and scholarly presentation of the case for an eight-hour day we have complete admiration. That his act in rendering this opinion and its accompanying award has materially advanced our national progress toward the eight-hour day, there can be no question. He has set down a marker on the road of progress.

"The eyes of man look toward tomorrow's sun, demanding a new light and a new warmth; the brain of man looks toward tomorrow's dawn, grasping a new concept; the soul of man yearns for a new freedom in the tomorrow toward which the eye looks and for which the brain plans. This universal expectation will not be denied. And it is by such markers as this just laid down by Judge Clark that we know they are not to be denied."

Clark was among the state's earliest advocates of a Workmen's Compensation Law. Committees of the General Assembly consulted him in the preparation of the act which was finally passed. After Congress passed the Safety Appliance Act, to protect employees from needless hazards, he promptly began urging its application and enforcement in North Carolina. The injury and death of so many employees engaged at work on railroads and in manufacturing plants were shocking to Clark, and prompted him to write, in a dissenting opinion: "It is a reproach to our civilization that any class of American workmen should, in the pursuit of a necessary and useful vocation, be subjected to a peril of life and limb as great as that of a soldier in time of war."

Further commenting, he stated that "a conservative estimate of the number of workmen killed or maimed in this country every year in industrial accidents is about 500,000. It is said that the total number killed and wounded in the Union Army during the Civil War was 385,325. In other words, the whole Confederate Army was unable to kill and cripple as many Union men in four years as are now killed and crippled in industrial employment in a single year." He reasoned, "We cannot expect this condition to improve if the courts can be induced to place the blame upon those killed and wounded, because in order to make a livelihood and with a purpose of obeying those for whom they labor, they venture in dangerous pursuits, while under such conditions the same courts relieve the master, who created the condition and gave the order, of all liability and blame whatsoever." In another opinion he wrote: "With the era of more just legislation in both this country and in England, and elsewhere, shortening the hours of labor for everybody, requiring sanitary provisions and safe appliances, labor has been encouraged and the progress of the world in a few years has more than equaled that of all the centuries that are dead. Justice to the laborer has been to the profit of the employer. The courts should not be less just than the laws."

2

Clark's sense of justice to labor did not carry with it a suggestion of injustice to others. Here, again, we have the application of his slogan, "The public welfare is the supreme law."

As early as 1903 he stated his formula and a prophecy: "If convinced that organized labor meditates no attack upon the rights of private property and no control of government in their own special interest, but that each man shall be free to own and enjoy that which he has honestly earned, then labor and the great bulk of the people—the farmers, the merchants, the professions, may unite and terminate the predominance which is given in practice, though not in our form of government, to aggregated consolidated wealth." His program for equal and exact justice to all carried no taint of a class spirit or what we now know as Bolshevism. Justice to the rights of property was quite as sacred with him. "There is no hatred of corporations as such; they are essential in the service of civilized life, nay indispensable, nor even against railroad corporations so far as they keep within the legitimate duties of their creation. . . . The opposition is not to them as servants of the public but as would-be masters of the people."

Clark's insistence upon justice to labor formed only a part of his liberal views and his program for the progress of mankind. As we have seen, the rights of women and children were made the special objects of his care, and the rights of minorities always found in him a champion and defender. His numerous opinions and writings upon this subject naturally attracted nation-wide attention and made of him an acknowledged leader among the conspicuous statesmen of his period, both in and out of the state. Clark's correspondence includes a number of letters from distinguished liberals, commending him for his progressive views on the living issues of the day and for his courage as a jurist in speaking out in favor of the forgotten man. One of these kindred spirits was Justice Brandeis. When he was given a testimonial dinner in New York, after his appointment to the Supreme Court of the United States, Clark was invited to attend and deliver the principal address, but other engagements prevented his acceptance.

Accordingly, it is no wonder that Clark was selected by the University of New York as one of America's distinguished jurists to serve as an elector in choosing illustrious citizens for its Hall of Fame, and that Senator Robert M. La Follette, in delivering a notable address in Raleigh in 1913, pronounced Chief Justice Clark a leader of the South in popular government and added: "I don't know whether you appreciate him or not, but the time will come when the people will see he is the best friend that North Carolina has had since it became an organized state."

CHAPTER XIX
PARTING SHOTS

"Justice delayed is justice denied."—Gladstone

ALTHOUGH THE PRESIDENT thought Clark too old in 1914 to be appointed to the Supreme Court of the United States, the people of North Carolina four years later elected him for the fifth time to the Supreme Court of his state. Still vigorous in mind and body, he continued his crusade for reforms, hoping to complete those unfinished while espousing new ones.

The noted lawyer and commoner, Cyrus B. Watson, said of him: "When Walter Clark is on the watch tower the people sleep in peace."

As we have seen, Clark throughout life manifested a passion for efficiency—in the army, on the plantation, at the bar, and upon the bench. His tireless efforts had resulted in accomplishing many reforms, but the one nearest to his heart—the administration of justice—had been grievously disappointing. Clark had done all that was humanly possible to speed up the administration of justice in North Carolina, to stop judicial hair-splitting, and to save the bench and bar from the continuing loss of prestige with the public. Other jurists and scholars, notably Justices Holmes and Brandeis, and Deans Pound and Wigmore, and Elihu Root, were by now voicing like warnings and pointing out the evils which were besetting both judge and lawyer alike. Clark resolved to speak to his brethren in a language that they could understand, and he did this in his farewell address to the North Carolina Bar Association in 1914 at its annual meeting at Wrightsville Beach.

"Under our system of practice and procedure a lawyer is trained to look backwards. He is like a surveyor running a line by stakes behind him. He searches for precedent, and unless he is an exceptional man the effect of such training is to make him reverence the opinion of some unknown judge, of unknown capacity, and of unknown bias, who happened to be a judge 100 or 200 or 300 years ago or more, when society was far less developed than now, instead of considering the views that would reflect the advanced thought of the times in which we live. But for the help derived from legislation, the course of judicial decisions would be as petrified as the laws of the Medes and Persians, or the mummies which rest beneath the Egyptian pyramids. Even in our legislation, progress is hampered by the fact that legislation is largely shaped by lawyers in the legislative bodies, and that even when progressive measures are passed they are taken on the judicial anvil and often hammered into unexpected shapes, and not infrequently are vetoed, by the most unprogressive members of our unprogressive profession, the judges. These members of our profession have usually attained at least middle age and their personal views of political economy not infrequently are taken by themselves as a true conception of the extent of the legislation which the constitution will permit Congress or the individual states to enact.

"Civilization is simply a search for greater efficiency. The great businesses of the world have revolutionized their methods and adopted better ones. Success depends upon it. Even the farmers are using improved machinery and better methods of planting and cultivation. The same is true of all callings and professions. In the medical profession and in chemistry these leaders who died fifteen years ago, could they return to life, would feel lost. Governments have improved their systems, armies have new weapons and improved systems of drill. Navies have thrown aside their obsolete vessels of war and have new systems of navigation. Even theology has taken a look ahead and has conformed to the discoveries in geology and astronomy, and has taken notice of the results of scientific investigation. In all the world there is but one profession which stands still, and that is ours. The most that we have done is to learn at last that our profession and the practice of law have not increased in efficiency and that popular disapproval of our obsolete methods is our portion beneath the sun."

Severe as this arraignment was, it was hardly comparable to the indictment which Dean Wigmore, of the Law Department of Northwestern University, incorporated in the preface of his monumental work on the *Law of Evidence* published in 1915, in which he elected to place most of the blame for the existing state of affairs upon the doorsteps of the judges. He declared that after perusing several thousand contemporary decisions he had formed the conclusion that most of the judges lacked acquaintance with legal science. Particularizing, he asserted that their knowledge of legal history was almost totally lacking; the philosophy and jurisprudence of the law were unknown to them; and there was no discrimination in the use of expository authorities. He concluded that this state of affairs was due to the judges' indifference to legal science, an indifference which they shared with most of the profession. "Another shortcoming," said he, "was undue servitude to the bondage of precedent, a fetish of immutability."

Dean Pound of the Harvard Law School, in several notable addresses, added his criticism. In his approach to the subject he was disposed to attach the blame to the judges and the law teachers. He summarized the defects of the law as taught and laid down by the courts as the sharp line between traditional and imperative elements in the law and the resulting attitude of teacher and text writer, court and practitioner, toward legislation. He declared, "It is not too much to say that they are bringing about an acute conflict between the law as it is taught and received and administered and those who are working for social progress." Referring to the conflict, he described it as that of a reactionary profession, zealously guarding a received tradition, fighting a retreat. He maintained that, consciously or subconsciously, legislation at variance with the received tradition is viewed with suspicion if not with hostility. He observed that the public is rightly dissatisfied with the jurists and "the jurists ought to be dissatisfied with themselves."

Although a distinguished teacher of law, Dean Pound made the admission that the conflict between the law and those who are working for social progress has its roots ultimately in the teaching of the law. Said he, "It is not a recall of judges or a recall of judicial decisions that should be invoked, but rather a recall of law teachers or at least a recall of a great deal of law teaching." He prophesied that the teaching of law and construing it as the judges think it should be construed, will bring about a continuing widening gulf between the law in the books and the law in action. One of his striking admonitions reads like a leaf taken from one of Clark's dissenting opinions: "Let us bestir ourselves to the end that taught law be that of living tissues and not that of dead fibre."

One of the strangest paradoxes in American history is that while the present system of courts in the United States is a copy of the English courts of 1775, yet after the English by their Judicature Act of 1873 completely abolished it and inaugurated a modern system of jurisprudence, American judges and lawyers still hold on to the old worn-out copy like grim death. A notable contribution to the thinking upon this subject is the study made by Caleb Perry Patterson, Professor of Government at the University of Texas, published in 1936. He spent a year in Great Britain devoted to the preparation of this work. Commenting upon the insistence of the American judge and lawyer upon perpetuating the old system of jurisprudence, which England itself had long discarded, and the refusal to modernize our own jurisprudence, he says: "To these chauvinistic legalists who think they are preserving American jurisprudence, when in fact they are maintaining medieval judicial institutions on American soil, it does not seem to occur that the choice lies between the medieval and the modern English judiciary. Since what we have is English, why oppose something that is English? . . . One system is as foreign as the other and the same reasons would hold for rejecting or adopting either."

None of these facts was new to Clark, since he began discussing them soon after he went upon the Supreme bench. In 1888 Lord Bryce published his *American Commonwealth,* which Clark took pains to commend to numerous members of the bar throughout the state. Discussing the backwardness of American judges and practitioners with respect to judicial reform, Lord Bryce wrote: "Thus one finds the same dislike to theory, the same attachment to old forms, the same unwillingness to be committed to any broad principle which distinguished the orthodox type of English lawyers in the first half of the last century. Prejudices survive on the shores of the Mississippi which Bentham assailed when those shores were inhabited only by Indians and beavers; and in Chicago, a place which living men remember as a lonely swamp, special demurrers, replications *de injuria,* and various elaborate formalities of pleading which were swept away by the English Common Law Procedure Acts of 1850 and 1852, flourish and abound to this day."

From the beginning of Clark's judicial career he cultivated the acquaintance of bright young men coming to the bar, and frequently wrote personal letters suggesting they read certain books, from which they would learn that the jurisprudence in England, from which we adopted our system, had long since inaugurated many reforms in the law and in the administration of it which were so badly needed in this country. The most notable of these books was Dicey's brilliant work, *Law and Opinion in England,* published in 1905 and republished in 1913. Dicey wrote that "under the Parliamentary Reform Acts 1867-1884 the Constitution of England had been transformed into a democracy; that the government of England was far less democratic than the government of the United States, but that the legislation of Congress is less socialistic than the legislation of the Imperial Parliament."

And he added, "nor in England are the laws tending toward socialism due to the political downfall of the wealthy class." One of the most significant statements contained in this volume and the one which Clark was fond of referring to was a quotation from Lord Bowen, whom he denominated one of the ablest and most enlightened of English judges: "It may be asserted without fear of contradiction that it is not possible in the year 1887 for an honest litigant in Her Majesty's Supreme Court to be defeated by any mere technicality, any slip, any mistaken step in his litigation. . . . The law has ceased to be a scientific game that may be won or lost by playing some particular move." Commenting, Dicey wrote: "Any critic who dispassionately weighs these sentences, knows their full meaning and remembers that they are even more true in 1899 than in 1887, will plainly understand the immensity of the achievements performed by Bentham and his school in the amendments of procedure—that is, in giving reality to the legal rights of individuals."

The delays in the administration of justice, occasioned by appellate courts' reversing the decisions of lower courts and sending the cases back for retrial on some flimsy error in procedure, had been abhorrent to Clark from the beginning of his judicial career. In a dissenting opinion, delivered in the last year of his life, he cited with approval an address of Elihu Root before the American Bar Association, in which the latter gave the kiss of death to the outworn stupid practices of appellate courts' granting new trials on technicalities and flimsy excuses. Said Root: "Every lawyer knows that the continued reversal of judgments, the sending of parties to a litigation to and fro between the trial courts and the appellate courts, has become a disgrace to the administration of justice in the United States. Everybody knows that the vast network of highly technical rules of evidence and procedure which prevails in this country serves to tangle justice in the name of form. It is a disgrace to our profession. It is a disgrace to our law and a discredit to our institutions."

For thirty years Clark had earnestly sought to remedy the evil practices here referred to. In a dissenting opinion in Pollard's case, Clark brought sharply to the attention of his associates on the bench and at the bar that justice demanded an end to litigation and that the court should abandon the practice of sending cases back for a retrial on immaterial technicalities. He boldly took the position: "The better thought of the age is that unless the verdict is clearly contrary to justice, no verdict in any case should be reversed on appeal."

To further his program of making the courts more efficient and responsive to public demands, Clark had long advocated vesting the rule-making power in the Supreme Court, so that all of the activities of the courts in the state might be co-ordinated under a responsible head, as had already been done in England. He also advocated the state's establishing a department of justice, which, acting in co-operation with the Supreme Court, would insure a speedy and intelligent administration of justice. Failing in these efforts, Clark, still true to his belief in the efficacy of pitiless publicity as a means of correcting evils and preventing wrongs, wrote in one of his dissenting opinions: "The surest way to insure relief of any grievance is to give publicity to the most glaring cases, at least that those seeking justice may receive it in accordance with the solemn pledge more than seven hundred years old—'to no man will we sell nor deny, nor delay justice.'"

Applying this philosophy and by way of illustration, he cited a number of cases, one the Penny case, which was an action against the railroad to recover damages for personal injuries, "where," said he, "the case had already been fifteen years in court, in which time four appeals had been taken to the Supreme Court, and for the fourth time a new trial was being given." Another case cited was Pettit against the railroad, seeking damages by a mother for the wrongful death of her child. Calling attention to the shocking delays of the court in that case, he said, "From the date of the death of the boy to the present time has been more than sixteen years. During that time approximately one hundred terms of court, with probably one hundred and fifty weeks of sessions, have been held in Edgecombe County, and there has been a change of personnel of the presiding judge more than thirty-two times. If the little boy (who was killed) had lived he would now be in his twenty-eighth or twenty-ninth year."

As a parting injunction to a stiff-necked and backward generation of lawyers, he wrote, "The law should express the best sentiment of the age. It should move, because all the world besides is moving. We should move up abreast of our age and not take our seats by the abandoned campfires of a generation gone before."

CHAPTER XX

PERSONALITIES AND POWER

"Let us have faith that right makes might; and in that faith let us to the end dare to do our duty as we understand it." —Lincoln

WHEN CLARK WAS A ten-year-old boy living in luxury at Ventosa, surrounded by cultured and wealthy kinspeople, James Buchanan Duke was born in a log cabin near Durham, North Carolina. Although coming from different sections of the state and from different social and economic strata, they were later to meet as friends.

Duke, without the pride of ancestry and denied even a high school education, fought his way up from a poor little farm in Orange County to the control of the American Tobacco Trust which ultimately dominated the tobacco industry of the world. Duke and Clark died within five years of each other, the one with an estate estimated to be worth more than a hundred million dollars; the other a comparatively poor judge. The Napoleon of industry and finance died in one of his many stately mansions; the judge, in a modest frame home on Halifax Street in Raleigh.

It was a whim of fate that these two men should have early met and consulted together as attorney and client, later to become antagonists in issues that shook the state and nation. Their differences were never personal, but each came to regard the other as a dangerous citizen—the one a ruthless industrialist, the other an apostle of injustice.

The original tobacco company, out of which grew the American Tobacco Trust, was organized by Washington Duke and his sons, James Buchanan, Benjamin, and Brodie. The father was uneducated but shrewd; Ben was kind and considerate; Brodie was the black sheep but a likable fellow; James Buchanan was masterful, resourceful, and ruthless—his father called him Buck and as Buck he was thereafter known.

The parent enterprise was given the name of W. Duke Sons & Company. The "company" was George W. Watts, a gentleman of wealth from Baltimore, who furnished the needed capital for the business. From the outset, Buck was recognized as the driving power, and the business grew rapidly, extending its sales throughout the nation. This company was the first to popularize cigarettes, while still manufacturing smoking and chewing tobacco with snuff as a sideline.

By 1880 Clark had established himself as an able, painstaking lawyer at the Raleigh bar, and in that year W. Duke Sons & Company employed him as its general counsel. Their correspondence shows that Clark selected attorneys to look after the concern's law business in other states while personally attending to its legal matters in North Carolina. This arrangement lasted until 1885, when he was appointed judge of the superior court.

It is a significant fact that in the years that followed, while Duke was engaged first in organizing a trust in the tobacco business of the world and later in creating a monopoly in the hydroelectric power business in Piedmont North Carolina, Clark, a Supreme Court jurist, was writing opinions for the Court and delivering addresses condemning trusts and monopolies and holding that the operation of public utilities should be under the strict supervision and control of the state. It was inevitable that a conflict between Duke's policies and Clark's philosophy would sooner or later occur. It finally came in 1918, when Duke had the Southern Power Company (now Duke Power Company) appeal to the North Carolina Supreme Court to overrule an opinion of Judge Shaw's, holding that the company had to furnish electric power and current to the North Carolina Public Service Company without discrimination in rates or service, subject to the regulation and control of the laws of the state.

In order to understand better the clash involving the imperious will of the utility magnate on one hand and the public law of the state on the other, it is necessary to review some of Clark's early judicial opinions.

The General Assembly of North Carolina in 1891 established the Railroad and Telegraph Commission, empowering it to regulate the rates of all public utilities in North Carolina. The railroads and other public service corporations fought the creation of the commission and afterwards, over a period of years, contested in the courts its jurisdiction and rulings.

Clark's tenure of office on the Supreme Court was contemporaneous with the litigation that followed. He was designated by the Court from the beginning to write the principal opinions dealing with this class of cases.

The first of these actions to come before him was an appeal by a telegraph company in 1895 challenging the ruling of the commission governing its service and rates. Clark wrote: "It is only by virtue of its franchise as a telegraph company that it can operate its lines at all. It cannot discriminate in favor of or against any customer. It cannot subtract itself from obedience to the rates prescribed by the authority of the state acting through the Commission by a contract giving one customer, the Railroad Company, preference in business and pleading that such business occupies the only wire it has. The discrimination is itself illegal."

A more far-reaching opinion was delivered by him in the Goldsboro Water Company case in 1898. His argument and conclusions in that case were founded upon the doctrine previously announced by the Supreme Court of the United States in the case of *Munn* v. *Illinois,* in which it was held that this country from its first colonization had regulated the charges of ferries, common carriers, hackmen, bakers, millers, public wharfingers, auctioneers, innkeepers, and many other matters of like nature. Adopting this opinion, Clark wrote: "Where the owner of property devotes it to a use in which the public has an interest, he in effect grants to the public an interest in such use and must to the extent of that interest submit to be controlled by the public." He elaborated the doctrine, declaring that the acceptance of a franchise carries the duty of supplying all persons along its lines, without discrimination; and the public is entitled to have the same service on equal terms and at uniform rates; that if this were not so, and that if corporations existing by the grant of public franchises and supplying the great conveniences and necessities of modern city life, as water, gas, electric light, streetcars, and the like, could charge any rates however unreasonable, and could at will favor certain individuals with low rates and charge others exorbitantly high rates or refuse service altogether, the business interests and the domestic comfort of every man would be at their mercy. They could kill the business of one and make alive that of another, and instead of being a public agency created to promote the public comfort and welfare, these corporations would be the masters of the cities they were established to serve. With prophetic insight he wrote: "A few wealthy men might combine and, by threatening to establish competition, procure very low rates which the company might recoup by raising the price to others not financially able to resist —the very class which most needs the protection of the law." He concluded with a warning: "The law will not and cannot tolerate discrimination in the charges of these quasi-public corporations. There must be equality of rights to all and special privileges to none, and if this is violated, or unreasonable rates are charged, the humblest citizen has the right to invoke the protection of the laws equally with any other."

In the face of these well established principles of law, Duke contended that his power company should not be amenable to these rules and that it had the right, by contract, to fix its own rules, rates, and condition of service. The power company's appeal in this case reached the Supreme Court in 1918, and the Chief Justice was soon to write the opinion. The facts found by the

Court in this case afforded a perfect basis for the application of his long-held philosophy, "the public welfare is the supreme law." These are the facts of the case which the Court found to be admitted or not denied: That the defendant power company was a public service corporation, and only by virtue thereof enjoyed and exercised the right and power of eminent domain; that it had a monopoly of the hydroelectric power supply and the markets in the territory through which its lines extended; that for more than ten years past it had been selling hydroelectric current to the plaintiff to be resold at retail to citizens at Salisbury, Spencer, East Spencer, High Point, and Greensboro, and also to the Southern Public Utilities Company (which the defendant substantially owned and controlled), to be resold at Charlotte, Winston-Salem, Reidsville, and other points, and had also been selling its current to the municipalities of Lincolnton, Shelby, and Newton, to be resold to their respective citizens; that its business had become affected with a public use and for that reason was subject to public regulation of its rates and conduct; that in 1914 it filed a statement with the Corporation Commission, denying that the commission had any authority to require it to file a schedule of its rates or to promulgate rules and regulations governing it, and expressly asserted this power to be in itself by saying: "Each case must be treated on its own peculiar circumstance, and the rates are subject to the reasonable rules and regulations of the Power Company's charter. The filing of these rates by this Company is in deference to the request of the Commission, and must not be treated or considered as done because any legal obligation is imposed upon it to file the same. This Company is advised that no legal obligation exists."

Acting upon this assumed power, it declined to sell power and current to any consumer for a period less than five years, and then only upon the terms which it saw fit to offer, under its assertion of absolute sovereignty and freedom from control by law.

On the question of discrimination in rates among its customers, the Court found as a fact that the defendant had entered into a long-term contract, extending to 1944, to furnish power to the Southern Public Utility Company (a corporation owned by it), which was engaged in precisely the same character of business as the plaintiffs, at a rate much less than those charged and demanded of the plaintiffs or any other consumer; that the defendant purchased its current from a wholly owned subsidiary at 4 mills per kw. h. under a long-term contract, but declined to allow the plaintiff to share in the water rate of 4 mills and demanded it pay 18 mills, or more than 470 per cent profit; that under the former ten-year contract between the parties, the rate was 11 mills, and upon the plaintiff's refusal to enter into a five-year contract at a much higher rate, the defendant threatened to cut off its supply of current and leave these cities in darkness.

The Court held upon this state of facts that the Power Company was engaged in a flagrant abuse of power and defiant denial of duty owed to the public, and manifested a wilful purpose on the part of J. B. Duke, its principal owner, to establish a power monopoly in North Carolina by using methods similar to those employed by him in building his tobacco monopoly, for which the Supreme Court of the United States had convicted him in 1911. The Court declared that it was of the highest importance that the claim of right of the defendant Southern Power Company to discriminate in the rates charged by it to purchasers under like conditions, should be clearly denied by the courts; that if the defendant was thus permitted to charge cotton mills, in which the owners of the defendant were interested, a rate of 11 mills, while it charged the plaintiff and other mills and industries in which it was not interested 18 mills, or a higher rate than it did others in like conditions, in a comparatively brief time the defendant would have the power to destroy, and thereby acquire the ownership of all the other cotton mills and industrial plants in the state, and thus create a cotton mill monopoly wherever its lines extend. The Chief Justice documented his opinion with historical facts, stating that, from an investigation made by Congress in the water power of the company, 94 per cent of the water power in North Carolina had been acquired by corporations which were either already owned or could soon be acquired by the Southern Power Company, or made subsidiary by the use of the same methods of underselling and acquisition of competitive plants by which the American Tobacco Company and the Standard Oil Company had acquired monopolies.

Wrote Clark: "The control of the defendant corporation is by the same men who organized the American Tobacco Company, which was ordered dissolved in the case of *U. S. v. American Tobacco Co.*, 221 U. S. 106 (October Term, 1910), in which the Supreme Court, in an opinion by Chief Justice White, held that J. B. Duke, the president of the tobacco trust, (and the president of this defendant company) was individually responsible for the violations of law committed by that concern."

Clark also called attention to the considerations enumerated by the Court in that case, which overwhelmingly established wrongful purpose and illegal combinations, among them these: "(c) By the ever present manifestation which is exhibited of a conscious wrongdoing by the form in which the various transactions were embodied from the beginning, ever changing, but ever in substance the same. Now the organization of a new company, now the control exerted by the taking of stock in one or another, or in several, so as to obscure the result actually attained, nevertheless uniform in their manifestations of the purpose to restrain others, and to monopolize and retain power in the hands of the few, who, it would seem, from the beginning contemplated the mastery of the trade, which practically followed. (d) By the gradual absorption of control over all the elements essential to the successful manufacture of tobacco products, and placing such control in the hands of seemingly independent corporations, serving as perpetual barriers to the entry of others in the tobacco trade...."

Clark further quoted from this opinion, in which it was said that the history of the combination was replete with demonstrations "of the existence from the beginning, of a purpose to acquire dominion and control of the tobacco trade, not by the mere exertion of the ordinary right to contract and to trade, but by methods devised in order to monopolize the trade by driving competitors out of business, which were ruthlessly carried out, upon the assumption that to work upon the fears or play upon the cupidity of competitors would make success possible."

Clark went on to say that the story of high finance and monopoly record, as shown in that case, was displayed along the same lines in the power enterprise; that in 1905 the same J. B. Duke and his associates, as disclosed by the undisputed facts in the record, incorporated the defendant company in New Jersey, in which state the American Tobacco Company and its subsidiary companies, or aliases, were chartered; that the defendants acquired water rights and built power plants on the Catawba and Broad rivers in South Carolina. Afterwards the same Duke and associates organized the Great Falls Power Company, also chartered in New Jersey in 1907, and as owners of the Southern Power Company, on March 1, 1910, sold to themselves, as owners of the Great Falls Power Company, the three hydroelectric plants which had been erected by the Southern Power Company. To take care of the cost of developing this property, the owners and promoters of the defendant power company placed a mortgage upon the same in the sum of $10,000,000, which it was alleged was substantially the cost of the property purchased and developed. In addition, they issued to themselves $6,000,000 of 7 per cent cumulative preferred stock and $4,000,000 of common stock, and substantially the same interest and men organizing the Great Falls Power Company as the holding company for the hydroelectric generating properties took over its part of the defendant company, and immediately executed a contract which provided that the Great Falls Power Company should furnish its hydroelectric current to the defendant for a long term of years at the rate of 4 mills per kw. h. The defendant company and its promoters, acting for themselves and for Great Falls Power Company, caused the latter company to issue $5,768,800 of 7 per cent cumulative preferred stock, and also a like amount in common stock, which was substantially all turned over to the defendant company and its promoters, who now own the same. Thereafter the same J. B. Duke and associates organized a subsidiary retail company, known as the Southern Public Utilities Company, which was principally owned by himself and immediate family and controlled by him. This company acquired a monopoly of the retail electric power business in Charlotte, Winston-Salem, and Reidsville. Thus these two corporations, under the same control, monopolized the wholesale supply of current and the retail distribution of it wherever a subsidiary company could get control of the municipal franchises.

Clark concluded: "It is unnecessary to trace the transactions of this company in all its manifestations, but enough has appeared to show that the existence and operation of a water power monopoly with power to discriminate in its rates would be a menace which neither the courts nor the public can disregard." He then observed: "The object of this action is not to declare or fix rates nor is it to have the rates declared exorbitant, however clearly this may appear, but to prevent that discrimination between the purchasers of its power, which is a method by which the Standard Oil Company, the American Tobacco Company, and all other trusts have crushed opposition and enlarged their power and increased their accumulations to a point which made them a menace to government by the people, and caused their dissolution by judicial decree."

It would be a reflection upon Duke's intelligence to assume that he thought his Power Company would be allowed to create a monopoly of hydroelectric power in western North Carolina, enjoy the right of eminent domain, and continue indefinitely to deny the authority of the state and its courts to regulate and control its rates and service to the public. But he knew from experience that justice was, for the most part, too slow to keep up with an imperious business man. He also knew from experience that a great fortune could be made from a monopoly by defying the law while fixing its own rules of the game before the public could secure relief through the courts. The American Tobacco Trust, a fresh example, was organized in 1890; yet it was twenty years later before the courts overtook it. There is a tradition that Duke told his lawyers, when organizing the Tobacco Trust, that he wanted it arranged so that it could be operated along the lines of the Standard Oil Company, and that if they could keep the courts off him for ten years, he would be satisfied.

Clark's opinion in the power case led to the decision of an important issue but it did not end the litigation. Later the case was removed to the United States Court, where it was not ended until six years after the litigation was begun. The United States Circuit Court of Appeals decided against the Power Company's contention, and it took the case finally to the Supreme Court of the United States. At the hearing before that Court, Chief Justice Taft asked if the Supreme Court of North Carolina had not found that this was a foreign corporation, enjoying the right of eminent domain granted by the state, and was discriminating among customers taking its current and power. When told that this was a fact, the Court manifested little further interest in the hearing and unanimously decided against the Power Company.

2

The Power Company, having lost its fight before the Supreme Courts, to fix its own rates, turned in 1920 to the Corporation Commission, whose authority it had flouted and defied in 1914, and asked that it fix an even higher rate to its consumers than the Company had ever charged.

To have an intelligent idea of the importance of this titantic struggle, it is necessary to know the history of Duke's acquisition of these properties and how they were organized and operated from the beginning, since these elements were used as a basis for his daring proposal to increase rates. It is also important to know Duke's method of building up his capital account, which constitutes a romance in high financing.

Around the turn of the century, the development of hydroelectric power had assumed national importance. North Carolina offered a more inviting field for such an enterprise than any other state in the Union. There were five main reasons for this: Here were located vast undeveloped water sites; these properties were remote and could be cheaply acquired; there were no coal deposits of importance in the state; here were already established many progressive towns and cities; and large manufacturing concerns and numerous textile mills already established were anxious to buy such current for power and lighting.

After the dissolution of the Tobacco Trust, Buck Duke, who had previously moved his residence to New York, returned to North Carolina and employed some of the riches accumulated through the Tobacco Trust in establishing a power monopoly in Piedmont North and South Carolina. Through several subsidiary corporations controlled and dominated by him and his family, he set about to acquire the most valuable water power sites in the Piedmont section of these states. Agents representing one or another of these corporations acquired these sites and adjacent lands along the rivers for storage basins, in most cases at prices usually paid for agricultural purposes.

The development and operation of these properties proved highly profitable from the outset. Duke secured contracts to sell power and current to a large number of towns, cities, and industrial consumers. A number of these contracts extended for a period of ten years. Notwithstanding these contractual obligations, in 1920 Duke caused the Southern Power Company to file with the North Carolina Corporation Commission a petition asking that the Company be allowed to cancel all of its outstanding contracts with consumers of current and power; and further that the commission fix a new schedule of rates which would yield a substantial return upon what the Company's engineers estimated it would cost at that time to replace the properties. This petition was predicated upon what was known among experts as the "replacement value theory," that is, that utilities should be allowed to capitalize on the high prices prevailing after the World War by writing up the asset values of their property to equal a sum which experts estimated it would then cost to purchase water rights and storage basins and to install the necessary machinery and equipment.

Many manufacturing concerns, municipalities, and other consumers filed protest, asserting that they had existing written contracts with the Power Company, extending for a number of years, which should be respected. The North Carolina Public Service Company, plaintiff in the suit above referred to and still pending against the Power Company, anticipating that the commission would allow an increase in rates, intervened in the proceedings and requested that if and when such an order was made it should include a provision directing the Power Company to furnish current and power to it upon like conditions and rates as it was furnishing current to other similar consumers, as had been expressly directed by the Supreme Court of the state. The commission's attention was also directed to the fact that the Power Company had removed the Public Service Company case to the United States Court, where the cost of continuing litigation would ultimately fall upon an innocent and helpless public. The commission disregarded this request and the plain duty which it owed to itself and the public, and treated the Court's decision as if it had never been made.

On the day fixed for the hearing, Buck Duke arrived in Raleigh in his private Pullman car, which he occupied as a residence throughout the proceedings. To see that the job was properly done he attended the sittings in person, accompanied by a bevy of noted attorneys and engineers. He offered evidence to show that the power sites and the storage basin lands along the rivers had been acquired at low prices and that the construction work had been very economically done. It was brought out that Duke had paid cash for it all and had taken bonds against the property for the full amount expended in acquiring and developing his power domain. The record evidence disclosed that the total investment which had been made was approximately $37,000,000 and that the contracts which had been entered into (some of them personally signed by him) were fixed to give a fair return on the capital actually invested. But, contended he and his lawyers, following the World War the prices of everything had gone up and he should now be allowed to establish by his engineers how much it would cost to replace these properties—land, water, and all. His experts with one accord testified that it would take about $75,000,000 to replace these properties. (It was not explained how the most valuable part of the assets, water power, could be replaced, since Duke already owned all of the valuable water sites in Piedmont North and South Carolina.) Having thus theoretically lifted these property values by their own bootstraps from $37,000,000 to $75,000,000, Duke demanded that the commission raise the schedule of rates to the public so that he and his associates could collect dividends on $75,000,000 instead of $37,000,000. The practical result of applying this "replacement value theory," as subsequent events showed, was to replace the water from the streams with $50,000,000 of watered stock and place an obligation upon the public to pay dividends forever on this unearned increment.

In the record made before the Corporation Commission, it appeared that the properties of the Power Company were embraced in two categories, one the valuable power sites and vast land holdings along the course of the rivers used as storage basins for the waters; the other the dams, generators, and transmission lines. Naturally, the extensive power sites and water basins were the most permanent and valuable assets of the corporation. The commission responded to the Power Company's contention by allowing it to cancel all existing contracts. It did not determine the actual hypothetical replacement value of the corporation's properties, but it did fix a very substantial increase of rates which the company was allowed to pass on to the consumers of current and power. The public regarded the new rates as presupposing a theoretical valuation of approximately $75,000,000, and, as we shall see later, Duke and his associates so regarded it and actually capitalized the increased earnings allowed by the commission's order, by issuing more than $50,000,000 of bonus watered stock to themselves.

Clark regarded the entire transaction as a flagrant disregard of the public welfare and in disobedience of the law. One of his comments was, "Jones is still required to pay the freight."

Clark did not live to see a published report of the United States Senate on Duke's high financing of these power properties. This story is graphically told in a report of the Federal Trade Commission, transmitted to the Senate in response to its resolution directing an investigation of the means and methods employed in building the Southern Power Company's empire. This report was published by the United States Senate, Seventieth Congress, 1st Session, 1933, in Document 92, Part 78. A digest of this report, made by a certified public accountant, shows, among other things, that from the inception of this enterprise to the date of the Senate's published report, Duke had organized and employed twenty-one corporations constituting the Duke Power group, all of which were principally owned and dominated by J. B. Duke; that from time to time the stock of these various companies was sold and purchased back and forth among the constituent corporations; that the surplus created by writing up the value of these properties was employed as a basis for issuing stock dividends to the Duke Power Company as the principal stockholder of the underlying companies; that the Duke Power Company then in turn issued stock dividends of its own from the surplus created by the receipt of the stock dividends from the underlying companies; it also created other surpluses from the valuation of investments in certain stocks, which it had acquired at less than par value, which were written up to equal the par value until finally the stock dividends issued by the Duke Companies amounted to $53,502,406.20 in par value. Of this amount, $32,931,739.41 was created by the valuation of stock dividends received by Duke Power Company from the underlying companies from inter-company profits on exchange of securities and from writing up securities to equal the par value thereof. The surplus from which the underlying companies declared the stock dividends was largely created by writing up the fixed assets of those companies. The grand write-up of values occurred in 1923, soon after the contest over the Corporation Commission's increase of rates was settled. The actual amount as shown by the Senate Report was $30,689,577.82, which, added to other write-ups as a basis for their future dividends, totaled $53,502,-406.20. The financial setup of the Duke Power Company, as reflected in the Senate Report of December 31, 1933, was a capital account of $151,000,000.00, which was divided into 1,500,000 shares of common stock of the par value of $150,000,000.00, and 10,000 shares of preferred stock with a par value of $1,000,000.00. As of that date there were outstanding 1,010,048 shares of common stock with a total par value of $101,004,800.00, and 2,838 shares of preferred stock with a par value of $283,800.00. The Senate's Report showed that 36.6 per cent of this stock was owned by the Duke Endowment Trust; 22.2 per cent by Doris Duke (four trusts). It will be observed that $36,000,000.00 of this stock conveyed by Duke to his Endowment Trust is considerably less than the write-up of the corporate values, which the Corporation Commission breathed life into by its order greatly increasing the rate authorized to be collected from the consuming public. It has been suggested that the future will raise the questions: Who supplied the assets for this foundation, Duke or the consuming public? Whose money is keeping it alive?

Since the foregoing was written, the Supreme Court of the United States, on November 22, 1943, refused to review a decision sustaining the action of the Federal Power Commission in valuing the Niagara Falls Power Company on the basis of its "actual legitimate original cost" instead of its "fair value."

Appealing from a decision by the Federal Circuit Court of Appeals in New York the company contended that its 1921 license from the Power Commission provided for a determination on the basis of "fair value." It asserted that this was repudiated by the Commission in 1942. The Commission allowed $24,680,680 as their actual legitimate original cost exclusive of certain items not in issue, and disallowed $15,537,943 on the ground that this amount represented "write-ups" transferred to the company's account when it was organized by a consolidation of predecessor companies in 1918.

CHAPTER XXI

"A BRAVE AND DETERMINED PEOPLE"

He who loves not his country can love nothing.—Byron

"I WANT YOU, the man who is accused of knowing everything about North Carolina—one of the greatest judges in the United States, who keeps up that high standard set by the fathers in civic, legislative and judicial deportment—to give me some information about the North Carolina troops in the Confederate Army." So wrote Congressman John W. Gaines of Tennessee to the Chief Justice in 1915.

This appreciation of Clark was no doubt inspired in part by the renown which had attended the publication of his *Histories of the Several Regiments and Battalions from North Carolina in the Great War of 1861-65*. This work, comprising five volumes, is regarded as the most complete history of its kind that has yet been compiled by any state, either North or South. A perusal of it gives a glimpse of the prodigious labor required in its preparation.

At the request of the state, but without any appropriation to defray the expenses, Clark, in 1895, began the task of compiling and editing this history. The means employed was to select as contributors those who were actually participants and could write from personal knowledge of themselves and their comrades, and describe the scenes of which they were eyewitnesses. The completion of the work required seven years. As the manuscripts came in, Clark personally read and diligently corrected all of them, comparing them with the original reports published by the government in *The Official Records of the Union and Confederate Armies*. As a further assurance of accuracy the sketches were printed in the newspapers of the state, and criticisms and corrections requested. From first to last, Clark estimated that he wrote, in connection with the preparation of this work, more than five thousand letters.

Those selected to write the histories represented every grade in the army from lieutenant general to private and included men who occupied civil office from United States senator and governor to constable. There are 254 of these histories, constituting about 4,000 pages in the five printed volumes. There are 165 pages in the three indexes. These indexes include more than 17,000 names, a large part of which are cited more than once. The work contains over 1,000 engravings with 32 maps.

As the state only obligated itself to publish the manuscript when finished, Clark assumed the additional burden of securing funds from those interested to take care of the expense of the engravings which went into the book.

When it is recalled that the task was performed by Clark while he was a member of the Supreme Court, between 1895 and 1902, the most active and turbulent period of his life, it taxes the imagination. But with him it was a labor of love to perpetuate the fame of the state and the bravery of his comrades in arms, as a living example, "as long as valor shall move the hearts of men, as long as the sacrifice of life for the good of one's country shall seem noble and grand."

The letter of Congressman Gaines is but an illustration of many similar letters found among Clark's correspondence. The preface to his history and numerous memorial addresses delivered by him here and there over the state throughout the years reveal many significant and interesting facts. "Such a record," declared he, "is only possible for a brave and determined people. There are those who will say that the cause of our war was slavery, and therefore it was unjust. After the lapse of more than half a century we can afford to speak plainly on the subject. Not one man in twenty in the South owned slaves, and those who served with our soldiers know well that they would not have fought to preserve that institution. It is also true that on the other side, the soldiery would not have gone into battle for the abolition of slavery, and ever indignantly denied such motive. In truth the soldiers of the South fought for independence, for the principle that every people had the right to govern themselves and to change their government at will. The soldiery of the North fought for the Union, and the Union only, because they believed that the preservation of liberty depended upon the continuance of the Union in its integrity, and that if this republic failed there would never be another. Yet we must admit that at the foundation of the desire for independence there was, and there had been from the beginning, a feeling that our right to maintain our own institutions, including, of course, that of slavery, depended upon our having an independent government secure from interference by the states of the North."

One of Clark's most interesting and significant observations, one which is quite apposite to the present conflict, stressed the deadly influence of unpreparedness. He pointed out the utter inability of people of both sections to understand the magnitude and the duration of the struggle before them, and he said that this lack of comprehension was aggravated by speakers on both sides who, in raising volunteers, declared that they would "contract to wipe up all the blood that would be spilled with a silk pocket handkerchief."

Clark likewise made a unique contribution to the economic aspect of the struggle, by revealing what he regarded as shortsightedness on the part of President Davis. "The Confederate Government," said he, "persistently refused, in the summer of 1861, to negotiate a loan of $600,000,000 which was tendered by capitalists in Europe, and President Davis gave positive instructions that in no event should more than $15,000,000 be accepted. If the loan had been taken, of the magnitude offered, the Confederacy would early have been supplied with ammunition, arms, provisions, and a navy, and the blockade later, to which we owed our defeat, would have been impossible." He made the further statement that "the European governments would have intervened if necessary to have preserved the investment of their capitalists in the $600,000,000 loan which would have been taken if secured on cotton."

Clark thought as did Pope: "Tho' triumphs were to gen'rals only due, Crowns were reserv'd to grace the soldiers too."

He called attention to the fact that in 1860 the census showed the total population of North Carolina to be less than a million, one-third of whom were Negroes; yet North Carolina sent more than 125,000 soldiers to the front, besides the home guards, who preserved order, guarded bridges, and at times strengthened the lines in North Carolina.

In one of his addresses he stated that the Federal records show that the Union, first and last, placed in line 2,850,000 men, while on the Confederate side, the records of which have been lost, the estimates are from 600,000 to 800,000; and he drew some striking comparisons. The magnitude of the Civil War, said he, could be judged by the numbers engaged on great historic fields. "Caesar, when he won the world's empire over Pompey at Pharsalia, commanded only 22,000 infantry and 1,000 cavalry. Napoleon won the mastership of France by his victory at Marengo with 21,000 men and the supremacy in Europe at Austerlitz with 80,000 men, and lost it at Waterloo where he commanded 65,000 men. We achieved our independence at Yorktown, where we captured 7,073 British with a loss in killed of 156 Americans and 85 French."

He further reminds us that in the Revolutionary War, in which we won our independence against the greatest power in the world, we left during the entire seven years only 1,735 men dead on the field of battle. In the War of 1812, our second war with Great Britain, we had only 1,235 killed outright, though that war saved us the entire country beyond the Mississippi; and in the war with Mexico, which brought us Texas, California, and the great territory lying between them, we lost only 1,047 men killed. In the

Civil War, he said, "North Carolina alone had 5,016 men killed in battle, 9,000 more died from wounds, and 29,000 from disease, making a total of 43,000 men (or one-third of the whole number of soldiers from this state) which North Carolina lost during the war, to say nothing of the wounded and crippled who survived."

Few authors have received more unstinted and universal praise than was given Clark as historian of the part which North Carolina took in this great drama of war. He had no apologies to make for his state. "If the cause finally failed, no blame can be laid upon a state which went into that war reluctantly but which, when it once entered, stinted neither in men, in courage, nor in supplies in its ardent support to the side which its people had espoused." With this as his text he incorporated in his history many striking facts in support of it.

On the cover of each volume of his histories he had imprinted in gold letters:

> "First at Bethel
> Farthest to the Front at Gettysburg
> And Chickamauga
> Last at Appomattox."

Of this he said, "The legend on the cover is no idle boast but is based upon evidence given herein that is deemed worthy to be presented to the great jury of the public and of posterity." And he added that Major Hale's history of the Bethel Regiment proves North Carolina's claim to be the first at Bethel, and the histories by Brigadier General Cox, Major General Grimes, and Colonel Frank Parker of the 30th Regiment abundantly establish that the volley of Cox's Brigade, of Grimes' Division, was the last at Appomattox. The last capture of guns by that gallant army was the taking of the four Napoleons by Roberts' North Carolina Cavalry Brigade the morning of the surrender. Davidson's history of the 39th Regiment, as well as Major Harper's of the 58th, and Colonel Ray's of the 60th, fully demonstrate that North Carolina soldiers were farthest to the front at Chickamauga, and they are corroborated by the report of C. A. Cilley, a staff officer of Vandeveer's Brigade, which faced North Carolinians on that well-fought field. The history of the 55th Regiment, by Adjutant C. M. Cook, shows that it went farthest to the front on the Cemetery Ridge at Gettysburg. Declared Clark, "The best proof of how far a line of battle went is where it left its dead and wounded. These derelicts, cast up by the blood wave of war, were found farthest in the front of that gallant regiment, and this is shown by the battlefield map prepared by the authority of the United States Government after years of careful investigation of official reports and living witnesses from both armies." A copy of this official map on a reduced scale is printed in the history.

With unbounded pride Clark incorporated Major Henry A. London's statement about the Battle of Gettysburg. Major London wrote: "At Gettysburg 2,592 Confederates were killed and 12,707 wounded; and 3,155 Federals were killed and 14,529 were wounded. The three brigades which lost more killed than any others in that battle were Pettigrew's North Carolinians. Pickett's Division alone lost 214 killed. The Twenty-sixth North Carolina Regiment under Pettigrew lost 86 killed and 502 wounded, which was the heaviest loss of any regiment in either army in any battle of the war."

Clark emphasized the fact that while North Carolina could not compare with Virginia in the role of high commanding officers, she furnished far more than her proportionate part of those who fought and died for the Lost Cause. Virginia's population was 1,600,000; her losses were 14,000. North Carolina's population was 960,000; her losses were 43,000. She was the last state, except her daughter Tennessee, to enter the conflict. Her population was one-tenth that of the states forming the Confederacy, yet she furnished one-sixth of the soldiers and one-fifth of the provisions and other supplies to the Confederate armies. She was the only state that operated blockade runners on the high seas throughout the war.

Clark includes in this work a story of the steamer "Ad-Vance," a blockade runner, and also the story of the cruiser "Shenandoah," which flew the Confederate battle emblem at her masthead until November 6, 1865, nearly seven months after Lee's surrender.

A striking and thought-provoking chapter in this work is the one written by Major W. A. Graham, a son of Governor Graham and a brother-in-law of Clark. He recounts that, after the battle at Bentonville, Governor Vance commissioned Governor Graham and Governor Swain to visit General Sherman's headquarters with a request for a personal interview, in the hope of suspending hostilities and saving the Capitol from destruction such as had occurred at Columbia, South Carolina, and at Fayetteville. The commissioners, after an unpleasant experience, reached General Sherman's headquarters, but were too late to return that night, and Governor Graham spent the night with General Sherman in his tent. The reply to Governor Vance was that General Sherman could not suspend hostilities but he enclosed the following orders of utmost significance to North Carolina:

"Headquarters Military Division of the Mississippi—In the Field, Gulley's Station, N. C., April 12th, 1865.

"All officers and soldiers of this army are commanded to respect and protect the Governor of North Carolina and the officers and servants of the State Government, the Mayor and civil authorities of Raleigh, provided no hostile act is committed against the officers and men of this army between this and the city.

W. T. Sherman,
Major-General Commanding.

"The train of cars now here in charge of Colonel James G. Burr of the staff of Governor Vance can pass to and from Raleigh, without let or hindrance until further orders. All guards and pickets will see that it is not interfered with or destroyed.

W. T. Sherman,
Major-General Commanding."

Governor Graham's daughter, Susan, who was then in her early teens, years afterwards recounted frequently to her children some of the stirring events of these momentous days. She recalled that Governor Vance came to her father's home at Hillsboro and remained there while the commissioners were conferring with General Sherman; and she told of an impressive incident that occurred while General Sherman was in Raleigh. He received a telegram, on April 14, announcing the assassination of President Lincoln but put the message in his pocket and did not then communicate its contents to his army, lest they should become enraged and inflict serious damage upon the Capitol.

A similar consideration was soon to be shown when General Sherman dictated the terms of General Johnston's surrender. But, unfortunately, the government in Washington, under the pernicious influence of the sadist, Thaddeus Stevens, repudiated it.

Chapter XXII
THE FULLNESS OF TIME

*"When to the sessions of sweet silent thought
I summon up remembrance of things past..."*
—Shakespeare

THE CHIEF JUSTICE was now approaching seventy-eight. His eye was not dimmed nor his natural force abated, but he realized that the camp fires were burning low. Like the Apostle Paul, he had the consolation that he had fought a good fight; that he had finished his course; and that he had kept the faith. For thirty-five years he had served as associate and chief justice of the Supreme Court.

Amid the sweet serenity of his books, he was "proud that he had learned so much and humble that he knew no more." The shelves of his library were filled with carefully selected books, old friends all read and none forgotten. But his greatest affection was for those which were the children of his own brain and the result of his own handiwork. There was *Clark's Code of Civil Procedure*, which over the years had meant so much to his brethren at the bar, to the judges, and to the administration of justice; there were the State Records of North Carolina in sixteen volumes which he had compiled without compensation at the request of the state; Constant's life of Napoleon in three volumes, translated by him and his wife from the French; and his favorite, the *Histories of the Several Regiments and Battalions from North Carolina in the Great War of 1861-65*, in five volumes, which he had compiled and edited to perpetuate the valor and glory of those with whom he had fought as a boy and those who had died in the Southern cause.

In one section of his library were eighty bound volumes of the *Reports of the Supreme Court*, which contained over 3,300 of his opinions, into which he had for thirty-five years poured his very soul. In orderly arrangement in a bookcase were more than ninety printed pamphlets and national magazines containing his addresses and articles, in which, together with his opinions, he had stated and expounded his philosophy of law and government and had earnestly sought to remove from government and the courts "the dead hand of the past." In the center of his library was a bust of Napoleon, which had stood there for half a century. Napoleon's career as a reformer and law-giver, until he re-established a monarchy, was an inspiration to Clark. There was a certain parallel in their lives: in war, the "Little Corsican"—the "Little Clark"; in law, the Code Napoleon—Clark's Code; in government, Napoleon battling to destroy autocracy—Clark fighting to banish special privileges, trusts, and monopolies.

His fearless challenge of trusts, monopolies, combines, and railroad abuses had been justified by subsequent events, so that not even an apologist for their ruthlessness and greed remained; married women had been emancipated and an enlightened public sentiment had forbidden the employment of infant children in industry, and many reforms in the practice and procedure of the courts had been accomplished under his leadership.

His repeated insistence over the years that "the public welfare is the supreme law" had given a new meaning and importance to the public welfare clause of the Constitution of the United States.

His technique of writing dissenting opinions, employing government statistics, scientific discoveries, and historical facts, was now followed by liberal justices of the United States Supreme Court.

It is an interesting fact that Clark's criticism of the "five old lawyers" on the Supreme Court (in his address at the University of Pennsylvania) for assuming to determine the economic life and public policy of the nation by declaring acts of Congress unconstitutional, for which he was roundly condemned by the reactionaries, has found increasing favor since his death, notably among justices of the Supreme Court.

Justice Frankfurter, in his lecture on "The Life of Justice Holmes and the Supreme Court," delivered a short while before he himself was appointed to the Supreme Court, said: "As late as 1905 the Supreme Court held it unconstitutional to limit the working hours of bakers to ten, and as recently as 1936 the Court adhered to its ruling that it was beyond the power of the states and of the nation to insure minimum wage rates for women workers, obviously incapable of economic self-protection. Every variety of legislative manifestation to subject economic power to social responsibility encountered the judicial veto."

Robert H. Jackson, while Attorney General of the United States and shortly before his appointment to the Supreme Court, in his book on *The Struggle for Judicial Supremacy,* wrote: "By 1933 the court was no longer regarded as one of the three equal departments among which the powers of government were distributed. . . . It took over into its control the whole range of the national economy. It tried to stem the increasing recession from Laissez Faire and to make its teachings a part of our constitutional law. . . . It conjured up such doctrines as 'freedom of contract' to defeat legislation, though the court later found that the Constitution did not mention it . . . and it did not put a curb on trusts but on the people."

Clark's correspondence reveals an intriguing story of the attitude of many prominent men who had once opposed him because they regarded his teachings dangerous. Associate Justice Brown was a member of the Supreme Court with Clark for fifteen years. Brown was generally regarded as the ablest exponent of judicial conservatism in the state, and his elevation to the bench was expected to prove a checkmate to the radical Clark. They had many judicial battles in conference but without personal bitterness. As the years passed and events changed, these great minds converged, until Brown wrote Clark, "I believe you and I agree in a majority of things nowadays." Near the close of Brown's career, he addressed a note to "Dear Chief Justice," sending an opinion which he had written, with the statement, "Under no circumstance would I have anything in an opinion of mine which is objectionable to you." Brown also enclosed a clipping of an interview between Mr. Epstein and Cardinal Gibbons. When Epstein congratulated the Cardinal upon looking well, he replied, "But it will not be long before the Heavenly Father takes me before him." "Pardon me, Your Eminence," said Mr. Epstein, "but in my judgment the Good Lord is too good a business man to let a gilt-edge bond like you go for eighty or ninety; he will keep you until you reach par at one hundred, and possibly until you are at a premium." Brown commented: "The enclosed clipping leads me to believe that for some reason the Lord will keep you here a long time."

Governor Morrison wrote: "I want you to let me say to you that I would rather have written into the Supreme Court reports of this state the great principles of justice and right that you have written than to have rendered any other service any other son of this state has ever given."

And Governor Gardner: "I think you have done more to impress yourself upon the constructive forces of North Carolina than any other man who ever lived in the state."

In the interim between Mr. Taft's service as President and as Chief Justice of the United States, he was entertained at a banquet in Durham, at which Judge Clark presided. Mr. Taft, in his address, jocularly remarked that he would not trust the Constitution with Judge Clark overnight. Clark's critics, choosing to miss the sense in the humor, broadcast this remark as an evidence of Taft's disapproval of Clark; they overlooked the obvious fact that Taft, while not agreeing with Clark in many things, had a high regard for him. Later, he wrote Clark from New Haven: "The American Bar Association is most anxious that you should be of its membership and attend its meetings. They are full of profit and pleasure. Besides, we want you with us. I wish you also to become the editor of the judicial section. May I ask as a personal favor that you afford me the opportunity of proposing you for membership?"

It was now a byword among the legal profession in North Carolina that most of Clark's dissenting opinions had already become the opinions of the courts, and that many of the reforms in law and procedure for which he had long fought had been enacted into law by the General Assembly. It has been given to few men so fully to realize the truth of the statement: "Time is God's mighty right arm of recompense."

A letter from the distinguished Chadbourne of the New York bar, a short time before Clark's death, commended his opinion construing the Federal Reserve Act, and concluded with the statement that when he was a student at Harvard Law School he was directed to read Clark's opinions as classics in expounding the law.

Dean Wigmore of the Northwestern University Law School urged him, though he was seventy-five years old, to deliver a course of lectures to his law class, while Dean Pound of the Harvard Law School joined in commending his learned opinions.

Invitations to deliver addresses before universities, bar associations, and law schools continued to the very end. The prophet was now not without great honor among the learned of his own North Carolina and the nation.

Professor William E. Dodd of the University of Chicago wrote: "You are about the only Judge of a high court I know who thinks seriously about social and political problems. It is a matter of great pride to me to be your friend and to point out to others that North Carolina probably has the ablest Chief Justice of any state in the Union. Your opinions are quoted by all the lawyers of liberal views I know—men like Roscoe Pound. I only wish you were endowed with perennial youth."

In a signed editorial in his magazine, Senator Robert M. La Follette wrote, after Clark's death: "My personal friendship for Judge Clark was a constant source of inspiration and encouragement. As a true citizen of the state and the nation, he was always a leader in the struggle against the evil forces that are ever seeking to undermine the foundations of democracy." He concluded: "Thousands of readers of *La Follette's* will mourn his loss because through the many articles which he had contributed to its columns, he had impressed himself upon the minds of the people of the nation over as one of the great leaders of progressive thought and an oustanding champion of the people against the ever-increasing encroachments of the Federal Judiciary."

The pseudo liberals in the state who did not have the will or the bravery to follow through with Clark excused themselves by saying the trouble with him was that he was twenty-five years ahead of his time. Strictly speaking, and from the record, it was more accurate to say that Clark, in his thinking and acting, was a third of a century ahead of his time. So far as the bench and bar were concerned, he was half a century ahead of his time.

In the closing years of his career, and occasionally afterwards, the chief criticism of him was that he was too ambitious. The record unquestionably discloses that he was a tremendously ambitious man. He seems to have been born with this quality. The vital question, however, is, were his ambitions purely selfish, or for others? We know that he was not ambitious to make money; that he deliberately gave up a lucrative law practice for a judicial career, which for many years after he went on the bench paid only $2,500 a year; that he did not try to save money by accepting free passes from railroad and steamboat companies after becoming a judge; that he never speculated and never engaged in outside business to make money. His only diversion was looking after the Ventosa plantation, which he operated, often at great inconvenience, with small profits, for the benefit of his brothers, sisters, and himself. There was never a time when he could not have left the bench and commanded a law practice that would have given him wealth, if possessions had been his passion.

2

The Chief Justice never doubted that future generations would vindicate his life's work. In the early spring of 1923 Clark and his son, John, were strolling through the cemetery in Raleigh. Their attention was attracted to several imposing monuments marking a grave here and there of a jurist or a statesman. The father said to the son: "When my days are over, I wish a simple marker placed over my grave. Whatever services I may have rendered to my countrymen during life will be cherished by them when I am gone. This is the only monument I care for." He repeated this wish in his last will and testament. A simple marker now indicates his grave.

In December, 1923, the Chief Justice visited for the last time Ventosa plantation. He carried with him, as had been his custom through the years, Christmas presents to the children of his tenants. There are still living on the plantation Negroes who have been there since the days immediately following the Civil War, who delight to recall circumstances connected with the Judge's occasional visits. They tell of Uncle Joshua, an old man who was a lay minister and who preached to the tenants. Clark would ask Uncle Joshua to repeat to him one of his last sermons, and would sit and listen. When the sermon was finished he would hand the old preacher fifty cents or a dollar, saying "A laborer is worthy of his hire."

The remaining tenants testify that Clark was always just in his dealings with them and treated them with uniform kindness and consideration. Old man Anderson Williams boasts of the fact that it was his pleasant duty to meet the judge at the train on these various visits, carry his valise, and wait on him while there. He remembers vividly the occasion of the Judge's last visit and recounts this incident: "We went to the train that afternoon and I carried the Judge's valise. As we arrived at the station the Judge said to me, 'Anderson, is there anything I can do for you?' I told him, Marse Judge, I have never asked you for much, but I shore would love to have an overcoat for the winter. The Judge took off the overcoat that he was wearing, handed it to me, and said, 'God bless you.' He then turned and went into the train."

On Saturday afternoon, May 18, 1924, Clark finished writing the last opinions of the Court which had been assigned him, and filed them neatly in his desk. Sunday morning he dressed as usual for church, but as the bells were ringing for the service a weariness overcame him and he lay down on his couch. The next morning about two o'clock a message was flashed to the press of the nation that Walter Clark, Chief Justice of the Supreme Court of North Carolina, was dead. The funeral cortege was composed of the Governor, Council of State, members of the Supreme Court, and a host of others. The active pallbearers were his five sons, two sons-in-law, and a nephew. At the head of the procession walked George Alston, who had been his trusted and faithful body servant during his entire thirty-five years service on the bench. It was fitting that the pomp and majesty of a great state should thus join with a lowly Negro servant in paying homage to a life that exalted the law, for Clark had often quoted Hooker: "Of Law there can be no less acknowledged than that her seat is the bosom of God, her voice the harmony of the world; all things in heaven and earth do her homage, the very least as feeling her care and the greatest as not exempted from her power."

The Chief Justice's body was placed in the rotunda of the State Capitol, where thousands of his fellow citizens passed his bier paying their respects to the last earthly remains of their valued friend and trusted judge. Distinguished citizens from every section of the state were present, and thousands of common people also had come for a last look at their friend. He had never mingled with them, but he had served them; he had never flattered them, but he had told them the truth; he had never preached to them, but he had fought their battles and they idolized him.

LIST OF WRITINGS

INDEX

SELECTED LIST OF WALTER CLARK'S WRITINGS
(Arranged chronologically under each head.)

I. Articles and Printed Addresses

THE AMERICAN LAW REVIEW

"The True Remedy for Lynch Law." November-December, 1894, pp. 801–7.

"The Progress of the Law." May-June, 1897, pp. 410–14.

"The Right of the Public to Regulate the Charges of Common Carriers and of all Others Discharging Public, or Quasi-Public Duties." September-October, 1897, pp. 685–700.

"Where Does the Governing Power Reside?" October, 1918, pp. 687–94.

"Centennial of the North Carolina Supreme Court (extracts from an address)." April, 1919, pp. 301–4.

"Can Shares of Stocks Be Exempted from Taxation, in the Hands of Shareholders?" September-October, 1920, pp. 689–704.

"Magna Carta and Trial by Jury." January-February, 1924, pp. 24–44.

"The Common Law. Address before the Law School of the University of North Carolina." May-June, 1924, pp. 450–68.

THE ARENA: A TWENTIETH CENTURY REVIEW OF OPINION

"The Telegraph and the Telephone Properly Parts of the Post Office System." March, 1892, pp. 464–71.

"The Election of Postmasters by the People." June, 1894, pp. 68–75.

"The Election of Senators and the President by Popular Vote, and the Veto." September, 1894, pp. 453–61.

"The Telegraph in England." August, 1895, pp. 372–75. Also in the *Congressional Record,* 54th Cong., 1st Sess., Senate Doc. No. 205.

"Should the Government Control the Telegraph?" December, 1895.

"The Land of the Noonday Sun—Anahauc—Mexico." February, 1896, pp. 349–60. (Illustrated. Frontispiece photograph of Walter Clark.)

"Mexico in Midwinter." March, 1896, pp. 523–43. (Illustrated with many full-page photographs.)

"The Land of the Noonday Sun—Mexico in Midwinter," April, 1896, pp. 697–723. (Illustrated.)

"Free Coinage Indispensable, but Not a Panacea." November, 1896, pp. 937–44.

"Maladministration of the Post-Office Department." May, 1897, pp. 947–55.

"The Rights of the Public over Quasi-Public Services." October, 1897, pp. 470–85.

"The Revision of the Constitution." February, 1898, pp. 187–98.

"How Can Trusts Be Crushed?" March, 1901, pp. 264–70.

"Why the Government Should Own the Telegraph and Telephone." November, 1901, pp. 519–20.

"Law and Human Progress." March, 1903, pp. 225–42.

"The Election of Federal Judges by the People." November, 1904, pp. 457–60. (Leading article, with a full-page picture of Clark.)

"'Aaron's Rod'; or Government by Federal Judges." November, 1907, pp. 479–81.

"All Americans of Royal Descent." December, 1907, pp. 628–31.

"Judicial Supremacy." February, 1908, pp. 148–55. (An editorial note preceding this article says that it is based upon an address before the Economic Club of Boston. Clark is characterized as "one of the strongest, clearest, and most fundamental thinkers and advocates of pure democracy in public life today.")

THE GREEN BAG: AN ENTERTAINING MAGAZINE FOR LAWYERS

"The Supreme Court of North Carolina." Three installments: October, 1892, pp. 457–74; November, 1892, pp. 521–40; December, 1892, pp. 569–91.

"Obituary of Augustus Summerfield Merrimon." December, 1892, pp. 605–7.

"Death Penalty by Burning at the Stake in North Carolina." April, 1896, pp. 149–50.

"The Supreme Court of Mexico and the Judicial System of That Country." May, 1896, pp. 203–8.

"The Vice-President: What to Do with Him." October, 1896, pp. 427–28.

"The Election of United States Senators by the People." January, 1898, pp. 4–6.

THE NORTH CAROLINA BOOKLET

"North Carolina Troops in South America. 'The Lost Battalion.'" October, 1904, pp. 3–17.

"Indian Massacre and Tuscarora War, 1711–'13." July 10, 1902, pp. 3–21.

"Journal of Colonel Richard Henderson Relating to the Transylvania Colony." January, 1904, pp. 12–31.

"Our State Motto and Its Origin." January, 1910, pp. 179–82.

"How Can Interest Be Aroused in the Study of the History of North Carolina?" (Address before the Teachers' Association, Wrightsville, N. C., June 12, 1901.) October, 1911, pp. 89–98.

"Roanoke Island." (Address delivered at the meeting inaugurated by the Literary and Historical Association, Manteo, N. C., July 24, 1902.) October, 1911, pp. 73–81.

"William Alexander Graham." July, 1916, pp. 3–16.

"Career of General James Hogan, One of North Carolina's Revolutionary Officers." October, 1911, pp. 105–10.

"Major General Stephen Dodson Ramseur." (Address delivered

at the presentation of the portrait of Ramseur, June 7, 1916.) October, 1916, pp. 69–75.

"Negro Soldiers." July, 1918, pp. 57–62.

"History of the Superior and Supreme Courts of North Carolina." October, 1918, pp. 79–104.

"General James Johnston Pettigrew, C. S. A." October, 1920–April, 1921, pp. 171–80.

OTHER PERIODICALS

"A Recovered Chapter in American History," *Harper's New Monthly Magazine,* October, 1896, pp. 753–58.

"The Election of United States Senators by the People," *Indianapolis Magazine,* July, 1897. Also in *Addresses and Articles, April–July, 1897,* pp. 119–23. See PAMPHLETS.

"Twelve Reasons Why the Telephone Should Be Restored to the Post Office," *New Time Magazine,* July, 1897. Also in *Addresses and Articles, April–July, 1897,* pp. 97–100. See PAMPHLETS.

"Open Letter to the Railroad Commission of North Carolina," *The News and Observer* (Raleigh, N. C.), July 13, 1897. Also in *Addresses and Articles, April–July, 1897,* pp. 101–18. See PAMPHLETS.

"Governmental Control of Railroads, Telegraphs, Telephones, and Express Companies," *The Coming Age,* April, 1900.

"Is the Supreme Court Constitutional?" *The Independent,* September 26, 1907.

"Government by Judges," *Ohio Law Review,* XI (1914), 485.

"Some Myths of the Law," *Michigan Law Review,* November, 1914, pp. 26–32. Also in the *Congressional Record,* 64th Cong., 1st Sess., Senate Doc. No. 449.

"Back to the Constitution," *Virginia Law Review,* February, 1915, pp. 214–26. Also in the *Congressional Record,* 64th Cong., 1st Sess., Senate Doc. No. 308.

"The Causes of Virginia's Greatness" (Address before the Literary Societies of the University of Virginia, June 14, 1915), *The Alumni Bulletin of the University of Virginia,* October, 1915.

"The Electoral College and Presidential Suffrage," *University of Pennsylvania Law Review,* June, 1917, pp. 737–47.

"Coke, Blackstone, and the Common Law," *Case and Comment,* April, 1918, pp. 861–72. Reprinted in the *Law Times* (London), September–October, 1918, pp. 393–94, 407–8, 421–22; reprinted also in the *Irish Law Times* (Dublin), October 12, 1918, pp. 250–52. See also PAMPHLETS.

"The Origin and Development of Law and Government," *Virginia Law Review,* November, 1920, pp. 103–9.

"Where Does the United States Supreme Court Get the Veto Power?" *The Locomotive Engineer Journal,* August, 1923.

CONGRESSIONAL RECORD

"The Legal Aspects of the Telegraph and Telephone," 54th Cong., 1st Sess., Senate Doc. 205. (*The American Law Review,* 1895.)

"The Telegraph in England." 54th Cong., 1st Sess., Senate Doc. 205. (*The Arena,* August, 1895.)

"Some Defects in the Constitution of the United States." 62nd Cong., 1st Sess., Senate Doc. No. 87. (Address to the Law Department of the University of Pennsylvania, April 27, 1906.)

"Government by Judges." 63rd Cong., 2nd Sess., Senate Doc. No. 610. (Address delivered at Cooper Union, New York City, January 27, 1914.) See also PAMPHLETS.

"Back to the Constitution." 64th Cong., 1st Sess., Senate Doc. No. 308. (*Virginia Law Review,* February, 1915.)

"Some Myths of the Law." 64th Cong., 1st Sess., Senate Doc. No. 449. (*Michigan Law Review,* November, 1914.)

PAMPHLETS. (These are available in the Library of the University of North Carolina.)

Everybody's Book. Some Points in Law of Interest and Use to North Carolina Farmers, Merchants, and Business Men Generally. Raleigh, N. C., P. M. Hale, 1882. Pp. 29. New Edition, revised, 1886. Pp. 45.

Address on the Life and Services of General William H. Davie, at the Guilford Battle Ground, July 4. Greensboro, N. C., Reece and Elam, Printers, 1892.

Addresses and Articles, April–July, 1897. Richmond, James E. Goode Printing Company, 1897. Pp. 172. (This contains seventeen articles and addresses, a few of which apparently have not been printed elsewhere.)

"Where Shall the Governing Power Reside?" (Address before the University College of Medicine, Richmond, Va., April 29, 1897.) In *Addresses and Articles, April–July, 1897,* pp. 3–19. See also *The American Law Review.*

"The Political Teachings of the Gospel." (Address before the Raleigh District Sunday School Conference, Franklinton, N. C., June 15, 1897.) In *Addresses and Articles, April–July, 1897,* pp. 44–57.

"The Right to Regulate Railroad Fares and Freight Rates." (Address before the Law Class of Wake Forest College, May 24, 1897.) In *Addresses and Articles, April–July, 1897,* pp. 20–43.

"Revision of the Constitution of the United States—Election of Judges, Senators and Postmasters by the People." (Address to the Bar Association of Tennessee at Nashville, July 30, 1897.) In *Addresses and Articles, April–July, 1897,* pp. 58–79.

Address by Hon. Walter Clark, Associate Justice Supreme Court of North Carolina, before the Eleventh Annual Convention of Railroad Commissioners, Held at Denver, Colo., August 10, 1899. (Published by the Interstate Commerce

Commission.) Washington, Government Printing Office, 1899. Pp. 18.

Old Foes with New Faces. (Address before the Bar Association of Virginia at Hot Springs, Va., August 25, 1903.) No imprint. Pp. 16.

Caldwell County, N. C., in the Great War of 1861-65. (Address on the Occasion of the Unveiling of the Monument to the Confederate Soldiers from Caldwell County at Lenoir, June 3rd, 1910.) Hickory, N. C., Clay Printing Co., 1910. Pp. 30.

The Gospel of Progress. (Address at Elon College, N. C., June 6, 1911.) No imprint. Pp. 12.

The Legal Status of Women in North Carolina, Past, Present and Prospective. (Address before the Federation of Women's Clubs, New Bern, May 8, 1913.) No imprint. Pp. 24.

Government by Judges. (Address Delivered at Cooper Union, New York City, January 27, 1914.) No imprint. 2nd ed. Pp. 24. See also Other Periodicals and Publications.

Equal Suffrage. (Address before the Equal Suffrage League of Virginia, at Richmond, Virginia, January 30, 1914.) No imprint. Pp. 18.

Address on Reform in Law and Legal Procedure. (Address before the North Carolina Bar Association at Wrightsville Beach, N. C., Tuesday, June 30, 1914.) Wilson, N. C., Wilson Stamp and Printing Co., 1914. Pp. 16.

Labor Day Address. (Delivered before the Trade Council of Wilmington, September 7, 1914.) Roanoke, Va., Industrial Era Print, 1914. Pp. 12.

"Thomas Ruffin," *Addresses at the Unveiling and Presentation to the State of the Statue of Thomas Ruffin by the North Carolina Bar Association. Delivered in the Hall of the House of Representatives, February 1, 1915,* pp. 7-23. Raleigh, N. C., Edwards and Broughton Publishing Co., 1915. (There is also a sketch of Thomas Ruffin in *The Green Bag,* October, 1892, pp. 467-74, as part of the article, "The Supreme Court of North Carolina."

Equal Suffrage. (Address before the Equal Suffrage League, Greensboro, N. C., February 22, 1915.) No imprint. Pp. 8.

The Legal Profession. Remarks of Chief Justice Walter Clark Accepting for the Court the Portrait of Hon. William T. Dortch, May 23, 1916. Raleigh, Edwards and Broughton Printing Company, 1916. Pp. 5.

Memorial Address upon the Life of General James Green Martin. (Delivered at Raleigh, N. C., May 10, 1916.) No imprint. Pp. 21.

Ballots for Both. (Address before the Equal Suffrage League, Greenville, N. C., December 8, 1916.) Raleigh, Commercial Printing Company, n.d. Pp. 16.

An Eight-Hour Day Decision: by Hon. Walter Clark, Chief Justice of the North Carolina Supreme Court, Acting as Umpire in the Case of Iron Molder's Union No. 364 (Wheeling, West Va.) versus the Wheeling Mold and Foundry Co. Washington, D. C., American Federation of Labor, [1918]. Pp. 8.

Coke, Blackstone, and the Common Law. (Reprinted from *Case and Comment*). Rochester, N. Y., Lawyers Cooperative Publishing Co., 1918. See also OTHER PERIODICALS.

II. GENERAL WORKS

The Code of Civil Procedure of North Carolina. By Walter Clark. Raleigh, Edwards and Broughton Printing Company, 1884, 1892; Goldsboro, N. C., Nash Brothers, 1900.

State Records of North Carolina. 16 vols. Collected and Edited by Walter Clark. Goldsboro, N. C., Nash Brothers, 1886-1907.

Recollections of the Private Life of Napoleon. Translated from French of L. C. W. Constant, by Walter Clark (with his wife).

SELECTED LIST OF WALTER CLARK'S WRITINGS 265

Histories of the Several Regiments and Battalions from North Carolina in the Great War 1861-'65. Written by members of the Respective Commands. Edited by Walter Clark. Published by the State. 5 vols. Vols. I, III, and IV, Raleigh, E. M. Uzzell, Printer, 1901; Vols. II and V, Goldsboro, N. C., Nash Brothers, Printers, 1901.

"Appeal and Error," 1300 pages, edited by Walter Clark. 1902. In the *Encyclopaedia of Law.*

"North Carolina in the Confederacy, 1861-1865." In *The South in the Building of the Nation* (12 vols. Richmond, Va., The Southern Historical Society, 1909), I, 483-97.

North Carolina Reports. Cases Argued and Determined in the Supreme Court of North Carolina. 164 vols. Annotated by Walter Clark. Reprinted by the State.

NOTE: Clark wrote a total of 3,235 opinions during his tenure on the Supreme Court Bench. Of these 2,682 were majority opinions of the Court; 182 were concurring opinions, and 371 dissenting opinions. These opinions appear in the printed reports of the Supreme Court beginning with 104 N.C. down to 187 N.C., both inclusive.

INDEX

Abernethy, W. E., 117
Adams, James Truslow, 29
Adams, John, 198
"Ad-Vance," blockade runner in Civil War, 245
Agrarians, 69-71
Agriculture, Clark's interest in, 52-53
"Airlie," home built by Clark family, 27, 35
"Albin," Clark estate at Scotland Neck, 25
Alderman, Edwin A., 118
Aldrich, Nelson W., Republican leader, 182
Allen, William A., a leader in impeachment proceedings, 127
Alston, George, Clark's servant, 175, 254
Altgeld, ex-Governor John P., commends Clark for speech, 98
American Bar Association, 64, 116, 192, 193, 220, 250-251
American Commonwealth, by Lord Bryce, quoted, 85-87, 219
American Federationist, praises Clark, 210-212
American Federation of Labor, Clark's opinions and speeches attract attention of, 206; praises Clark for supporting eight-hour day, 210-212
American Law Review, The, welcomes contributions from Clark, 66; Clark writes article for, 67, 94; attacks Federal railway receiverships, 90, 159, 205
American Tobacco Company, tobacco farmers resent, 70; dissolved, 98, 99; opposes Clark, 130; Clark points out abuses of, 152; supports Simmons, 184; organization of, 223-224; Clark compares Southern Power Company with, 228 ff.
Anderson, General George B., 10-11
Andrews, Colonel A. B., railroad policy of, 91-92; and impeachment proceedings, 128
Antietam. *See* Sharpsburg
Arena, The, Clark contributes articles to, 67, 74, 93-94, 189-190, 194
Armistead, Lieutenant Colonel F. S., 16
"Assumption of Risk," 171
Astor, John Jacob, 92
Atlantic and Great Western Canal, 46
Atlantic and North Carolina Railroad, litigation over, 142 ff.
Atlantic Coast Line, consolidation of, 87; opposition to Clark, 130
Aurelius, Marcus, 189
Austria, opposed to tobacco trust, 152
Aycock, Governor Charles B., rejects proposed lease of Atlantic and North Carolina Railway, 142-143; applies for bench warrant against McBee and Finch, 143 ff.; candidate for U. S. Senate, 177 ff.; sketch of, 177-178; Clarence Poe marries daughter of, 188; death of, 184, 189

Bailey, Josiah William, and Kilgo-Clark controversy, 117-118; opposes Clark in election for Chief Justice, 130
Baker, General L. S., 17
Baltimore Convention, 185
Bancroft, George, 26
Baptists, fight State support of higher education, 104-105, 106-107
Bass, Professor, Clark studies under, 31, 32-33
Battle, Judge William H., Clark reads law under, 15, 39

267

Battle, Senator Jacob, 160
Beard, Charles A., and Clark's views on Federal judiciary, 193, 196-197
Belmont Select School, Clark enters, 33-34
Bennett, Colonel, 11, 72
Bentham, Jeremy, philosophy of, 80-82, 84, 219, 220
Bentonville, battle of, 20-21
Bethel Regiment, 243
Beveridge, Albert, 198
Bible, Clark a student of, 77
Biblical Recorder, 117, 130
Bill of Rights, Clark on, 195
Blackstone, Sir William, 80, 82
Blounts, Clark related to, 42
Blue Book, published by Kilgo, 119
Bonaparte, Napoleon, Clark's interest in, 34; Constant's life of translated by Clark and his wife, 66, 246; quoted, 161, 169; size of armies, 242; Clark compared with, 248
Bowen, Lord, quoted, 220
Branch, General L. O'B., 11
Brandeis, Judge Louis D., adopts Clark's technique of writing opinions, 64; attacks railroad monopolies in *Other People's Money,* 89-90; agrees with Clark in publicity as a remedy for social and industrial diseases, 94; and demand for reform in government, 180; Clark in communication with, 204; Clark invited to deliver principal address at dinner in honor of, 214; warns against evils besetting judges and lawyers, 215
Branson, W. H., sued for libel, 119
Brittain, E. E., acts as editor of *News and Observer,* 186
Broadfoot, Charles W., 16
Brougham, Lord, 82
Brown, George H., elected justice of State Supreme Court, 154, 155; prevents publication of address denouncing Clark, 192-193; attitude towards Clark, 249-250
Brown, Judge Henry B., Clark quotes, 67
Brown, Rome G., denounces Clark, 192-193

Bryan, William Jennings, one line of Clark's ancestors connected with, 42; and National Convention of 1896, 73-74; admires Clark, 74; defeated for presidency, 85; ridiculed by Kilgo, 104; favors Clark for president of the United States, 179; Simmons tries to prevent endorsement of for the presidency, 181; attacks Simmons editorially, 182-183; Simmons machine opposes, 185; favors Clark's appointment to U. S. Supreme Court, 191; Clark corresponds with, 204; mentioned, 180
Bryan and Statton Commercial College, Clark enrolls in, 40
Bryce, Lord, author of *American Commonwealth,* quoted, 85-87; on American jurisprudence, 219
Bryson, Captain Walter, 8
"Bull Frog, The," essay by Clark, 33
Burr, Colonel James G., 245
Busbee, Fabius H., selected to lead campaign against Clark in contest for Chief Justice, 133-134; friendship with Clark ends, 140
Butler, Marion, a leader of the Populist Party, 69, 181
Byrd, Colonel William, 28

Caldwell, J. P., editor of the *Charlotte Observer,* 70
Caldwell, Judge, 90
Campbell, Lord, quoted, 82
Cape Fear and Yadkin Valley Railroad, absorbed by Southern and the Atlantic Coast Line, 87-89
Cardozo, Judge Benjamin, 77
Carlyle, Thomas, quoted, 150
Carnegie, Andrew, 179
Carpetbaggers, 72
Carr, Julian S., 117
Catt, Mrs. Carrie Chapman, consults Clark, 168; eloquence of, 170
Chadbourne, William M., commends Clark's opinion construing Federal Reserve Act, 251
Charlotte Observer, 70, 110, 178, 187
Chesterton, G. K., quoted, 76-77

INDEX 269

Child labor, Clark opposes, 170 ff., 248
Christian Advocate, 118
Christian Education, Its Aims and Superiority, pamphlet issued by Kilgo, 103-104
Cilley, C. A., 243
Civil War, Clark on, 240 ff.
Clark, Anna M., dies in infancy, 49
Clark, Colin, marries Janet McKenzie, 23; Clark fond of visiting, 31; Clark borrows cash from, 36; Clark's attachment to, 39; places claim against government, 41; death of, 42
Clark, Mrs. Colin, employs Clark as counsellor and business adviser, 42
Clark, General David (Clark's father), takes pride in Ventosa, 3; commissioned brigadier general in the North Carolina Militia, 13; urged by Clark not to enter service, 13-14; education of, 26; marries Anna Maria Thorne, 26; lover of fine horses, 31; purchases body servant for Clark, 34; surrenders management of plantation to Clark, 35; gives Clark plantation, 36
Clark, David McKenzie (Clark's grandfather), settles in Plymouth, 23 ff.; marries Louise Norfleet, 25
Clark, David (Clark's son), 49
Clark, Ed, 36, 40
Clark, Eugenia Graham, 49
Clark, John Washington, 49
Clark, John, 252
Clark, Susan Washington, 49
Clark, Thorne McKenzie, 49
Clark, Walter (Clark's son), 49
Clark, Walter McKenzie, ancestry, 23 ff.; birth, 26; childhood years and early education, 30 ff.; body servant purchased for, 34; as Confederate soldier, 4 ff.; at battle of Sharpsburg, 5 ff.; receives slight wound, 8, 11-12; writes parents, 14-19 *passim;* enters University of North Carolina, 14-15; elected major, 15, 16; commands post, 17 ff.; at battle of Bentonville, 20-21; returns to Ventosa, 19 ff.; assumes responsibility of rehabilitating family plantation, 35 ff.; contributes articles to *Raleigh Sentinel,* 37-39; had studied law at University of North Carolina, 39-40; goes North to study law, 40-41; reading, 41; begins practice of law, 42 ff.; family connections of, 42; defeated in contest for legislature, 42; made chairman of judiciary committee, 43; urges support of State University, 43; challenges Pugh to duel, 43 ff.; courtship and marriage, 47-49; purchases control of *Raleigh News,* 51; elected member of State Executive Committee, 51; writes and annotates Code of Civil Procedure, 51; becomes friend of Josephus Daniels, 53; as superior court judge, 54 ff.; personal appearance and habits, 60; ability as judge, 60 ff.; as associate justice of Supreme Court, 60 ff.; judicial opinions of, 63 ff.; begins compiling and editing State Records of North Carolina, 66; urges government ownership of telephone and telegraph, 67-69; renominated Supreme Court judge, 69-71; urged to accept nomination for governor, 72-73; philosophy of, 75 ff.; and trusts, 85 ff.,98-100; fights railroad monopoly, 87 ff.; Denver speech of attracts national attention, 97-98; and Kilgo-Gattis trials, 102 ff.; and impeachment proceedings against Judges Furches and Douglas, 122 ff.; and contest for Chief Justice, 129 ff.; whispering campaign launched against, 132 ff.; writes notes to Governor Russell, 132 ff.; prevents larceny of Atlantic and North Carolina Railroad, 142 ff.; advocates new social and economic order, 147 ff.; attacks unequal distribution of wealth, 149 ff.; becomes Chief Justice, 154 ff.; relations with associate justices, 155 ff.; writes history of Supreme Court, 159; fights for women's rights, 161-169; opposes child labor, 170-173; defends minorities, 173-176;

attitude toward Jews, 173-175; and Simmons, 177 ff.; becomes candidate for U. S. Supreme Court, 177 ff.; deserted by *News and Observer*, 184 ff.; appreciation of in *Arena*, 189-190; appointment to U. S. Supreme Court urged, 190-191; denounced at meeting of North Carolina Bar Association, 192-193; advocates abolition of life tenure for Federal judges, 193 ff.; attitude toward labor, 206 ff.; elected to Supreme Court for fifth time, 214; urges reform in American legal and judicial system, 215 ff.; employed as general counsel of W. Duke Sons & Co., 224; early judicial opinions of involving public utilities, 225-226; opposes efforts of J. B. Duke to build power monopoly in state, 226 ff.; begins compiling and editing *Histories of the Several Regiments and Battalions from North Carolina in the Great War of 1861-65*, 239; on bravery of South during Civil War, 240 ff.; publications by, 247-248; and Napoleon, 248; total accomplishments of, 247 ff.; visits Ventosa for last time, 253-254; death, 254

Clark, Mrs. Walter McKenzie (Susan Washington Graham Clark), courtship and marriage, 47-49; birth and education, 48-49; father of, 48, 49; mother of, 49; home life of, 49-50; death of, 50; joins Clark in translating life of Napoleon, 66; Col. A. B. Andrews a groomsman at marriage of, 91; recalls Sherman's stay in Raleigh, 246

Clark, William A. Graham, 49

Clarke, John H., appointed to U. S. Supreme Court, 191

Clay, Henry, 67

"Cleveland Democrats," 69

Cleveland, Grover, quoted, 85-86; 87

Code Napoleon, 248

Code of Civil Procedure, Clark writes and annotates, 51, 62; Clark's attitude toward, 60-61; importance of, 248; compared with Code Napoleon, 248

Columbian Law School, Clark completes law course in, 40

Commentaries on the Laws of England, Blackstone's, 80

Commoner, Bryan's, 179

Confederacy, war of, 4 ff.; refuses to negotiate loan, 241; losses of, 241

Congressional Record, Clark's addresses on Constitution printed in, 194

Connor, H. G., associate justice of the Supreme Court, asks Clark to befriend Josephus Daniels, 53; and impeachment proceedings, 128; becomes associate justice, 154; sketch of, 155-156

Constant, L. C. W., author of life of Napoleon, 66, 246

Constitution of 1868 (N. C.), and women's property rights, 163

Constitution, U. S., Clark's attitude toward, 193 ff.; Clark's address on at the University of Pennsylvania, 194 ff.

Cook, Adjutant C. M., 244

Cooper Union, Clark delivers address at, 194, 203

Corporation Commission, Southern Power Company challenges authority of, 227; Southern Power Company petitions for permission to cancel contracts, 233 ff.

Corwin, Professor Edward S., of Princeton, quoted, 200

"Court week," 54-55

Cox, Brigadier General W. R., 243

Craig, Locke, and impeachment proceedings, 127; candidate for governor, 181

Craven, Dr. Braxton, 121

Crawford, L. W., editor of the *Christian Advocate*, 118

Criminal law, Clark as administrator of, 62-63

Crowell, Dr. J. F., offers presidency of Trinity College to Clark, 103

Curran, John P., 170

INDEX   271

Daniels, Josephus, forms friendship with Clark, 53; and Kilgo, 107, 118; Josiah Bailey on, 117; covers McBee trial, 144; cited for contempt, 146; attacks Simmons machine, 181 ff.; attitude of toward W. W. Kitchin, 184; on Simmons' candidacy for U. S. Senate, 184; deserts Clark, 185 ff.; elected national committeeman, 186; Clark accuses of desertion, 186 ff.; breach with Clark comes to light, 187 ff.
Davidson College, 65
Davidson, John M., author of history of 39th Regiment, 242
Davis, Jefferson, 16, 21, 241-242
Davises, Clark related to, 42
Day, Captain W. H., named as Clark's second, 44, 45, 46; Clark's friendship for, 46; selected to lead assault against Clark in contest for Chief Justice, 133-134; ends friendship with Clark, 140; defends McBee, 144
Declaration of Independence, Clark on, 153, 194, 195
"Defects in the United States Constitution," title of Clark's address at the University of Pennsylvania, 194
Democratic Convention. *See* State Convention
Democrats, and election of 1896, 71 ff.; and impeachment proceedings, 122 ff.; and 1902 election of chief justice, 129 ff.; and political contest of 1898 and 1900, 180-181; of 1908, 181; of 1912, 177 ff.; *passim*
DeRosset, Colonel W. L., 7
Devin, Judge, on Clark's memory, 158-159
Dicey, Albert V., author of *Law and Opinion in England*, 168, 219-220
Dillon, Judge, 90
Disraeli, 174
Dissenting opinions, Clark's technique in, 63-64, 248
Dodd, William E., admires Clark's ability as judge, 251
Douglas, Robert M., State Supreme Court justice, impeachment proceedings against, 122 ff.; Clark accused of instituting impeachment proceedings against, 131; retired, 154
Douglas, Stephen A., 202
Dred Scott case, 202
Duke, B. N., and Kilgo trial, 113, 115, 119; one of organizers of American Tobacco Company, 223
Duke, Brodie, 223-224
Duke, James Buchanan, organizes American Tobacco Company, 98-99, 223-224; Aycock on, 179; sketch of, 223-224; and power companies, 224 ff.; held individually responsible for monopoly, 229; incorporates American Tobacco Company in New Jersey, 230; takes advantage of law's delay to amass fortune, 231, 232
Duke, Washington, serenaded by Kilgo, 108, 112; one of organizers of American Tobacco Company, 223-224
Duke Power Company, litigation over, 224 ff.
Duke University, Kilgo correspondence at, 108. *See also* Trinity College
Dukes, and Kilgo, 104, 105, 110, 116
Durham Daily Sun, 108
Durham, banquet held at, 249

Editor in Politics, by Josephus Daniels, 118, 119, 184, 187
Eight-hour day, Clark's battle for, 209 ff.
Eleanor of Provence, 165
Elizabeth, Queen, 165
Ellis, Governor John W., 4
Elon College, Clark delivers address at, 207-208
England, Clark visits, 52, 53; government ownership of communications in, 67-68; women's rights in, 167-168; judicial system of, 59, 80-81, 199, 218 ff.
Epstein, anecdote about, 250
Equal Suffrage League of Virginia, Clark addresses, 169
Europe, Clark travels in, 52-53

Faircloth, Judge W. T., 123
Federalists, 198
Federal judges, Clark's attitude toward, 192 ff.
Federal Trade Commission, and Duke Poser Company, 236
Fellow-Servant law, 206
Fifth Battalion Junior Reserves, Clark elected major of, 15
"Five Elderly Lawyers," 199, 201, 203
Finch, K. S., and railroad conspiracy, 143, 145
Fleming, Lieutenant Greenlea, 11
Flower, Benjamin O., editor of *Arena*, estimate of Clark by, 189-190
"Forgotten man," Clark on, 95-97
Forum, The, quoted, 67
Fourteenth Amendment, 200-201
Fowle, Governor Daniel G., appoints Clark to Supreme Court, 54, 59
France, opposed to tobacco trust, 152
Frankfurter, Justice Felix, on Clark, 154; quoted, 249
Fredericksburg, battle of, 12
Freeman, Douglas Southall, on Lee, 11
Free passes, controversy over, 90 ff., 97, 130, 135
Freight rates, Clark on, 96-97
Furches, Daniel M., impeachment proceedings against, 122 ff.; impending retirement of, 129; Clark accused of instituting impeachment proceedings against, 131
Fusionists, in election of 1896, 71-72; and impeachment proceedings, 122; and political contest of 1912, 180 ff.

Gaines, Congressman John W., asks Clark for historical information, 239, 240
Garber, Dr. Paul N., on Kilgo, 105, 107-108
Gardner, Governor O. Max, pays tribute to Clark, 250
Gaston, Judge William, 154
Gattis, Rev. T. J., and Kilgo controversy, 114 ff.
General Assembly (N. C.), sells railroad to private interests, 51; Clark prepares bill for, 93-94; and impeachment proceedings, 122 ff.; grants right of suit to married women, 166; Mrs. Carrie Chapman Catt addresses, 170; enacts progressive measures, 181; establishes Railroad and Telegraph Commission, 225; *See also* Legislature
George, Henry, 39, 153
George, Lloyd, 39
Gerry, Elbridge, 197
Gettysburg, heroism of North Carolina troops at, 243, 244
Gibbons, Cardinal, anecdote about, 250
Gladstone, William E., 83
Glenn, Governor Robert B., opposes fusion, 71-72; mentioned, 56
Goldsboro Water Company case, Clark's opinion in, 225 ff.
Goldsmith, Oliver, 49
Gompers, Samuel, attitude of towards Clark, 206
Gospel of Progress, Clark speaks on at Elon College, 207-208
Graham, Susan Washington. *See* Clark, Mrs. Walter McKenzie
Graham, Governor W. A., sketch of, 48-49; visits General Sherman, 245-246
Graham, Major W. A., contributes chapter to Clark's history, 245-246
"Grandfather clause," 127
Grant, U. S., 21, 200
Graves, Professor Ralph H., 33
Grays, Clark related to, 42
Great Falls Power Company, litigation over, 230 ff.
Green Bag, The, Clark contributes articles to, 66, 159
Greensboro News, 187
Grimes, Major General Bryan, 243
Guthrie, Major William A., Populist nominee for governor, 73

Hale, Major E. J., 243
Halifax, Clark builds law office at, 42
Hamilton, Alexander, 195
Hampton, General Wade, 19-20

INDEX

Hanna, Mark, 85
Harlan, Judge John M., 203-204
Harper, Major G. W. F., 243
Harper's Ferry, 5, 6
Hartsuff, General, 10
Harvard Law School, 217, 251
Hill, General A. P., 11
Hill, General D. H., 6, 10
Hill, Judge, T. J., candidate for Chief Justice, 132, 138
Hilliards, Clark related to, 42
Hinsdale, J. W., defends McBee, 144
Histories of the Several Regiments and Battalions from North Carolina in the Great War of 1861-65, compiled and edited by Clark, 239 ff., 247
History, Clark's fondness for, 79
History of the Dividing Line Between Virginia and North Carolina, 28
Hitler, Adolph, 173
Hoke, Judge W. A., on Clark, 61; presides at Kilgo-Gattis trial, 120; becomes associate justice, 154, 155; sketch of, 157-158; concurs with Clark in dissenting opinion, 164
Hoke v. *Henderson,* 123-124, 125, 128
Holmes, Lieutenant General T. H., 13, 16
Holmes, Judge Oliver Wendell, 64, 80, 215; Frankfurter's lecture on, 249
Holt, Colonel E. J., 134
Holt, J. A., 117
Holt, Governor Thomas M., associated with Clark in buying control of *Raleigh News,* 51
Hood, W. S., 10
Hooker, Richard, 254
"Hope," Clark's essay on, 34
Hot Springs, Va., Clark delivers address at, 149-153
Howie, Captain Sanford G., 9
Hydroelectric power, development of in North Carolina, 233

Impeachment trial, 122 ff.
International Exposition of Vienna, 46
Interstate Commerce Commission, 95
Italy, opposed to tobacco trust, 152

It's a Far Cry, by Judge Robert W. Winston, 90
Ivanhoe, 174

Jackson, Andrew, 79, 202
Jackson, Robert H., author of *The Struggle for Judicial Supremacy,* 249
Jackson, Thomas Jonathan (Stonewall), Clark marries relative of, 12; mentioned, 6, 9-10
James, William, 76, 116
Jarvis, Thomas J., 117, 118
Jefferson, Thomas, 41, 79, 83, 104, 106, 153, 193, 198, 201, 202
Jews, Clark's defense of, 173 ff.
Jhering, Rudolf von, quoted, 81
Johnson, Cave, 67
Johnson, Samuel, 80
Johnston, General Joseph E., 19, 20-21, 42, 245
Jones, Rev. Sam, influence of on Kilgo, 105-106
Judges, and administration of justice, 215 ff.
Judicature Act of 1873, 218
Junior Reserves, 15, 16, 20-21
Jurney, Rev. N. M., and Kilgo trial, 113
Justice, Clark's efforts to speed administration of, 215 ff.

Kilgo, Rev. John C., controversy of with Clark, 102 ff.; sketch of, 103 ff.; trial of, 112 ff.
King, R. N., 121
Kingsbury, Dr. T. B., 109
Kinston Free Press, 108
Kitchin, Claude, sketch of, 138, nominates Clark for chief justice, 138-140
Kitchin, W. H., 138
Kitchin, Governor W. W., candidate for U. S. Senate, 177; sketch of, 178; elected governor, 181; platform of, 183; attitude of Josephus Daniels toward, 184; health wrecked, 189
Kossuth, Louis, 79

Labor, Clark's views on, 152, 206 ff.
Lacy, Ben, 134
La Follette, Senator Robert M., and

Theodore Roosevelt, 180; has Clark's addresses on Constitution printed in *Congressional Record*, 194; Clark corresponds with, 204; pays tribute to Clark, 214, 251-252
La Follette's, 251-252
Law and Opinion in England, by Albert V. Dicey, 219-220
Law library, Clark encourages collection of, 160
Law of Evidence, by Dean Wigmore, 217
Lawyers, and administration of justice, 215 ff.
Lee, Robert E., 4-21 *passim;* 244
Legal Tender Act, 200
Legislature, urged to tax unimproved land in article by Clark, 39; Clark defeated in contest for, 42; and University of N. C., 43; Clark halts improvident undertaking of, 51; and railroads, 93 ff.; and impeachment proceedings, 122 ff.; Simmons' machine accused of influencing, 182
"Life of Justice Holmes and the Supreme Court, The," lecture by Felix Frankfurter, 249
Lincoln, Abraham, 4, 62, 79, 83, 95, 152, 202, 246
Lincoln, Levi, 198
"Little Clark," Clark's nickname, 4
London, Clark visits, 52, 53
London, Major Henry A., 244
Longstreet, General James, 6, 12
Lorimer, Senator, 182
Luther, Martin, 100

McBee, V. E., and railroad conspiracy, 143 ff.
McClellan, General George B., 6
MacDonald, Flora, 23
McIver, Dr. Charles D., 117, 137-138
McKenzie, Episcopal clergyman, settles at Plymouth, 23
McKenzie, Janet, marries Colin Clark, 23
McKenzies, Clark related to, 42
McRae, Judge James C., declines to run against Clark, 59

Madison, James, 196, 197, 198
Magazine of American History, 66
Manassas, Second Battle of, 5, 12
Mansfield, Lord, 82
Marbury v. *Madison*, 198-199
Markham, S. P., 120
Marshall, John, 198, 199
Methodist Church, Clark's activities in behalf of, 52
Methodists, Anna Clark joins, 30; Clark addresses Sunday School convention of, 78-79; and Kilgo-Gattis Controversy, 116-117; of North Carolina, and Kilgo, 103
Mexico, Clark visits, 74
Miller, Judge, 90
Miller, James H., indicted for maintaining a gambling house, 56-57
Minorities, Clark defends, 173-176
Molders vs. the Wheeling Mold and Foundry Company, Clark's opinion in, 210-212
Montgomery, Judge W. A., and impeachment proceedings, 122, 124, 125; retires from Supreme Court, 154
Montgomery, Judge W. J., and Kilgo-Gattis controversy, 109
Morgan, J. P., 87, 90, 91, 101, 179
Morning Post, Kilgo's speech published in, 119; and impeachment proceedings, 128; opposes Clark, 130; sides with McBee, 144
Morrison, Governor Cameron, pays tribute to Clark, 249
Moseley, E. A., secretary to Interstate Commerce Commission, writes to Clark, 209
"Mudcut Letters," 51
Mullen, J. M., Clark forms law partnership with, 42
"Mullet Road, The," 142
Munick case, Clark's opinion in, 174-175
Munn v. *Illinois*, 225

Nash and Pollock, Misses, Susan Graham attends school of, 48
National Democratic Committee, 186-187

INDEX 275

National Democratic Convention, Clark's name presented for vice president, 73
National League of Women Voters, Clark becomes counseller of, 168
National War Labor Board, Clark selected as umpire for, 209-210
Negroes, at Ventosa, 28-29, 252-253; Clark defeated on account of vote of, 42; Clark saves from disastrous credit system, 52; during Reconstruction, 71; vote of, 92, 127; and Governor Russell, 133; Clark's regard for, 175-176; and Fourteenth Amendment, 201
Neverson, Clark's body servant, 5, 12, 15, 17, 21, 34, 175
New Deal, 149, 152
New York University, honors Clark, 214
News and Observer, The, publicizes Clark's opinions, 53; and Kilgo-Gattis controversy, 106, 107, 121; *Raleigh Post* strives to discredit, 128, 130; reports railroad scandal, 146; hails Clark's opinion in *Rea v. Rea,* 161-162; attacks Simmons Machine, 181 ff.; critical of W. K. Kitchin, 184; fails to support Clark's campaign for U. S. Senate, 185 ff.
North Carolina, losses of in Civil War, 242-243
North Carolina Bar Association, 159, 192-193, 215-217
North Carolina College for Negroes, 175
North Carolina Historical Commission, 65
North Carolina Public Service Company, 224, 234
Norfolk Journal, 43
Norfleet, Louise, marries David McKenzie Clark, 25
Norfleet, Marmaduke, 24-25
Norfleets, Clark related to, 42
Northwestern University, 217, 250
"Notes By the Way," Clark's article in *Roanoke News,* 43, 44

Odell, W. R., 119
Official Records of the Union and Confederate Armies, The, 238
Oglesby, Rev. A. G., 112
"Old Court," 158
"Old Foes with New Faces," Clark's address at Hot Springs, Va., 149-151
Osborne, Judge, 58
Other People's Money, by Judge Brandeis, 89, 180
Overman, Senator Lee S., 188, 194
Owen, Senator, has Clark's addresses on Constitution printed in *Congressional Record,* 194

Page, Rev. Mr., 109
Page's Railroad, 130
Palfrey, General Francis W., 9
Parker, Colonel Frank M., 243
Parliament, and women's rights, 167
Patterson, Caleb Perry, studies English legal and judicial system, 218-219
Payne-Aldrich Tariff Bill, 182
Pearson, Judge Richmond M., 154, 162
Penney case, 221
Penrose, 182
Pettigrew, Colonel J. Johnston, 4
Pettigrew's North Carolinians, at Gettysburg, 244
Pettit case, 172-173, 221-222
Pickett's Division, at Gettysburg, 244
"Pleas of Contributory Negligence," 171
Plymouth, Clark in command of post at, 17
Poe, Clarence, Clark writes to, 187-188; marries one of Aycock's daughters, 188
Polk, Colonel L. L., a leader of Populist party, 69
Pollard's case, Clark's opinion in, 221
Pope, Alexander, quoted, 242
Populism, Clark accused of, 75, 131
Populists, endorse Clark's nomination to Supreme Court, 69-71; and Colonel Andrews, 92; and Russell, 133; aid Democrats, 180, 181
Pou, Edward W., and free-pass abuse, 90-91
Pou, James H., chairman of Democratic State Executive Committee, 73; and

free-pass abuse, 90-91; urges appointment of Clark to U. S. Supreme Court, 191
Pound, Roscoe, 154, 215, 217-218, 250
Pritchard, Judge Jeter, 146
Progressive Farmer, The, 69, 187
Prospect Hill, Clark born at, 26
Pugh, H. P., challenged to duel by Clark, 43-46, 76
Purnell, Judge Thomas R., and railroad conspiracy, 143 ff.

Ragan, John H., 98
Railroad and Telegraph Commission, and passenger fares, 97; established by General Assembly, 225
Railroad Commissioners, Clark addresses in Denver, 95 ff.
Railroads, Clark crusades against abuses of, 87 ff.; conspiracy of, 142 ff.
Raleigh and Gaston Railroad, 46, 91
Raleigh *Morning Post*. See *Morning Post*
Raleigh *News*, Clark purchases control of, 51
Raleigh *Sentinel*, 37-39, 43
Ransom, General Matt W., 5, 10
Ransom, General Robert, 10, 12
Ray, Colonel James M., 243
Rea v. Rea, 161-162
Reading, Clark's, 41
Reconstruction, Clark on, 37-39
Reece, Joe, 209
"Replacement Value Theory," 234, 235
Reports of the Supreme Court, 247-248
Republicans, 69, 70, 92, 131, *passim*
"Revision of the Constitution; Election of Judges and Senators by the People," title of Clark's address before Tennessee Bar Association, 194
Ridgeway, Clark attends school in, 31-33
Riverside Plantation, 36, 43
Roanoke News, 43
Roanoke River, 24, 27-28, 29, 30
Roberts, General W. P., 243
Rockefeller, John D., 117, 179
Rogers, Rowan, 121
Roosevelt, Franklin D., 193, 203

Roosevelt, Theodore, 86, 179-180, 192, 204-205, 209
Root, Elihu, 215, 220
Rountree, George, 127
Roustan, Madame, Susan Graham attends school of, 48-49
Ruffin, Hannah, marries Marmaduke Norfleet, 24-25
Ruffin, Judge Thomas, 56, 154, 159; doctrine of, 123-125
Russell, Governor Daniel L., and whispering campaign against Clark, 132 ff.; Clark writes notes to, 132 ff.; Republican nominee for governor, 73; mentioned, 128, 131, 142

Safety Appliance Act, 209
Savage, W. E., 44, 45
Scales, Governor Alfred M., 54
Schenck, Judge David, 56, 66
Scotland Neck, 24, 25, 42
Seaboard Air Line Railroad, consolidation of, 75, 87; opposes Clark, 130
Seawell, Judge A. A. F., 170
Sharpsburg, Clark at battle of, 5 ff.
Shaw, Judge T. J., 120, 225
Shell-Fish Commissioner, and impeachment proceedings, 122 ff.
"Shenandoah," cruiser in Civil War, 245
Shepard, Dr. J. E., president of North Carolina College for Negroes, 175-176
Sherman Antitrust Act, 86, 98, 99, 100, 130, 152
Sherman, General W. T., in Georgia, 19; at Bentonville, 20-21; visited by Graham and Swain, 245-246
Shiras, Judge George, 200
Simmons, Furnifold M., advises Clark to accept nomination to Supreme Court, 70; and Kilgo-Gattis controversy, 118-119; and impeachment proceedings, 127, 128; dislikes Clark for criticizing big interests, 130-131; and Senatorial campaign of 1912, 177 ff.
Simon, Sir John, Clark writes to, 164-165

INDEX 277

Simonton, Judge, Charles H., 88
"Sissy," 117, 118
Skinner, Harry, 193
Smith, Ed Chambers, 145-146
Smiths, Clark related to, 42
Snyder, H. N., 105
Sorrell, J. P., 121
Southern Power Company, litigation over, 224 ff.
Southern Public Utilities Company, and development of power monopoly, 227, 228, 231 ff.
Southern Railway, consolidation of, 87; political influence of under management of Colonel Andrews, 91-93; opposes Clark, 130; supports Simmons, 184; McBee connected with, 143
Southgate, James H., and Kilgo-Gattis controversy, 110-112, 113
Spencer, Samuel, tries to buy railroad, 88
Standard Oil Company, as monopoly, 96, 99, 229, 231, 232
State Convention (Democratic), 1894, 70-71; 1896, 71 ff.; 1902, 137 ff.; 1896, 72-73; 1912, 185
State League of Women Voters, Clark becomes legal adviser to, 168
State Literary and Historical Association, Clark addresses, 147-149
State Records of North Carolina, Clark begins compiling and editing, 66, 247
Stevens, Thaddeus, 40, 245
Stone, Judge Harlan F., 64, 191
Stuart, General J. E. B., 6, 12
Superior Court, Clark as judge of, 54 ff.
Supreme Court (State), Clark licensed by, 42; Clark argues cases before, 46; cites Clark's Code of Civil Procedure, 51; Clark appointed to fill vacancy on, 54; elected to, 59; Clark's ability as member of, 60 ff.; Clark renominated for, 70; renders opinion in Kilgo-Gattis trial, 120; and impeachment proceedings, 122 ff.; and contest for chief justice, 129 ff.; Clark nominated chief justice of, 140; and railroad conspiracy, 142 ff.; Clark as chief justice of, 154 ff.; *passim*.

Supreme Court and the Constitution, by Charles A. Beard, 193
Supreme Court (U. S.), Clark's appointment to urged, 190-191; Clark's views on, 192 ff.; Clark's views referred to in debates over, 193; bill, defeated, 203; Clark advocates vesting rule-making power in, 221; doctrine of in *Munn* v. *Illinois*, 225
Swain, Governor, 15, 245-246
Swindell, Dr. F. D., 109

Taft, William Howard, and Supreme Court, 204; and Duke Power Company, 232, attends banquet in Durham, 250; has high regard for Clark, 250-251; wants Clark to join American Bar Association, 250-251
Taney, Judge Roger B., 202
Telegraph, Clark advocates government ownership of, 67-69
Telegraph Company, Clark rules against discriminatory practices of, 225
Telephone, Clark advocates government ownership of, 67-69
Tennessee Bar Association, 194, 205
Tew, Colonel C. C., 4, 11, 22
Tew's Military Academy, 3, 5
Thompson, Cyrus, 117
Thompson, Judge Seymour, editor of *The American Law Review*, 159, 205
Thorne, Anna Maria, marries David Clark II, 26
Thorne, Dr., 26
Tournament, Clark meets Susan Graham at, 47-48
Trade Council, Clark addresses, 296-207
Trinity College, Clark invited to address, 65; Clark sought for presidency of, 65; Clark delivers commencement address at, 77-78; and Kilgo-Gattis Controversy, 102 ff.
Trusts and Utilities, Clark's early judicial opinions relating to, 225 ff.
Tumulty, Joseph P., 187

U. S. v. *American Tobacco Company*, cited by Clark, 229-230
University College of Medicine, Clark addresses, 83-84, 94-95
University of Chicago, 117
University of North Carolina, Clark studies law at, 39-40; Clark urges support of, 43; confers degree of Master of Arts on Clark, 46; Clark invited to address, 65; confers degree of Doctor of Laws on Clark, 65; and Kilgo, 109; Clark addresses law class at, 167; mentioned, 118
University of Pennsylvania, Clark addresses, 194 ff., 247
University of Texas, 218

Vance, Governor Zebulon B., 17, 245, 246
Vanderbilt, William H., 91
Vanderbilt University, 116-117
Vandeveer's Brigade, 244
Van Wycks, the, 26
Ventosa, ancestral home of Clarks, 3, 21-22, 26, 27-31, 35, 52, 223, 252, 253
Vine Hill Academy, Clark sent to school at, 31

Wake Forest College, 65, 79, 100-101
Walker, Judge Platt D., becomes associate justice, 154, 155; sketch of, 156-157
Walters, Harry, tries to buy railroad, 88, 89
Ward v. *Odell*, 171
Washington, Clark's stay in, 40, 42
Washington, Susannah Sarah, 49
W. Duke Sons and Company, 224
Watlington, "Colonel," anecdote about, 58
Watson, Cyrus B., nominated for governor, 73; and Kilgo-Gattis controversy, 120, 121; on Clark, 224
Watts, A. D., Simmons' political manager, 182; sketch of, 185; takes charge of administration of patronage, 188; and Dr. George T. Winston, 189
Watts, George W., 224
Webb, Rev. R. S., and Kilgo, 107
Webster, John R., and Kilgo trial, 109, 114
Weeks and Foster, Clark enters law offices of, 40
Weldon, Clark at, 17-18
"Where Shall the Governing Power Reside," Clark's address at University College of Medicine, Richmond, Virginia, 83-84
White, Judge Edward D., 229-230
Wigmore, Dean John H., on defects in legal system, 215, 217; urges Clark to give course of lectures, 251
Williams, Anderson, anecdote about, 253-254
Wilson, Woodrow, urged to appoint Clark to U. S. Supreme Court, 191; selects Clark as an umpire for National War Labor Board, 209-210; mentioned, 179, 183, 185, 187, 197
Wilson, James, 197
Winston, Dr. George T., 66, 189
Winston, Robert W., author of *It's a Far Cry*, counsel for Kilgo and Duke, 120; relates anecdote on free-pass abuse, 90-91
Wofford College, 105
Woman's College, 137
Woman's Suffrage, Clark enlists in cause of, 168-170
Women, Clark's defense of, 161 ff.
Workmen's Compensation Law, Clark an early advocate of, 212-213

Yancey County, Clark quotes note of mountaineer from, 137
Yarborough House, Clark halts gambling in, 56-57

www.ingramcontent.com/pod-product-compliance
Lightning Source LLC
Chambersburg PA
CBHW021355290426
44108CB00010B/257